AS G

X-MEN

MONSTROUS

Writer: **Daniel Way**

Pencilers: **Jason Pearson** with **Sara Pichelli** (#36-37)
and **Nick Bradshaw** (#39 & #41)

Inkers: **Karl Story**
with **Sara Pichelli** (#36-37) and **Nick Bradshaw**
with **Norman Lee, Jay Leisten & Craig Yeung** (#39 & #41)

Colorists: **Sonia Oback** (#36-37) and **Rachelle Rosenberg** (#39 & #41)

Letterers: **VC's Cory Petit, Joe Caramagna & Clayton Cowles**

Cover Art: **Jason Pearson** (#36-37 & #39) and **Salvador Larroca & Guru eFx** (#41)

Associate Editor: **Daniel Ketchum**

Editors: **Nick Lowe & Axel Alonso**

STRANGE TALES #89

Penciler: **Jack Kirby**

Inker: **Dick Ayers**

COLLECTION EDITOR: JENNIFER GRÜNWALD • ASSISTANT EDITORS: ALEX STARBUCK & NELSON RIBEIRO
ITOR, SPECIAL PROJECTS: MARK D. BEAZLEY • SENIOR EDITOR, SPECIAL PROJECTS: JEFF YOUNGQUIST • SENIOR VICE PRESIDENT OF SALES: DAVID GABRIEL
SVP OF BRAND PLANNING & COMMUNICATIONS: MICHAEL PASCIULLO • BOOK DESIGN: JEFF POWELL

EDITOR IN CHIEF: AXEL ALONSO • CHIEF CREATIVE OFFICER: JOE QUESADA • PUBLISHER: DAN BUCKLEY • EXECUTIVE PRODUCER: ALAN FINE

NISHING X-MEN VOL. 7: MONSTROUS. Contains material originally published in magazine form as ASTONISHING X-MEN #36-37, #39 and #41; and STRANGE TALES #89. First printing 2012. ISBN# 978-0--5115-9. Published by MARVEL WORLDWIDE, INC., a subsidiary of MARVEL ENTERTAINMENT, LLC. OFFICE OF PUBLICATION: 135 West 50th Street, New York, NY 10020. $16.99 per copy in the U.S. and $18.99 in Canada (GST #R127032852); Canadian Agreement #40668537. **Printed in the U.S.A.** ALAN FINE, EVP - Office of the President, Marvel Worldwide, Inc. and EVP & CMO Marvel Characters DAN BUCKLEY, Publisher & President - Print, Animation & Digital Divisions; JOE QUESADA, Chief Creative Officer; TOM BREVOORT, SVP of Publishing; DAVID BOGART, SVP of Operations & Procurement, Publishing; AN JAYATILLEKE, SVP & Associate Publisher, Publishing; C.B. CEBULSKI, SVP of Creator & Content Development; DAVID GABRIEL, SVP of Publishing Sales & Circulation; MICHAEL PASCIULLO, SVP of Brand Planning mmunications; JIM O'KEEFE, VP of Operations & Logistics; DAN CARR, Executive Director of Publishing Technology; SUSAN CRESPI, Editorial Operations Manager; ALEX MORALES, Publishing Operations Manager; LEE, Chairman Emeritus. For information regarding advertising in Marvel Comics or on Marvel.com, please contact John Dokes, SVP Integrated Sales and Marketing, at jdokes@marvel.com. For Marvel subscription ies, please call 800-217-9158. **Manufactured between 4/4/2012 and 4/23/2012 by R.R. DONNELLEY, INC., SALEM, VA, USA.**

8 7 6 5 4 3 2 1

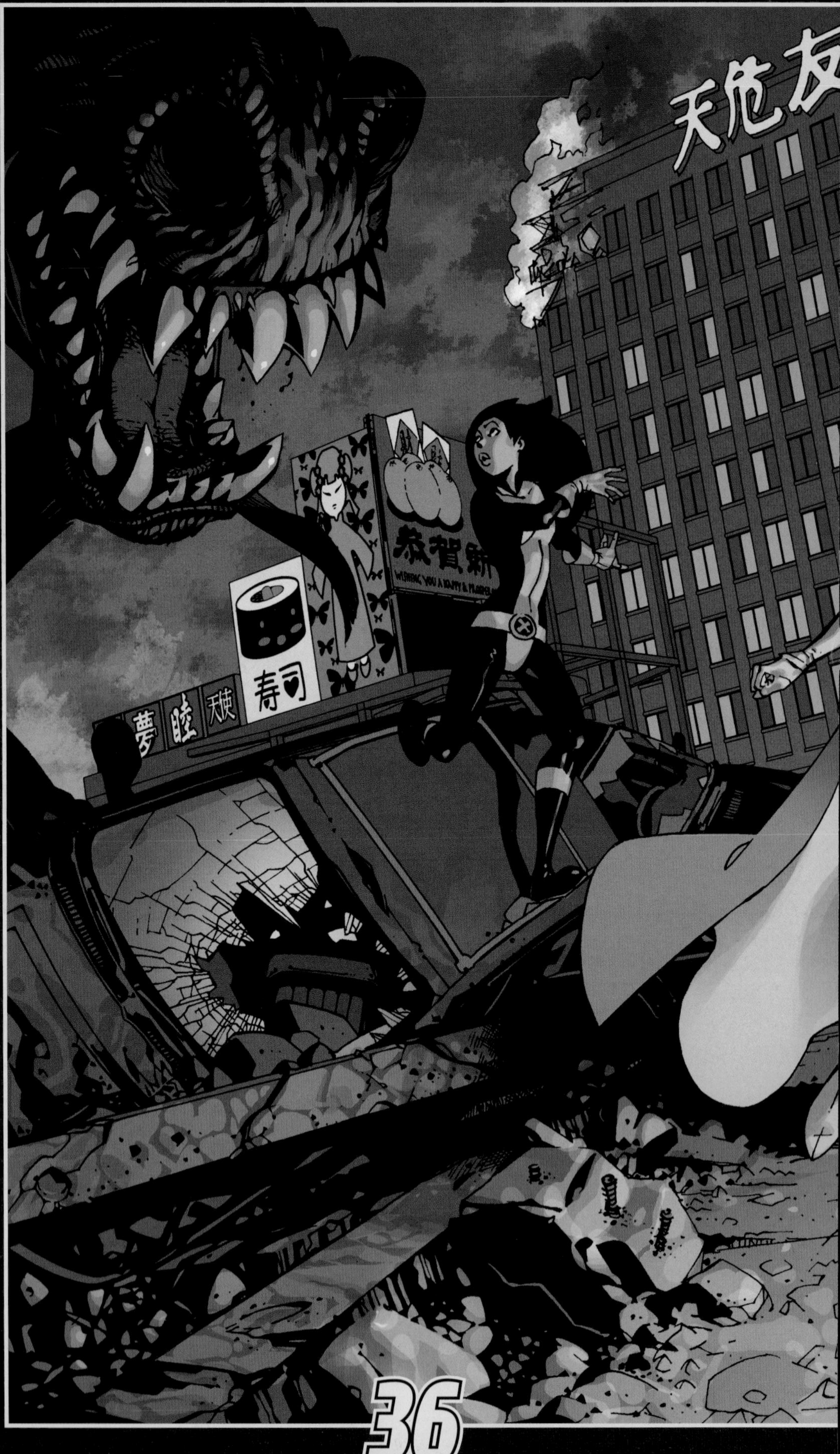
天危友
恭賀新
寿司

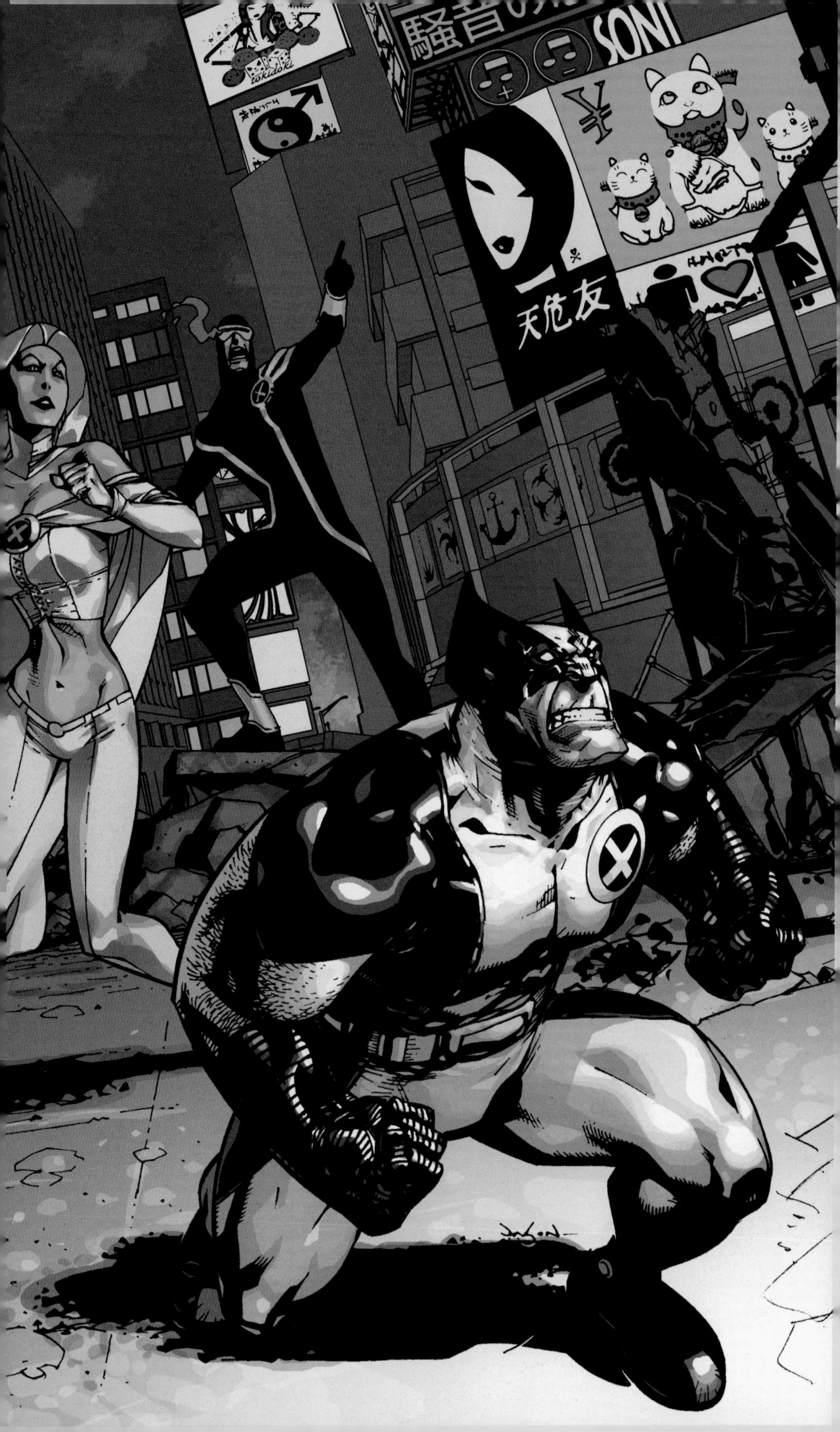
SONI
tokidoki
天危友

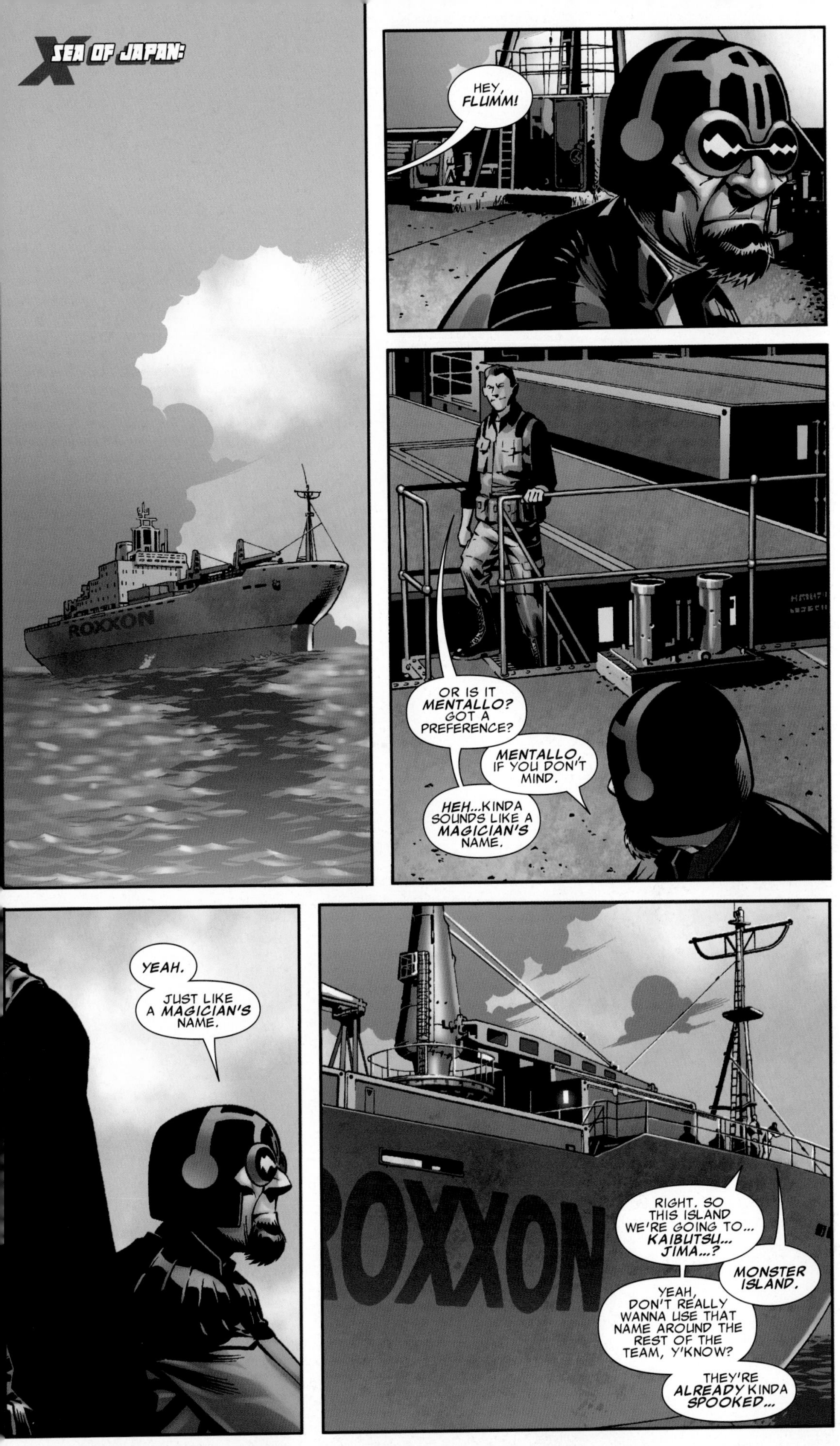
SEA OF JAPAN:
ROXXON
HEY, FLUMM!
OR IS IT MENTALLO? GOT A PREFERENCE?
MENTALLO, IF YOU DON'T MIND.
HEH...KINDA SOUNDS LIKE A MAGICIAN'S NAME.
YEAH.
JUST LIKE A MAGICIAN'S NAME.
ROXXON
RIGHT. SO THIS ISLAND WE'RE GOING TO... KAIBUTSU... JIMA...?
MONSTER ISLAND.
YEAH, DON'T REALLY WANNA USE THAT NAME AROUND THE REST OF THE TEAM, Y'KNOW?
THEY'RE ALREADY KINDA SPOOKED...

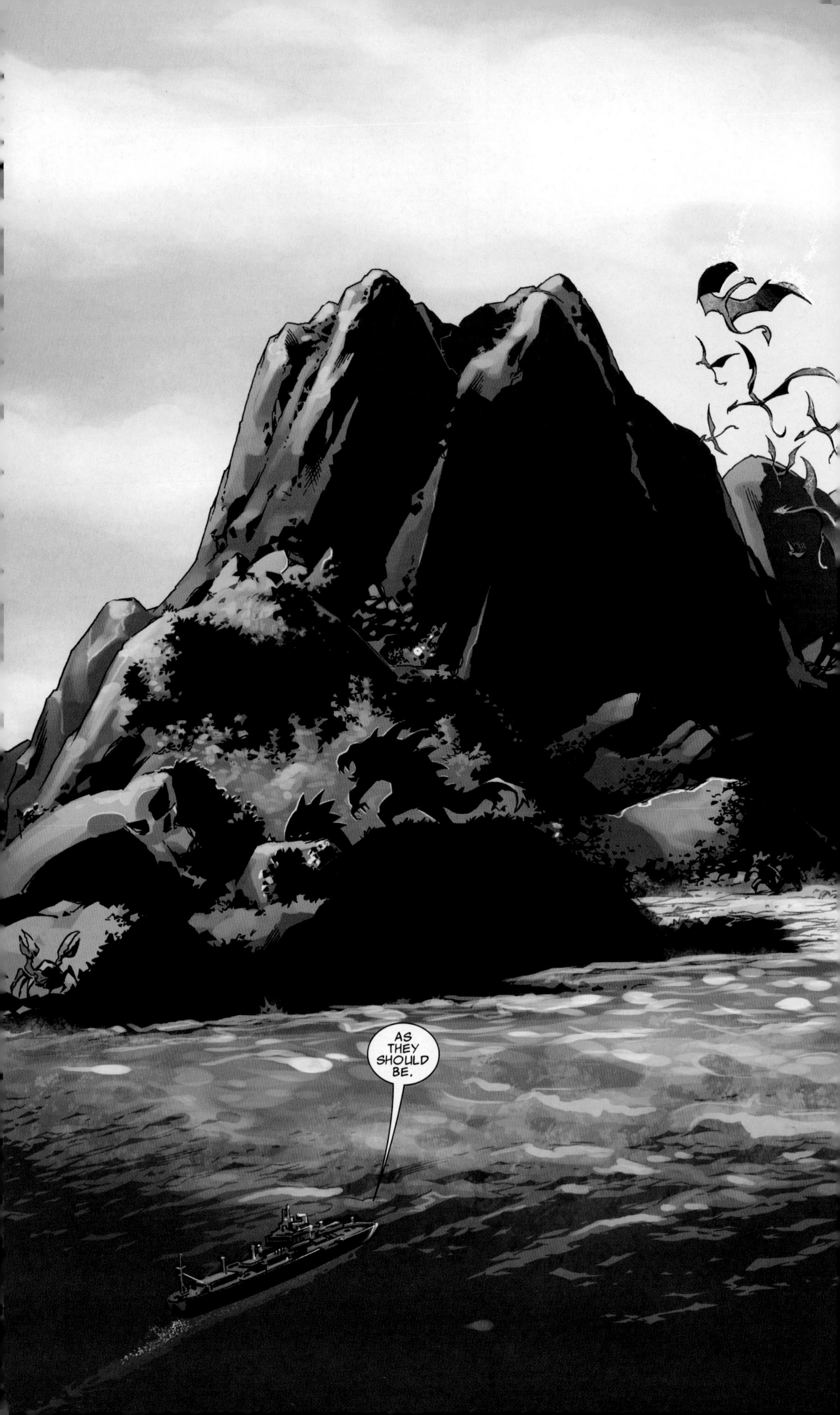
AS THEY SHOULD BE.

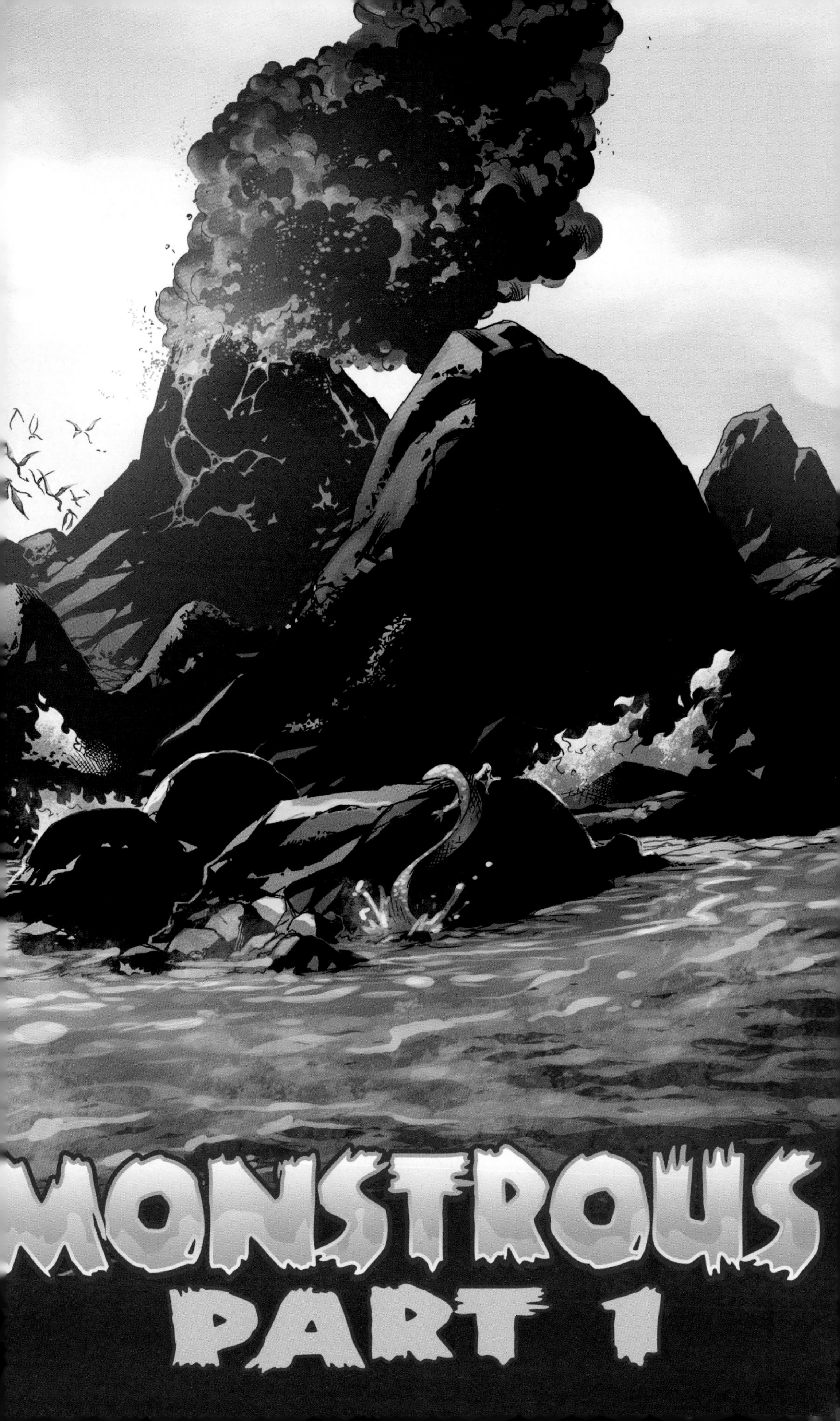
MONSTROUS
PART 1

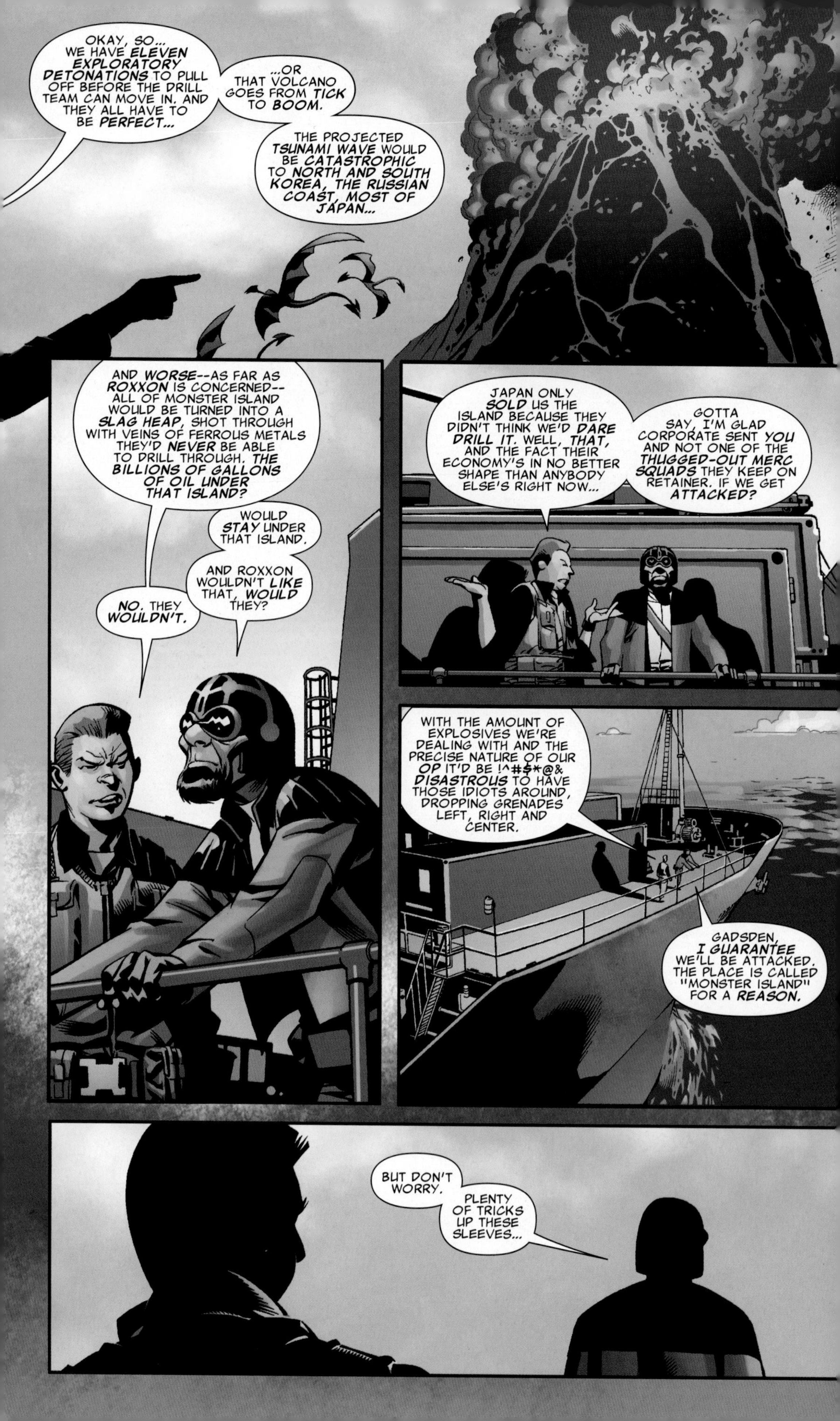
OKAY, SO... WE HAVE ELEVEN EXPLORATORY DETONATIONS TO PULL OFF BEFORE THE DRILL TEAM CAN MOVE IN. AND THEY ALL HAVE TO BE PERFECT...
...OR THAT VOLCANO GOES FROM TICK TO BOOM.
THE PROJECTED TSUNAMI WAVE WOULD BE CATASTROPHIC TO NORTH AND SOUTH KOREA, THE RUSSIAN COAST, MOST OF JAPAN...
AND WORSE--AS FAR AS ROXXON IS CONCERNED--ALL OF MONSTER ISLAND WOULD BE TURNED INTO A SLAG HEAP, SHOT THROUGH WITH VEINS OF FERROUS METALS THEY'D NEVER BE ABLE TO DRILL THROUGH. THE BILLIONS OF GALLONS OF OIL UNDER THAT ISLAND?
WOULD STAY UNDER THAT ISLAND.
AND ROXXON WOULDN'T LIKE THAT, WOULD THEY?
NO. THEY WOULDN'T.
JAPAN ONLY SOLD US THE ISLAND BECAUSE THEY DIDN'T THINK WE'D DARE DRILL IT. WELL, THAT, AND THE FACT THEIR ECONOMY'S IN NO BETTER SHAPE THAN ANYBODY ELSE'S RIGHT NOW...
GOTTA SAY, I'M GLAD CORPORATE SENT YOU AND NOT ONE OF THE THUGGED-OUT MERC SQUADS THEY KEEP ON RETAINER. IF WE GET ATTACKED?
WITH THE AMOUNT OF EXPLOSIVES WE'RE DEALING WITH AND THE PRECISE NATURE OF OUR OP IT'D BE !^#$*@& DISASTROUS TO HAVE THOSE IDIOTS AROUND, DROPPING GRENADES LEFT, RIGHT AND CENTER.
GADSDEN, I GUARANTEE WE'LL BE ATTACKED. THE PLACE IS CALLED "MONSTER ISLAND" FOR A REASON.
BUT DON'T WORRY.
PLENTY OF TRICKS UP THESE SLEEVES...

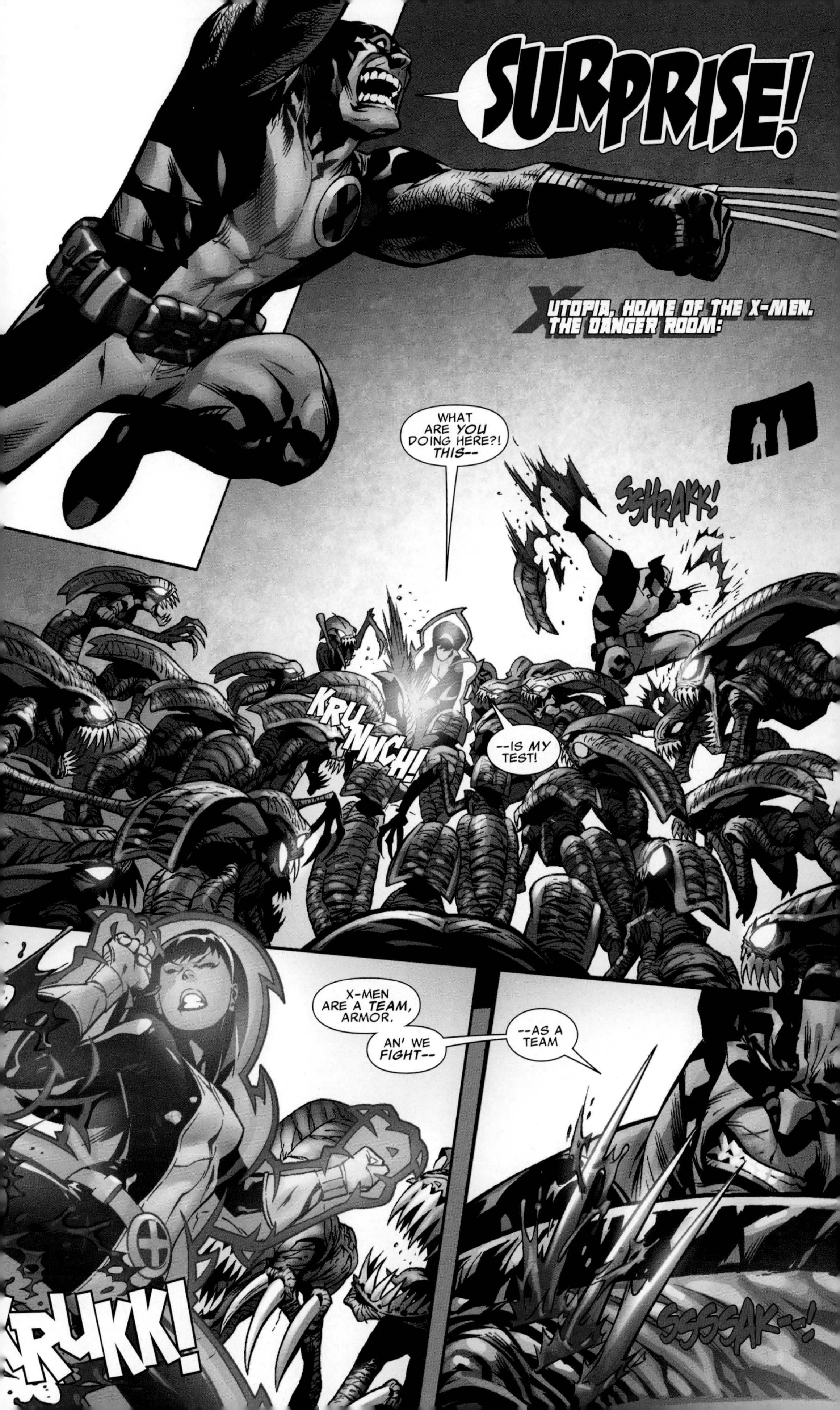
SURPRISE!
UTOPIA, HOME OF THE X-MEN. THE DANGER ROOM:
WHAT ARE YOU DOING HERE?! THIS--
SSHRAKK!
KRUNNCH!
--IS MY TEST!
X-MEN ARE A TEAM, ARMOR.
AN' WE FIGHT--
--AS A TEAM
RUKK!
SSSSAK--!

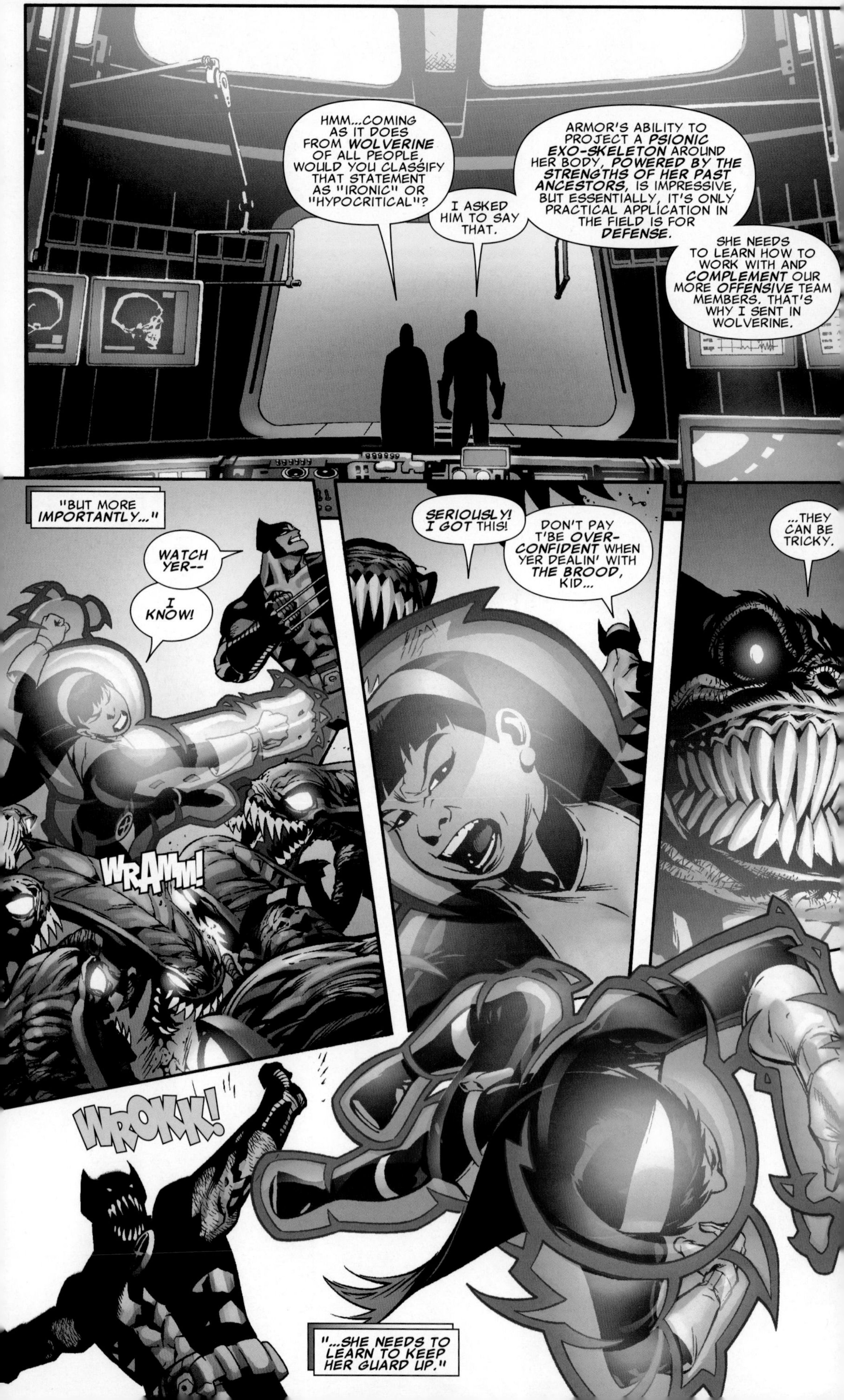
HMM...COMING AS IT DOES FROM WOLVERINE OF ALL PEOPLE, WOULD YOU CLASSIFY THAT STATEMENT AS "IRONIC" OR "HYPOCRITICAL"?
I ASKED HIM TO SAY THAT.
ARMOR'S ABILITY TO PROJECT A PSIONIC EXO-SKELETON AROUND HER BODY, POWERED BY THE STRENGTHS OF HER PAST ANCESTORS, IS IMPRESSIVE, BUT ESSENTIALLY, IT'S ONLY PRACTICAL APPLICATION IN THE FIELD IS FOR DEFENSE.
SHE NEEDS TO LEARN HOW TO WORK WITH AND COMPLEMENT OUR MORE OFFENSIVE TEAM MEMBERS. THAT'S WHY I SENT IN WOLVERINE.
"BUT MORE IMPORTANTLY..."
WATCH YER--
I KNOW!
WRAMM!
SERIOUSLY! I GOT THIS!
DON'T PAY T'BE OVER-CONFIDENT WHEN YER DEALIN' WITH THE BROOD, KID...
...THEY CAN BE TRICKY.
WROKK!
"...SHE NEEDS TO LEARN TO KEEP HER GUARD UP."

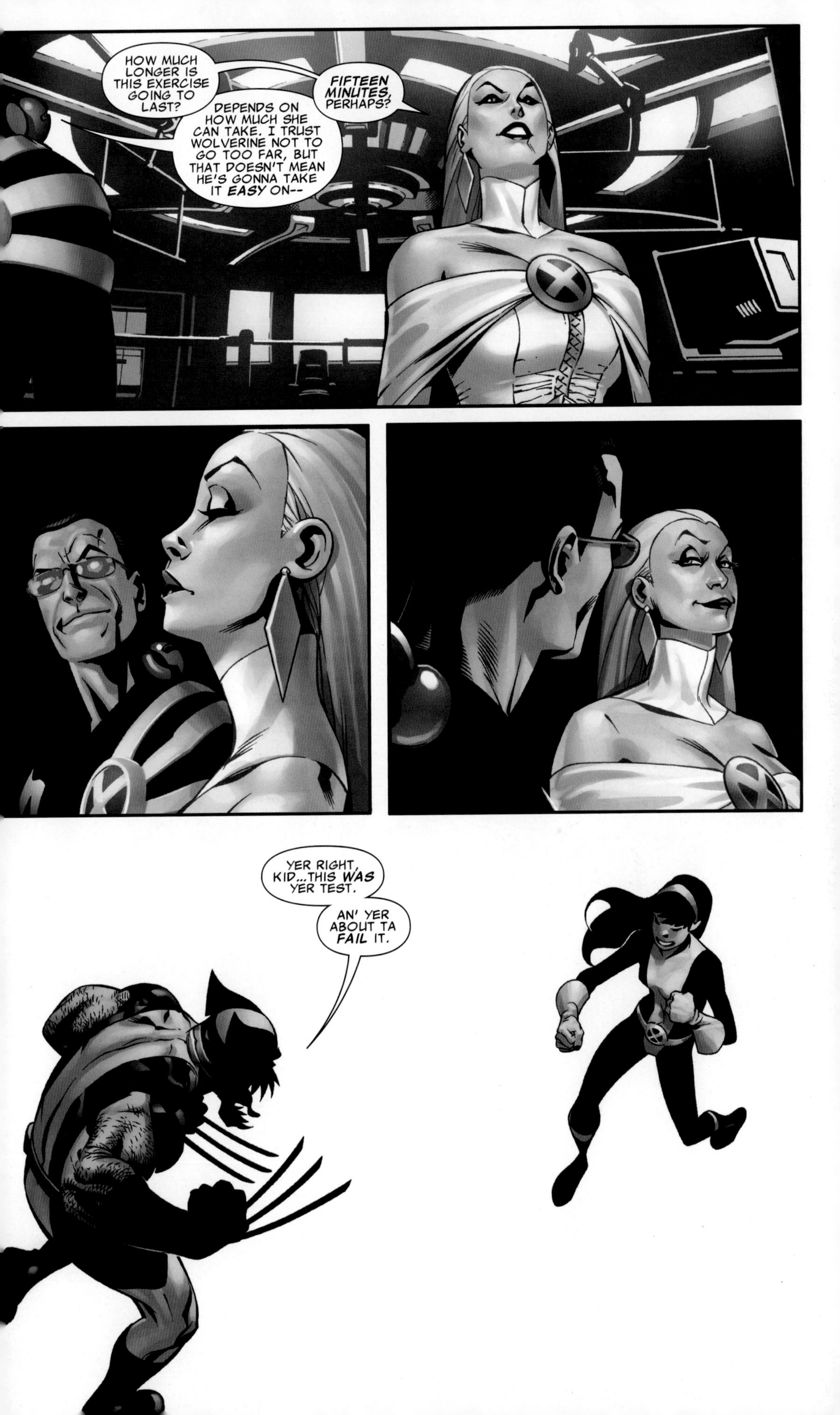
HOW MUCH LONGER IS THIS EXERCISE GOING TO LAST?
FIFTEEN MINUTES, PERHAPS?
DEPENDS ON HOW MUCH SHE CAN TAKE. I TRUST WOLVERINE NOT TO GO TOO FAR, BUT THAT DOESN'T MEAN HE'S GONNA TAKE IT EASY ON--
YER RIGHT, KID...THIS WAS YER TEST.
AN' YER ABOUT TA FAIL IT.

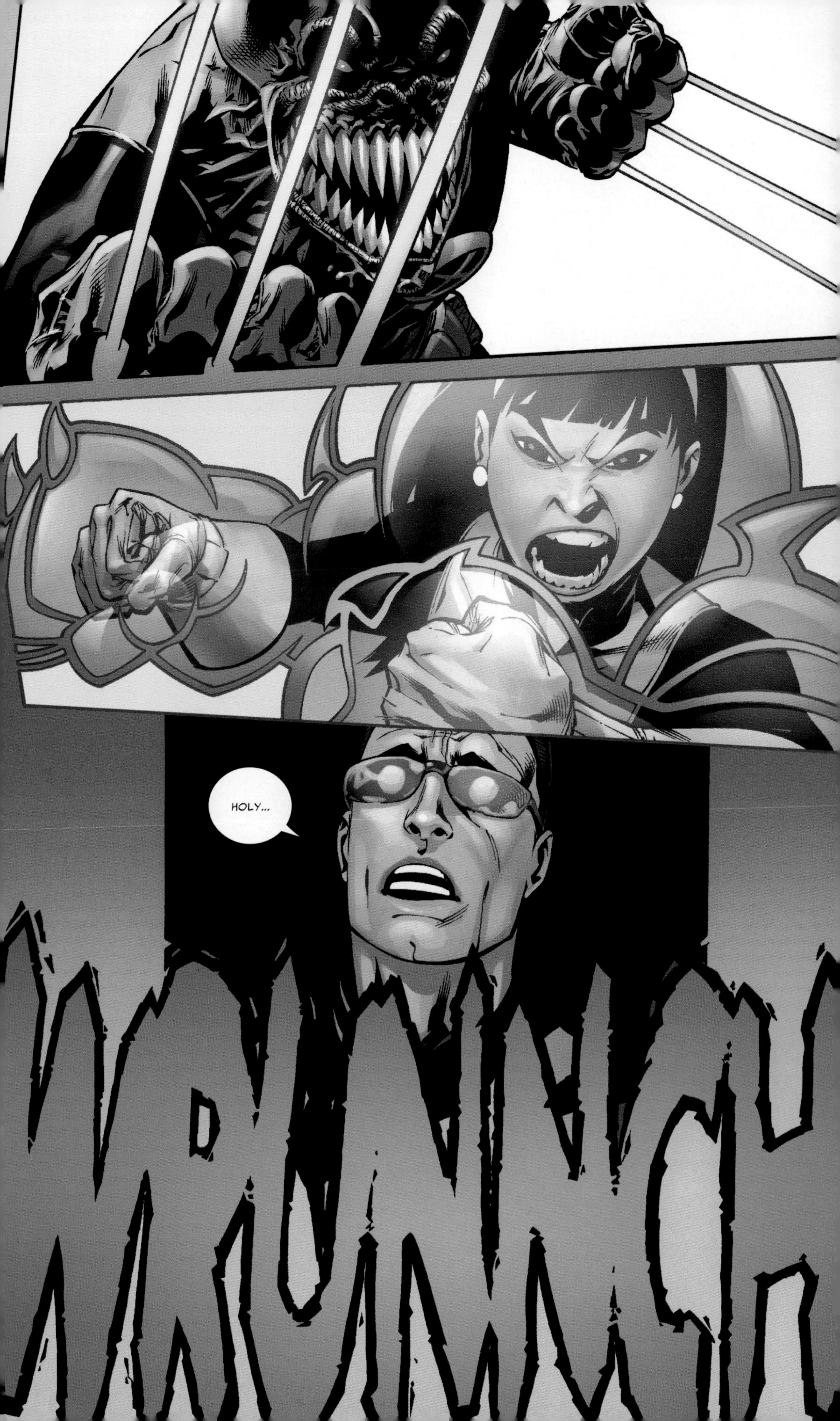
HOLY…

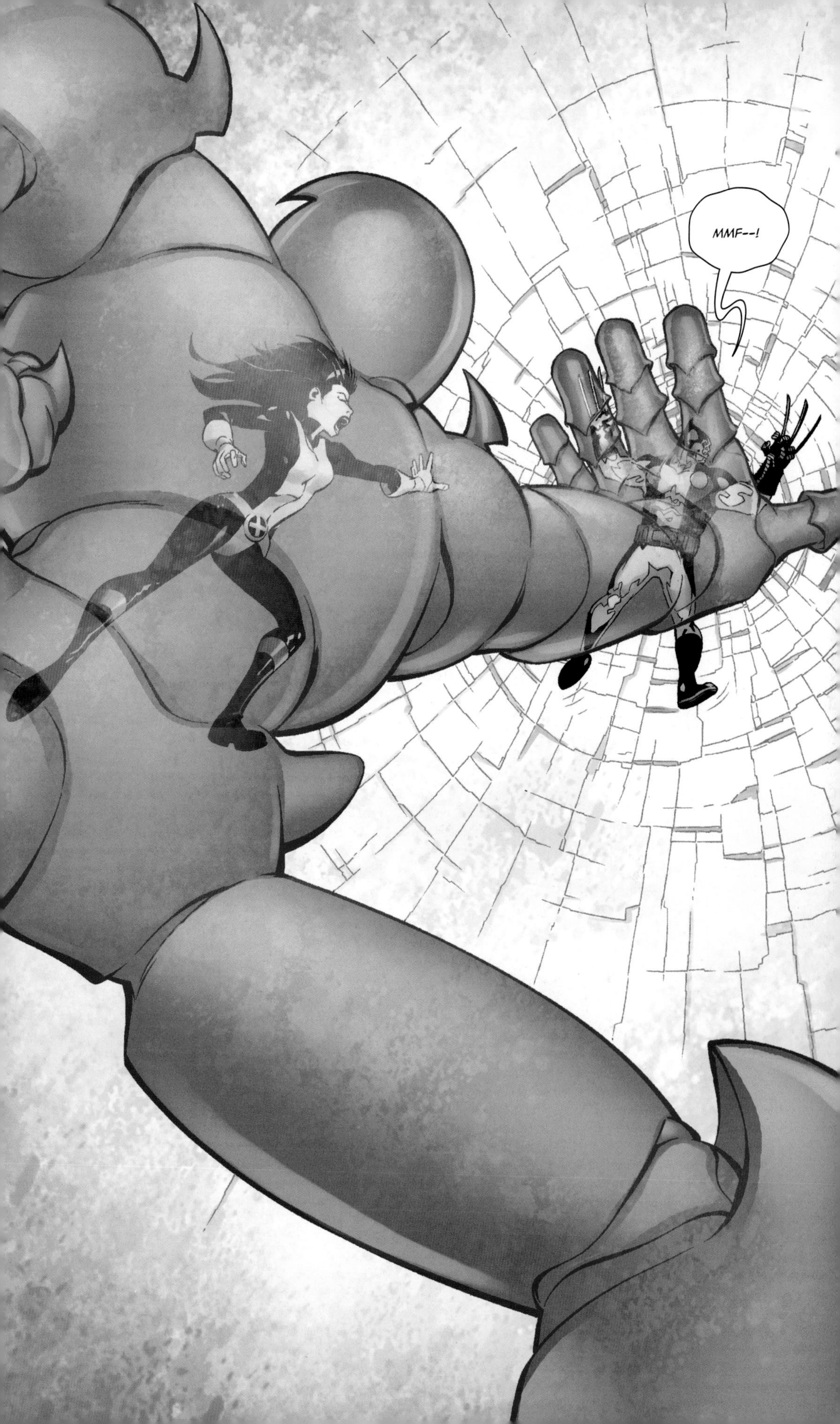
MMF--!

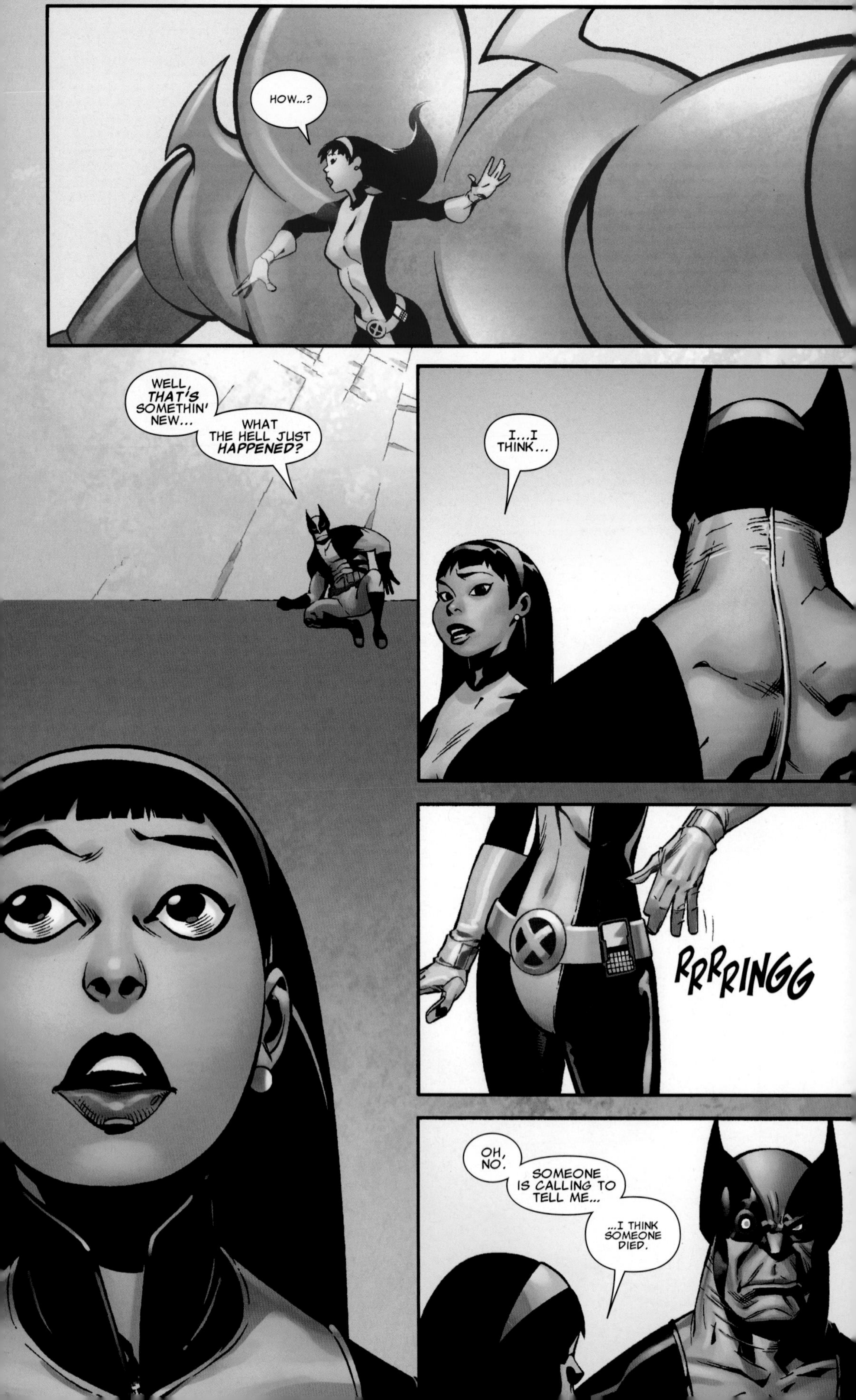
HOW...?
WELL, *THAT'S* SOMETHIN' NEW...
WHAT THE HELL JUST *HAPPENED?*
I...I THINK...
RRRINGG
OH, NO.
SOMEONE IS CALLING TO TELL ME...
...I THINK SOMEONE DIED.

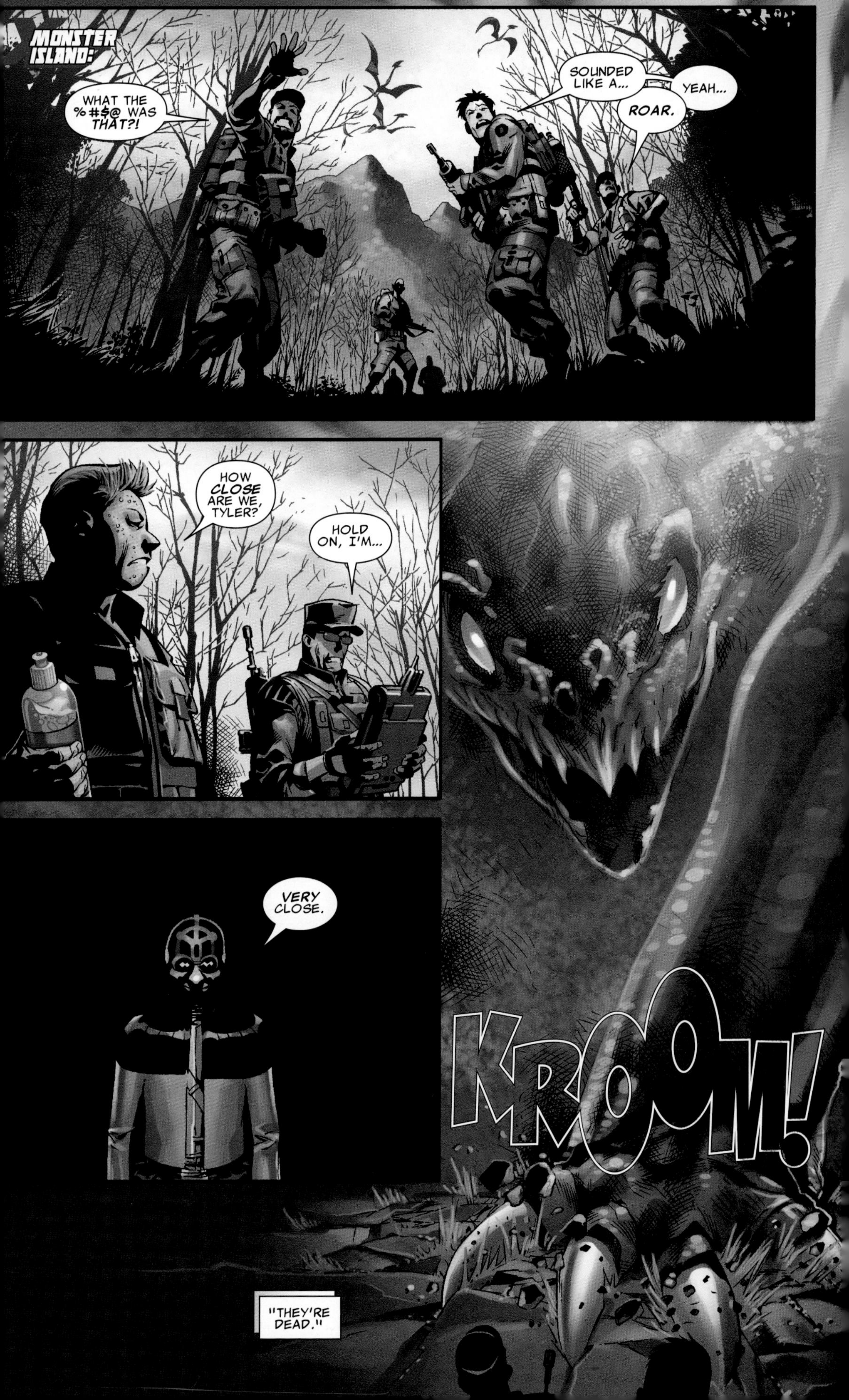
MONSTER ISLAND:
WHAT THE %#$@ WAS THAT?!
SOUNDED LIKE A...
YEAH...
ROAR.
HOW CLOSE ARE WE, TYLER?
HOLD ON, I'M...
VERY CLOSE.
KROOOM!
"THEY'RE DEAD."

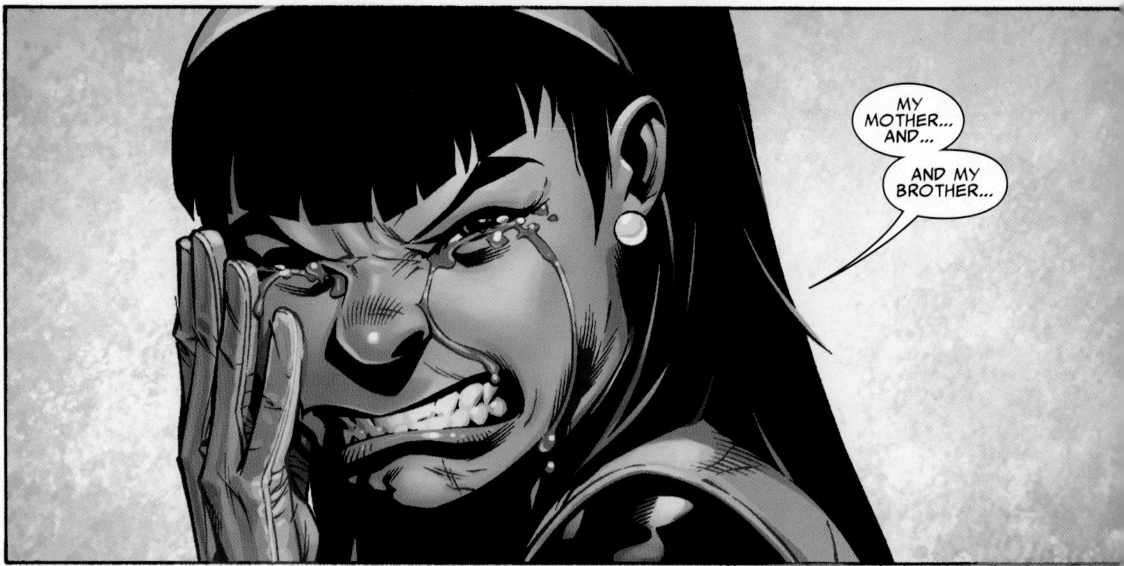
MY MOTHER... AND...
AND MY BROTHER...

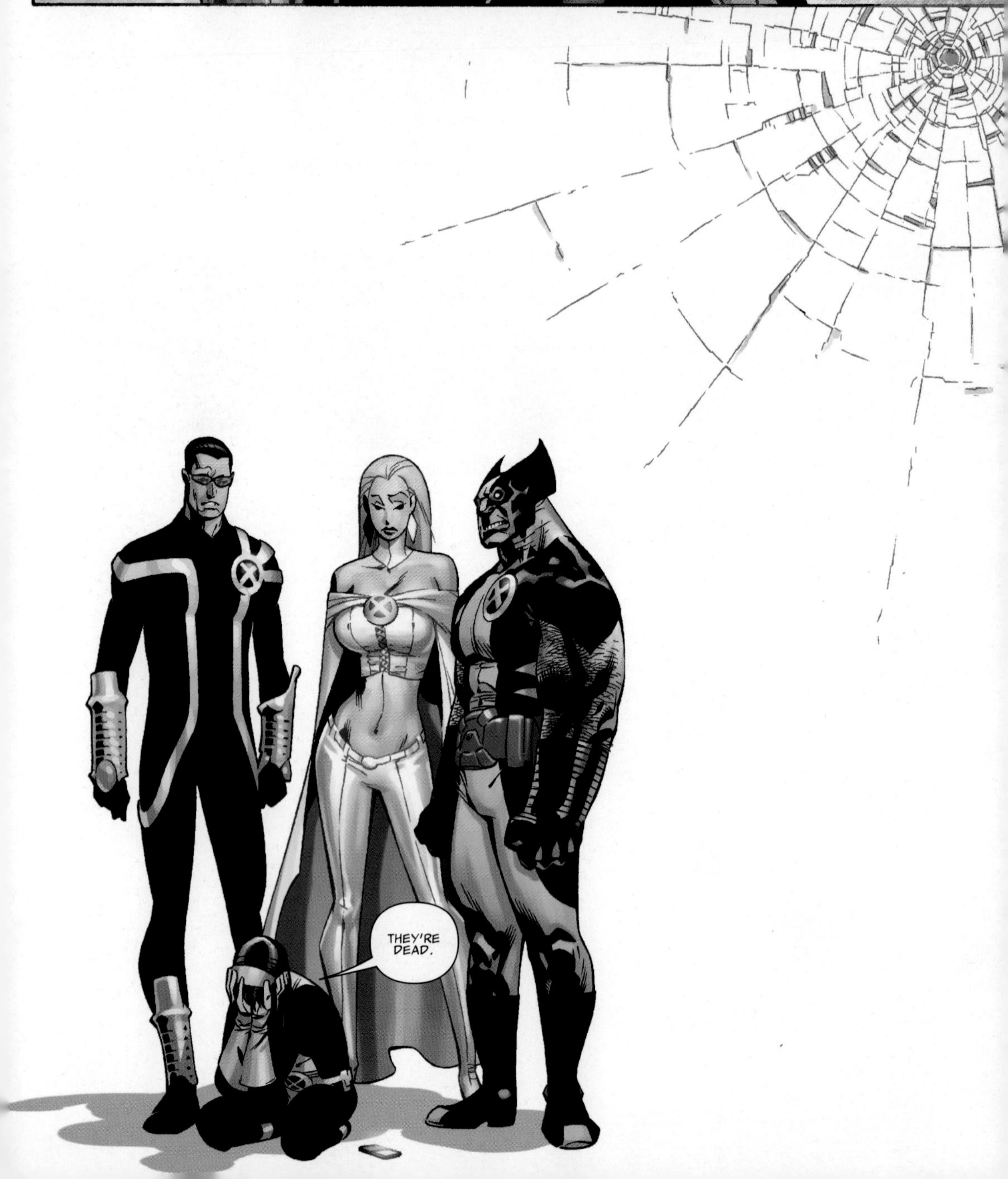
THEY'RE DEAD.

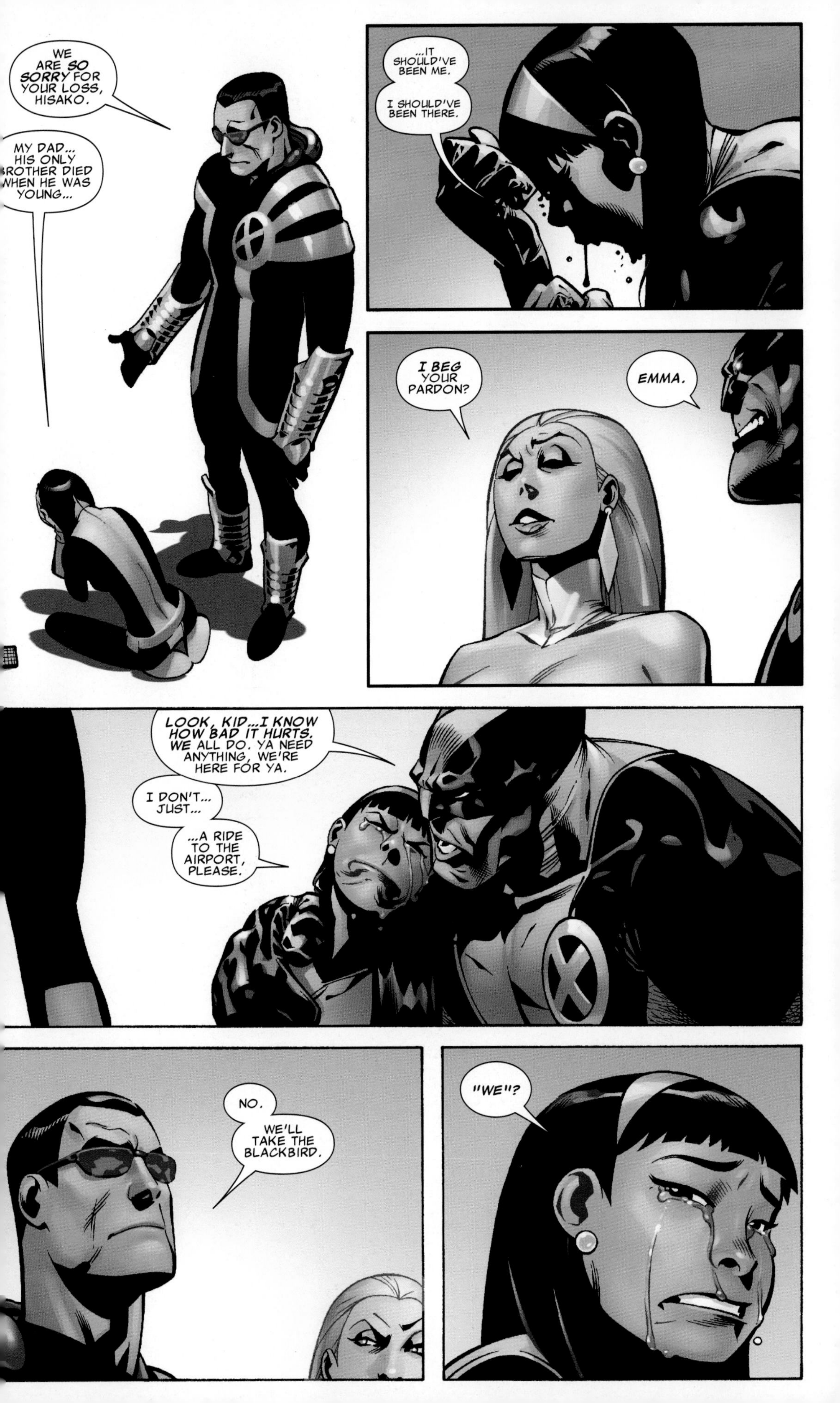

WE ARE SO SORRY FOR YOUR LOSS, HISAKO.
MY DAD... HIS ONLY BROTHER DIED WHEN HE WAS YOUNG...
...IT SHOULD'VE BEEN ME.
I SHOULD'VE BEEN THERE.
I BEG YOUR PARDON?
EMMA.
LOOK, KID...I KNOW HOW BAD IT HURTS. WE ALL DO. YA NEED ANYTHING, WE'RE HERE FOR YA.
I DON'T... JUST...
...A RIDE TO THE AIRPORT, PLEASE.
NO.
WE'LL TAKE THE BLACKBIRD.
"WE"?

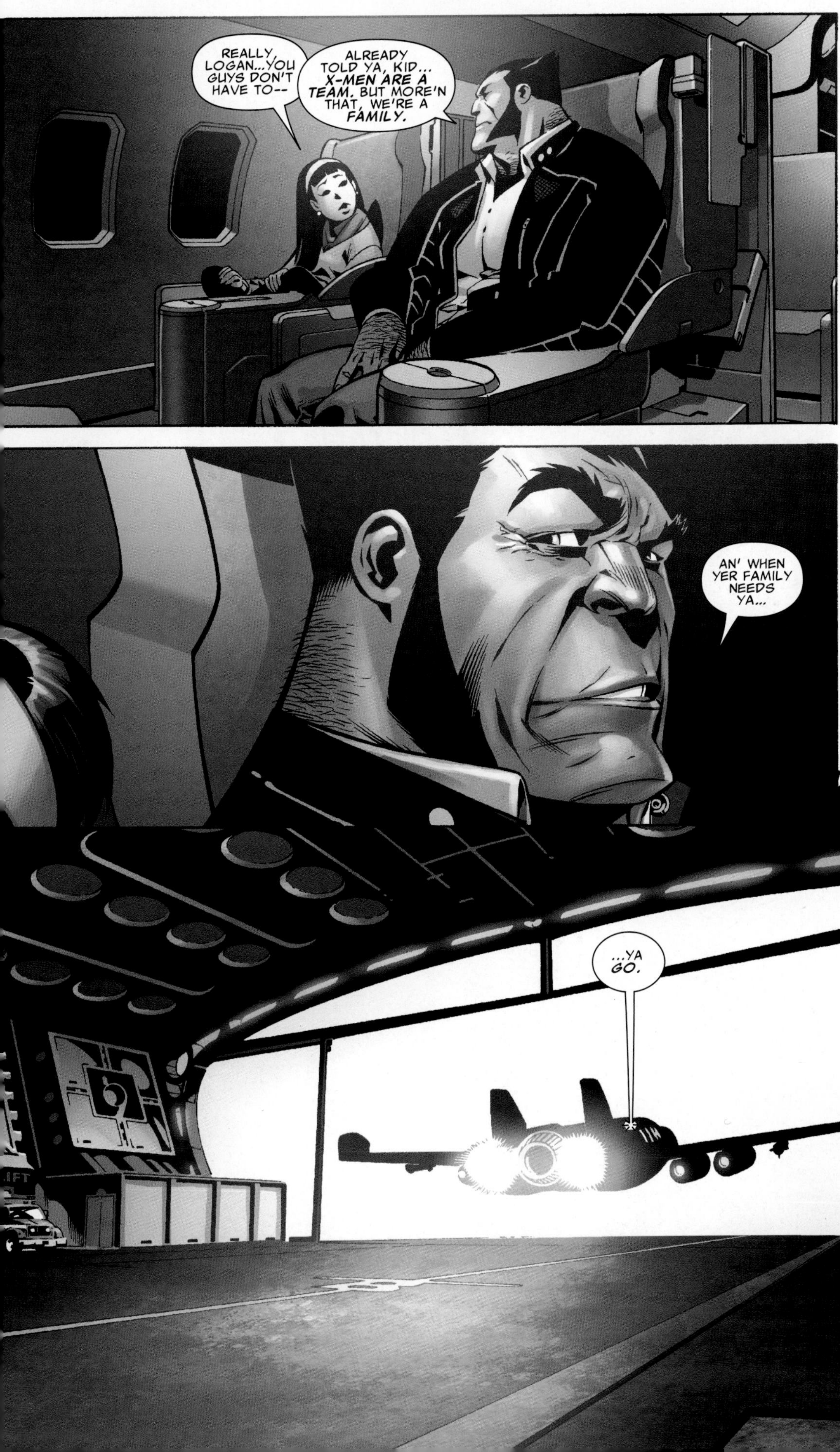
REALLY, LOGAN...YOU GUYS DON'T HAVE TO--
ALREADY TOLD YA, KID... X-MEN ARE A TEAM. BUT MORE'N THAT, WE'RE A FAMILY.
AN' WHEN YER FAMILY NEEDS YA...
...YA GO.

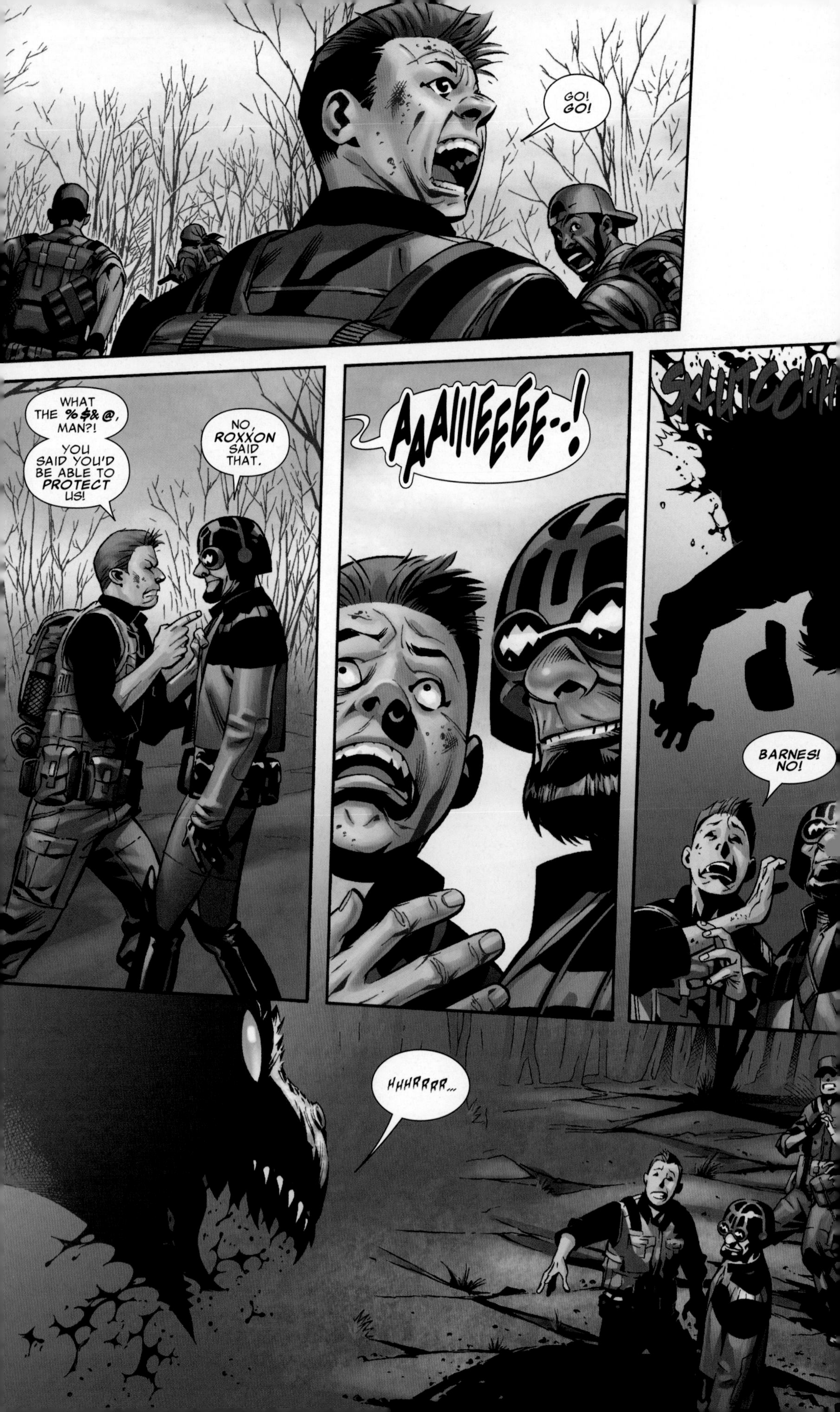
GO! GO!
WHAT THE %$&@, MAN?!
YOU SAID YOU'D BE ABLE TO PROTECT US!
NO, ROXXON SAID THAT.
AAAIIIEEEE--!
SKLITCCHH
BARNES! NO!
HHHRRRR...

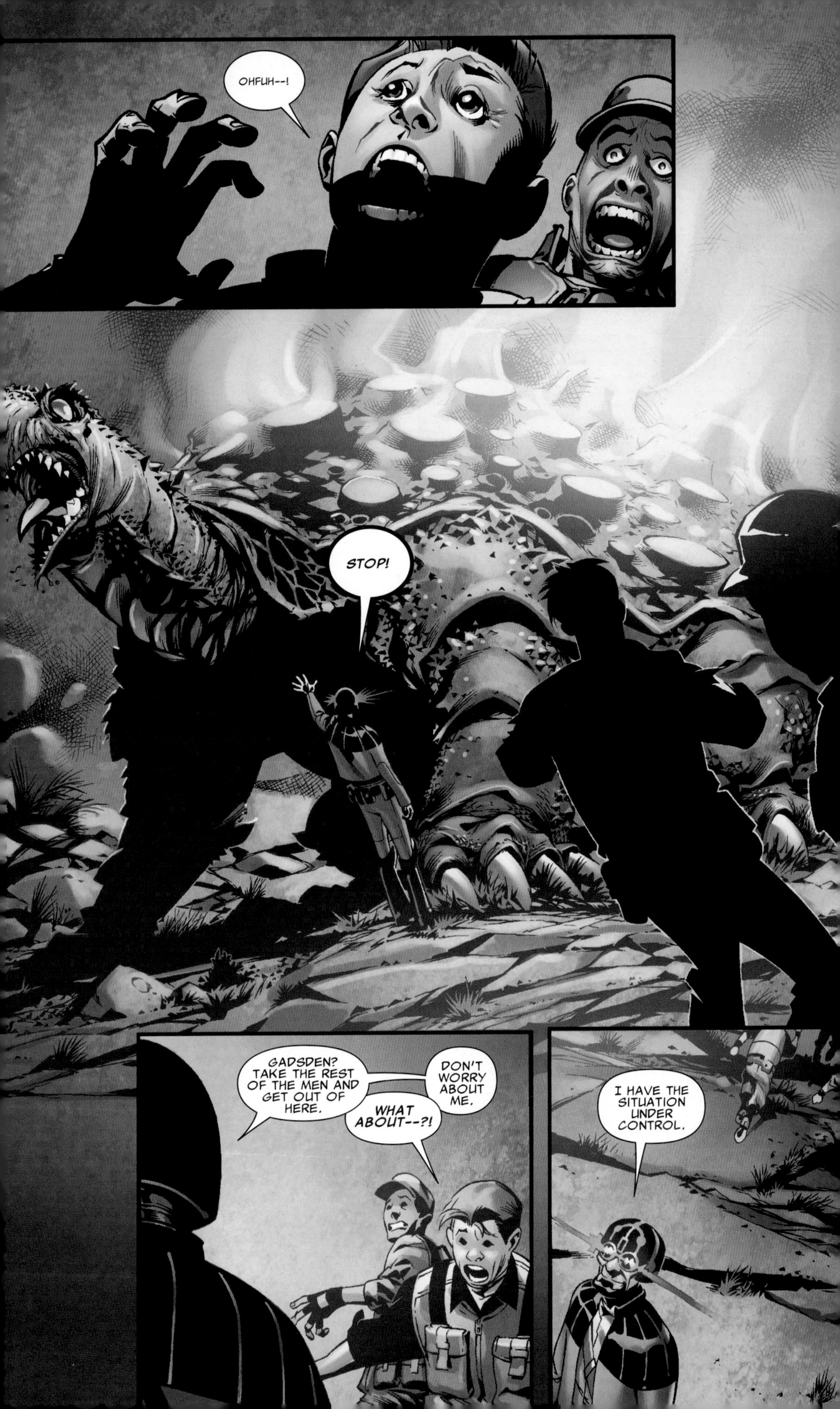
OHFUH--!
STOP!
GADSDEN? TAKE THE REST OF THE MEN AND GET OUT OF HERE.
DON'T WORRY ABOUT ME.
WHAT ABOUT--?!
I HAVE THE SITUATION UNDER CONTROL.

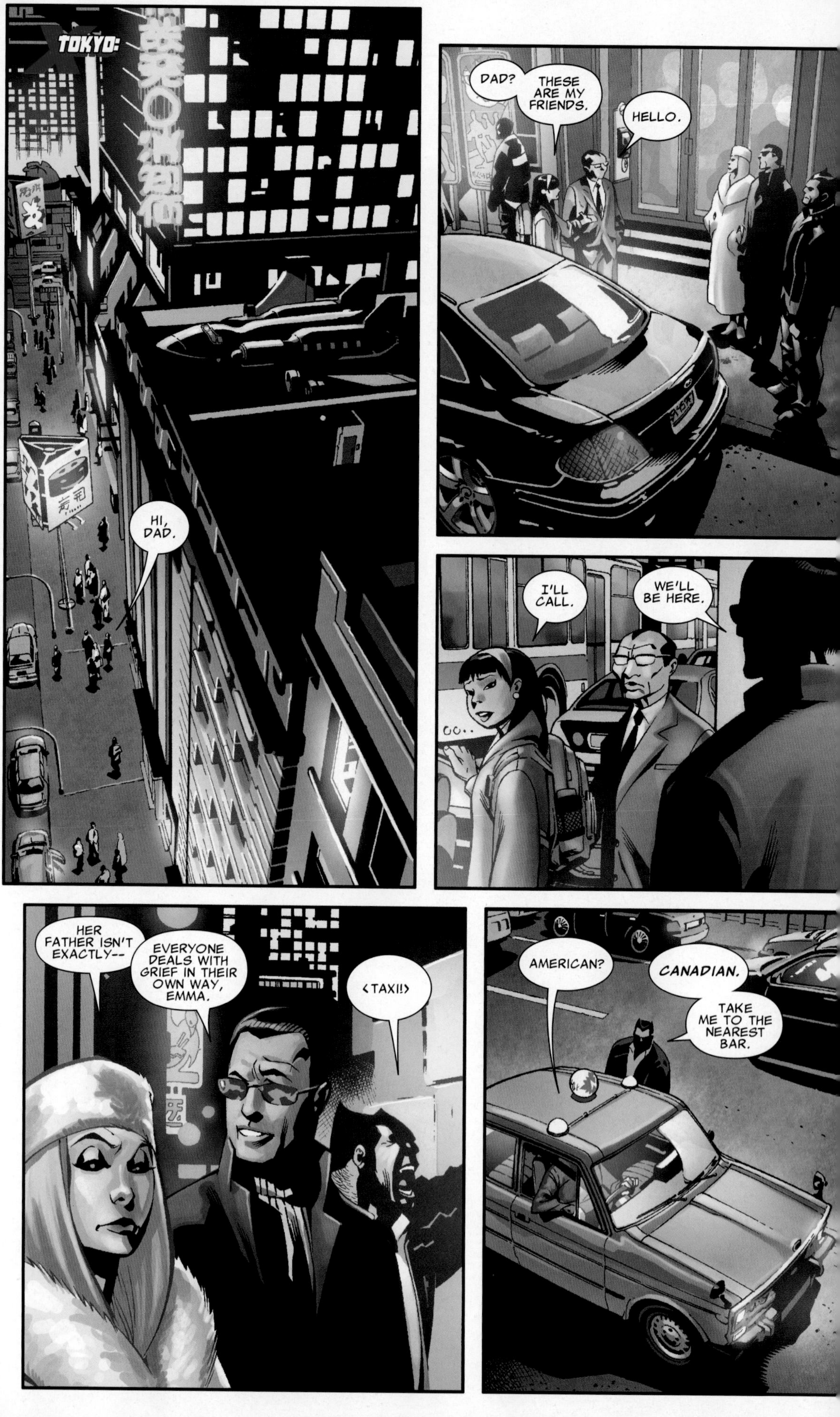
TOKYO:
HI, DAD.
DAD?
THESE ARE MY FRIENDS.
HELLO.
I'LL CALL.
WE'LL BE HERE.
HER FATHER ISN'T EXACTLY--
EVERYONE DEALS WITH GRIEF IN THEIR OWN WAY, EMMA.
‹TAXI!›
AMERICAN?
CANADIAN.
TAKE ME TO THE NEAREST BAR.

MENTALLO! COME IN!

WHERE ARE YOU?! WE MADE IT BACK TO THE BOAT!

CONGRATULATIONS.

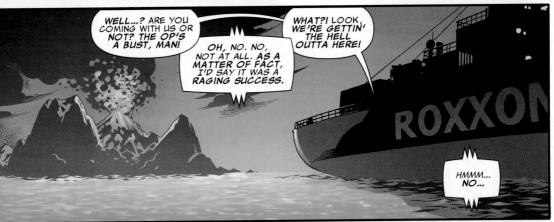

WELL...? ARE YOU COMING WITH US OR NOT? THE OP'S A BUST, MAN!

OH, NO. NO, NOT AT ALL. AS A MATTER OF FACT, I'D SAY IT WAS A RAGING SUCCESS.

WHAT?! LOOK, WE'RE GETTIN' THE HELL OUTTA HERE!

ROXXON

HMMM... NO...

...I'M AFRAID YOU'RE WRONG ABOUT THAT, AS WELL.

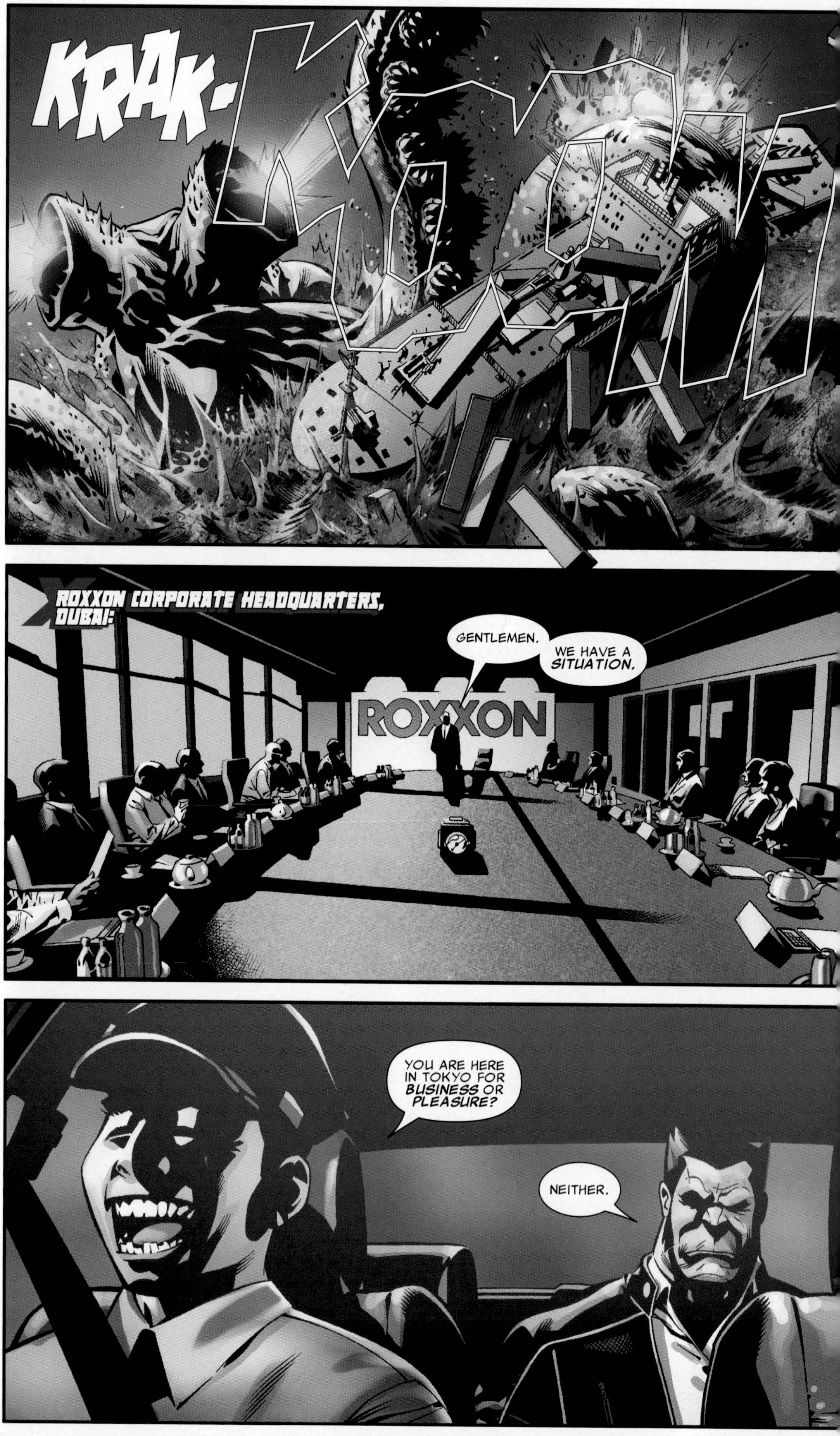
KRAK-KOOOM
ROXXON CORPORATE HEADQUARTERS, DUBAI:
ROXXON
GENTLEMEN.
WE HAVE A SITUATION.
YOU ARE HERE IN TOKYO FOR BUSINESS OR PLEASURE?
NEITHER.

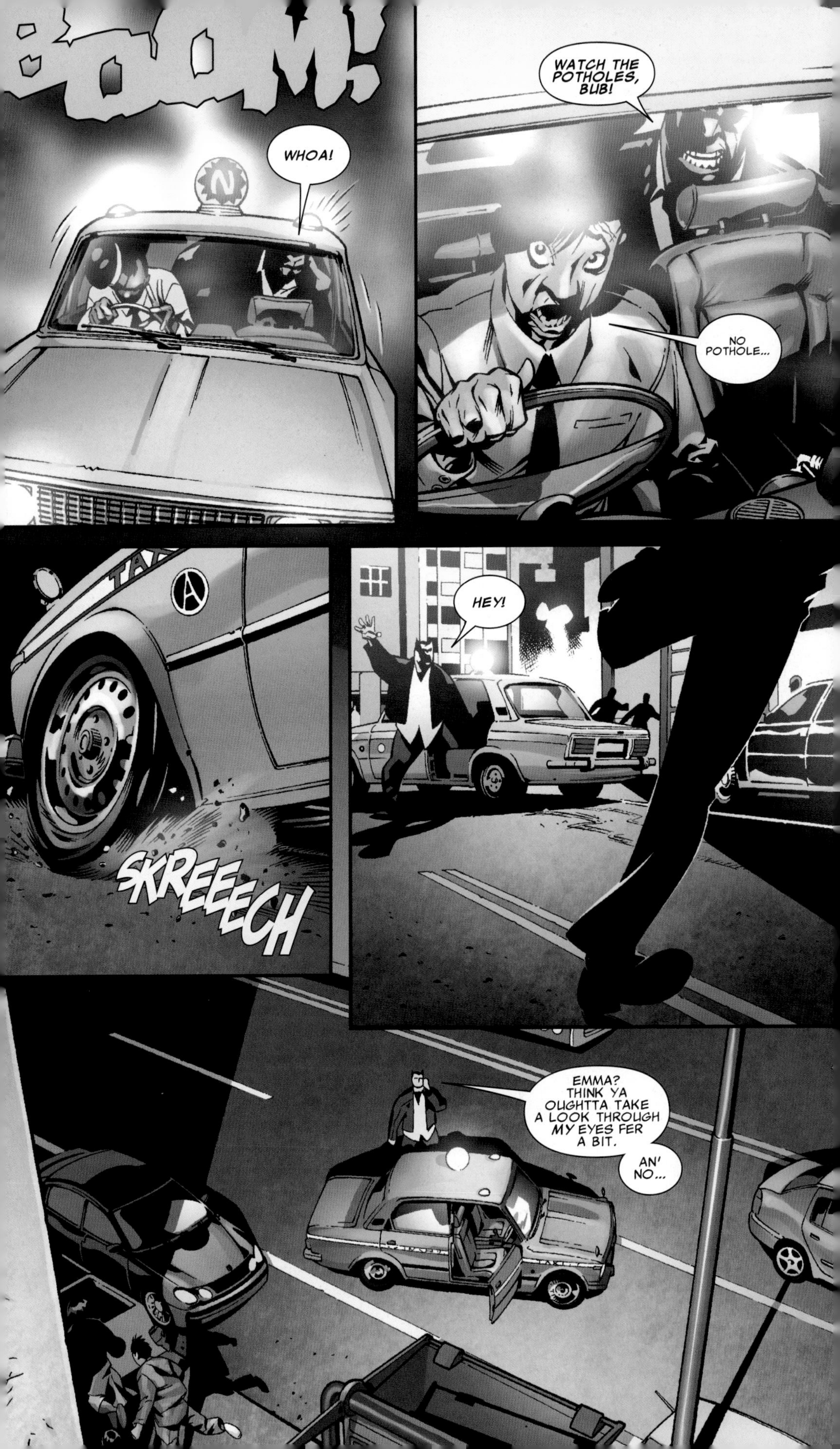
BOOM!
WHOA!
WATCH THE POTHOLES, BUB!
NO POTHOLE...
SKREEEECH
HEY!
EMMA? THINK YA OUGHTTA TAKE A LOOK THROUGH MY EYES FER A BIT.
AN' NO...

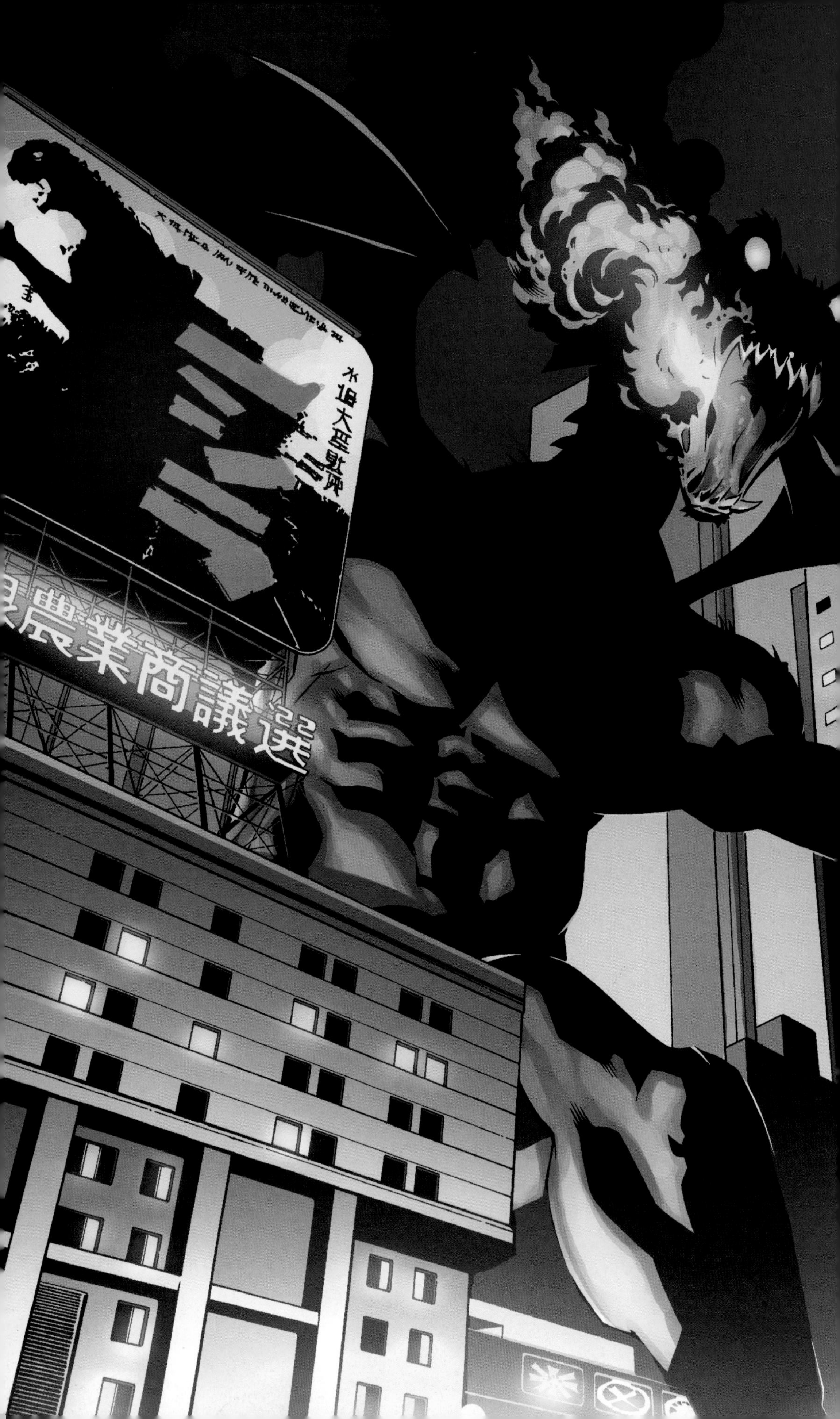
農業商議選

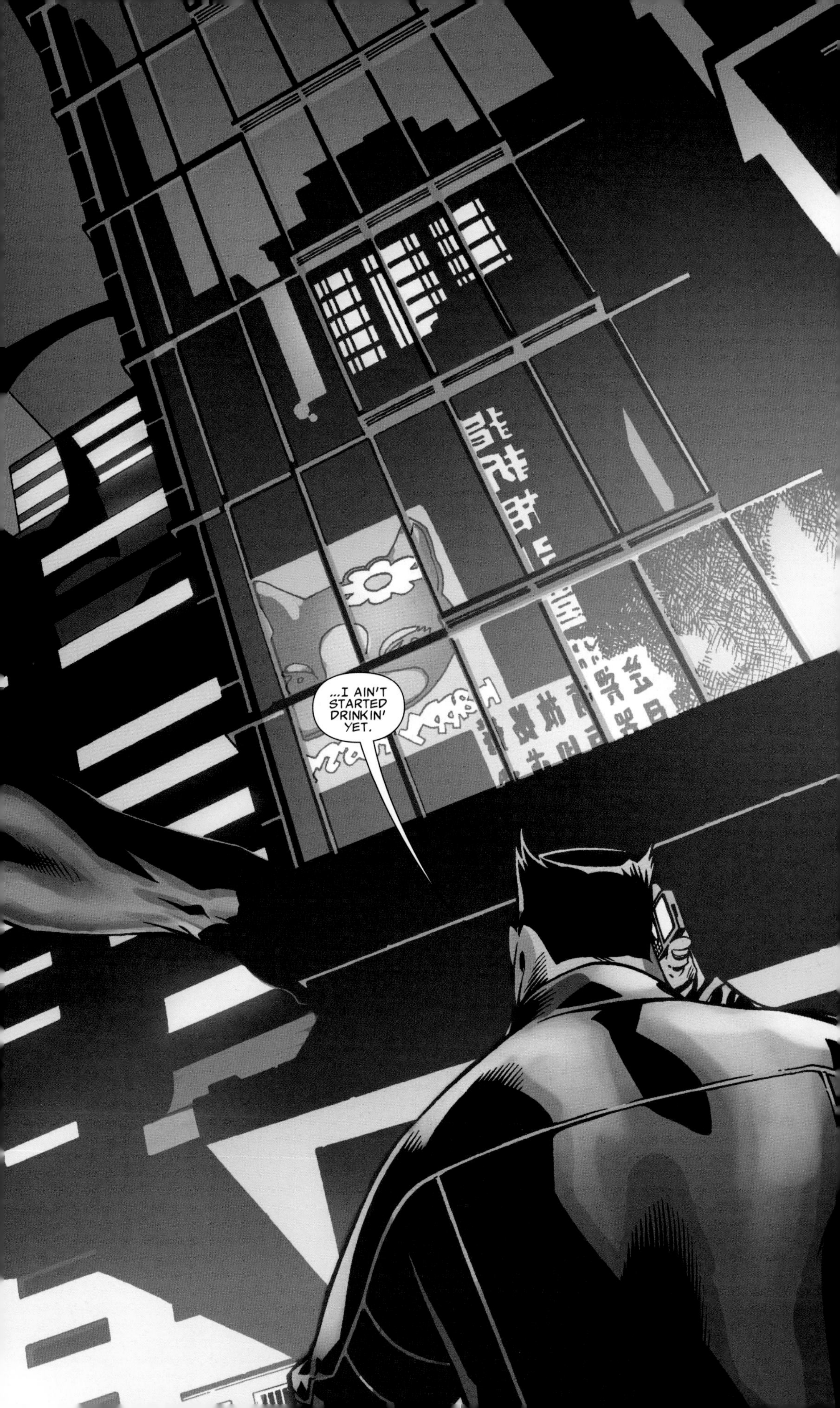
...I AIN'T STARTED DRINKIN' YET.

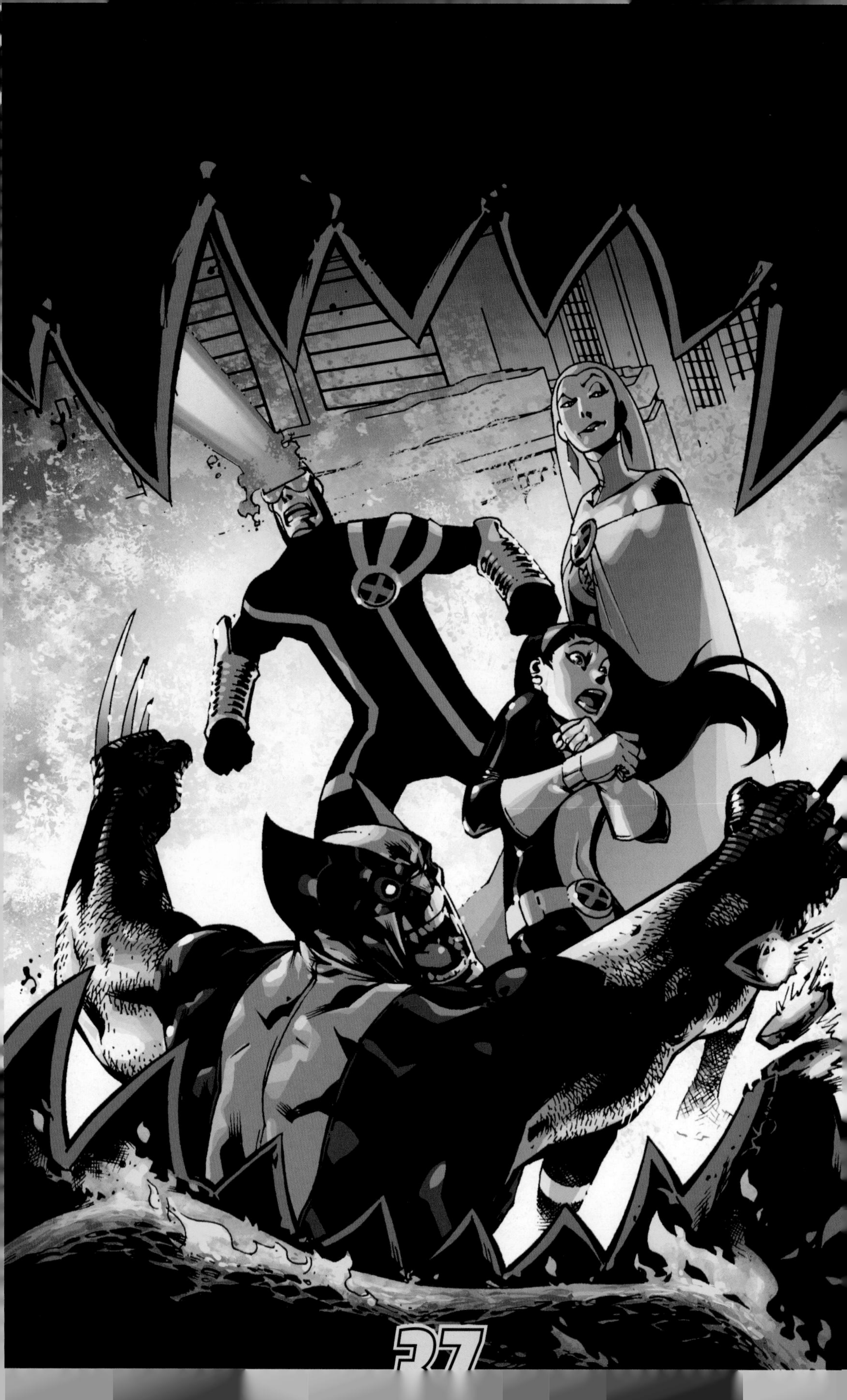
37

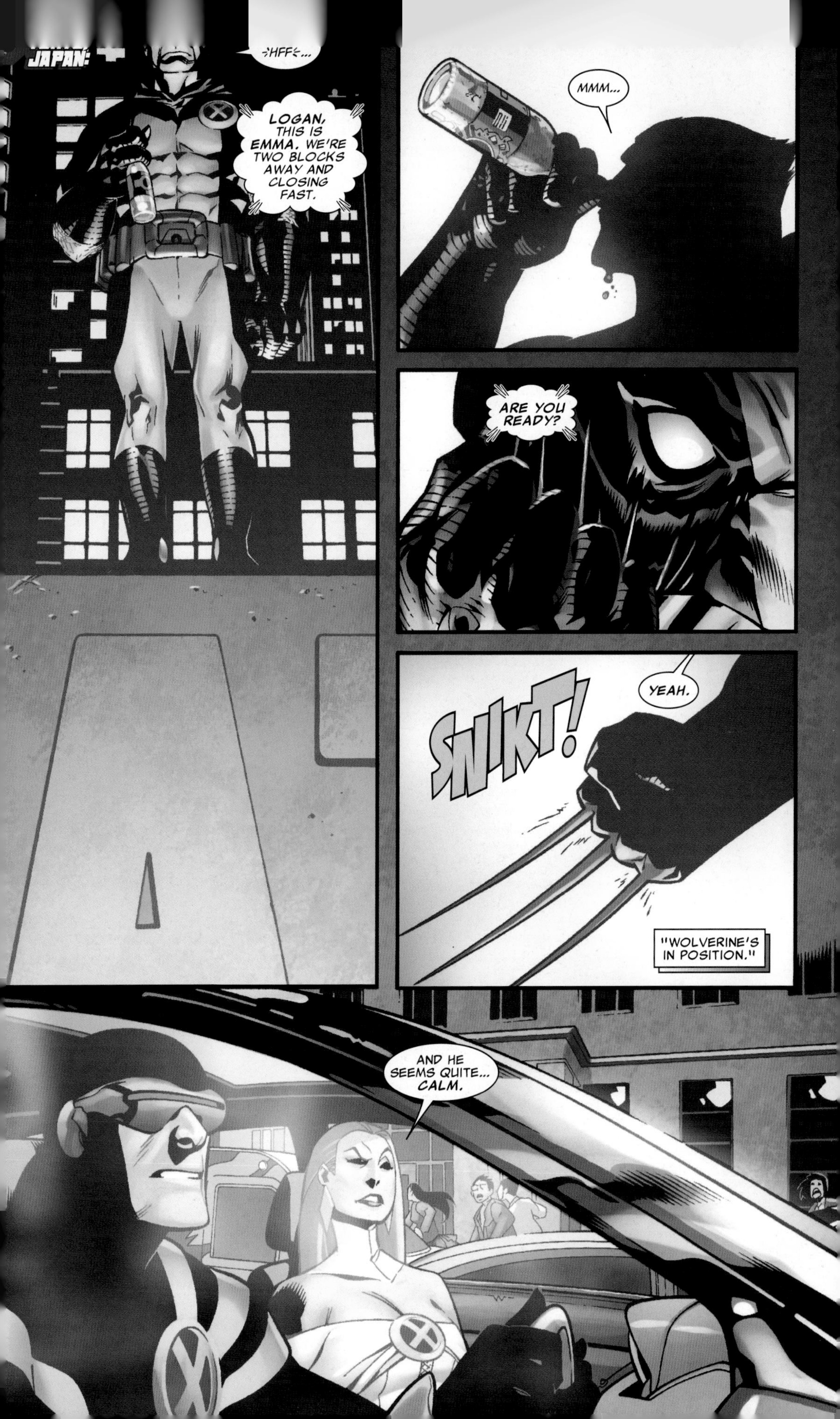
JAPAN:
HFF...
LOGAN, THIS IS EMMA. WE'RE TWO BLOCKS AWAY AND CLOSING FAST.
MMM...
ARE YOU READY?
YEAH.
SNIKT!
"WOLVERINE'S IN POSITION."
AND HE SEEMS QUITE... CALM.

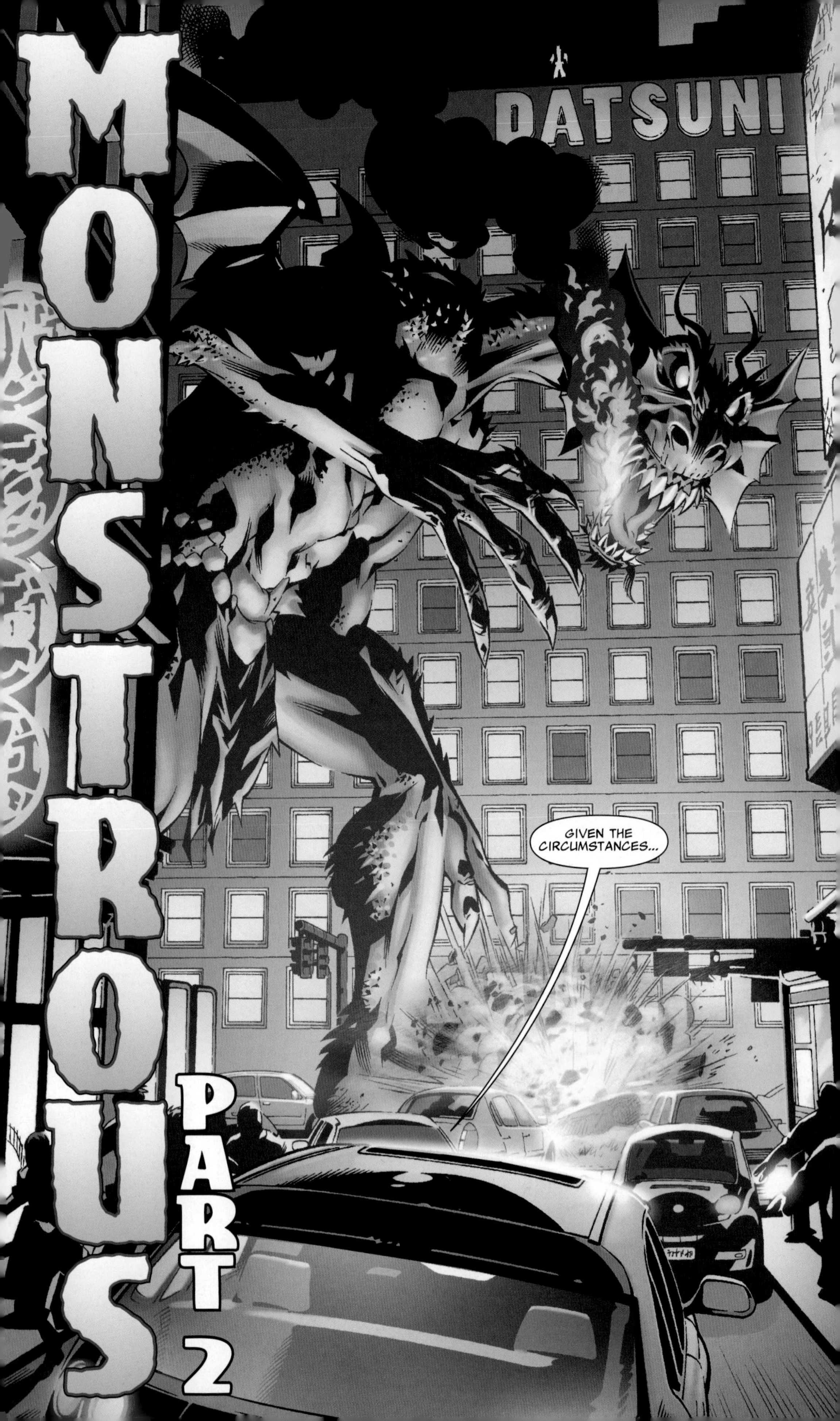
MONSTROUS
PART 2
DATSUNI
GIVEN THE CIRCUMSTANCES...

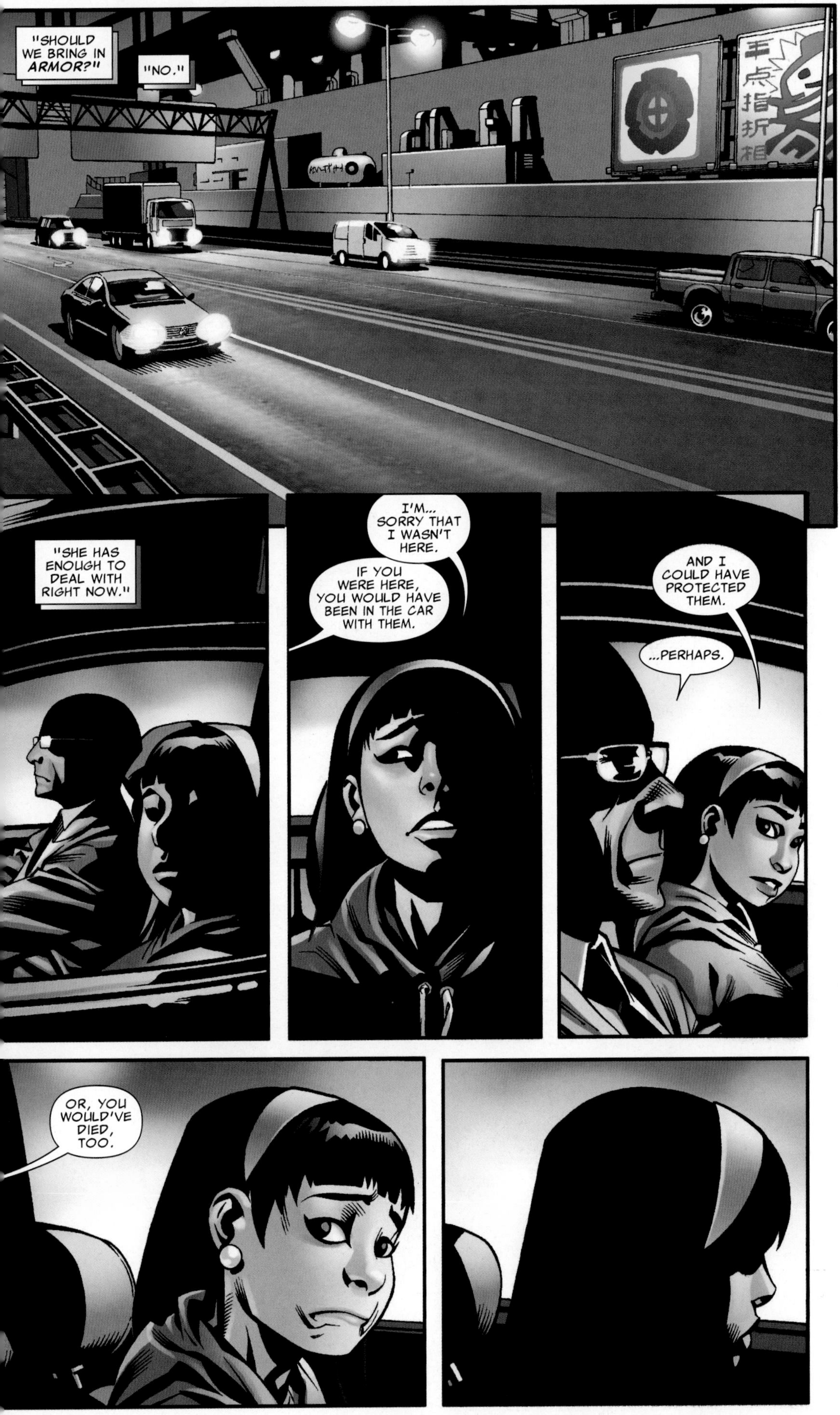

"SHOULD WE BRING IN *ARMOR?*"
"NO."
"SHE HAS ENOUGH TO DEAL WITH RIGHT NOW."
I'M... SORRY THAT I WASN'T HERE.
IF YOU WERE HERE, YOU WOULD HAVE BEEN IN THE CAR WITH THEM.
AND I COULD HAVE PROTECTED THEM.
...PERHAPS.
OR, YOU WOULD'VE DIED, TOO.

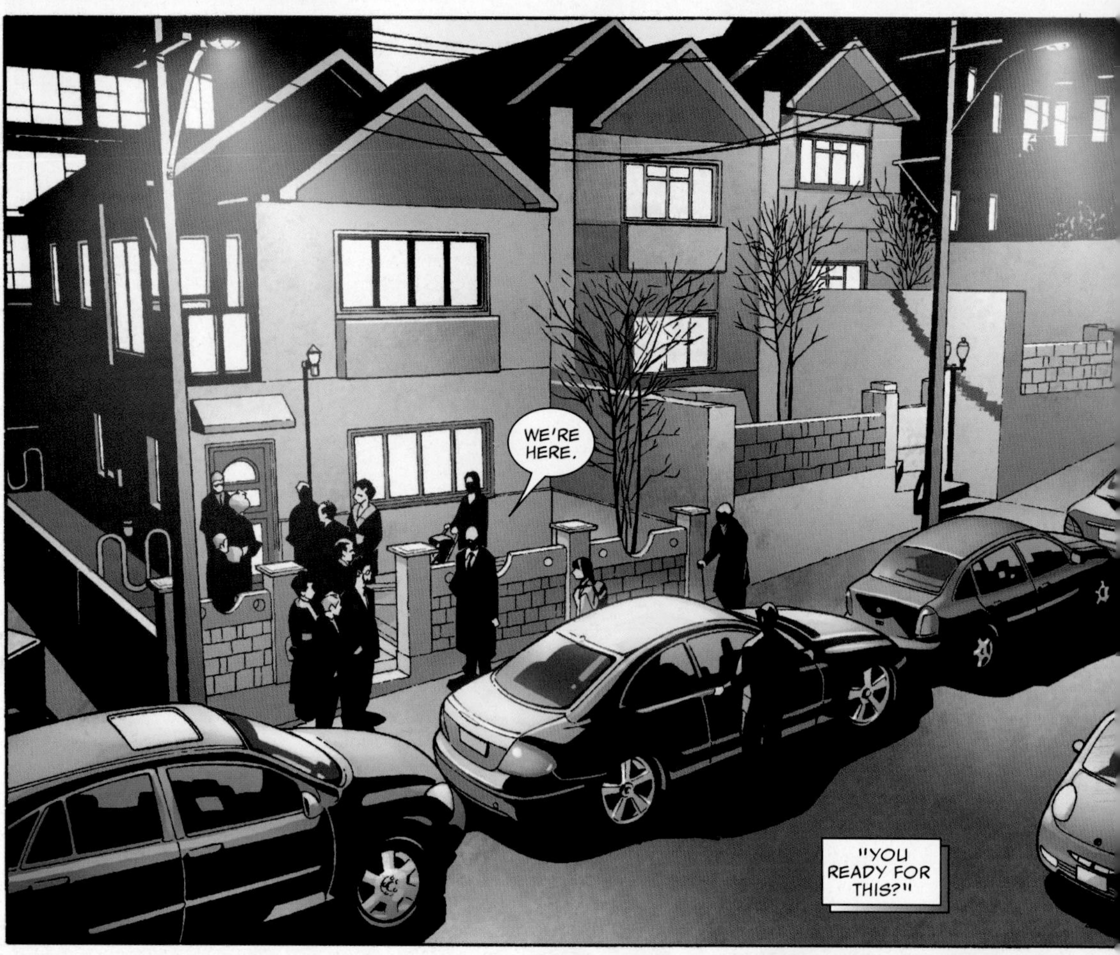
WE'RE HERE.
"YOU READY FOR THIS?"

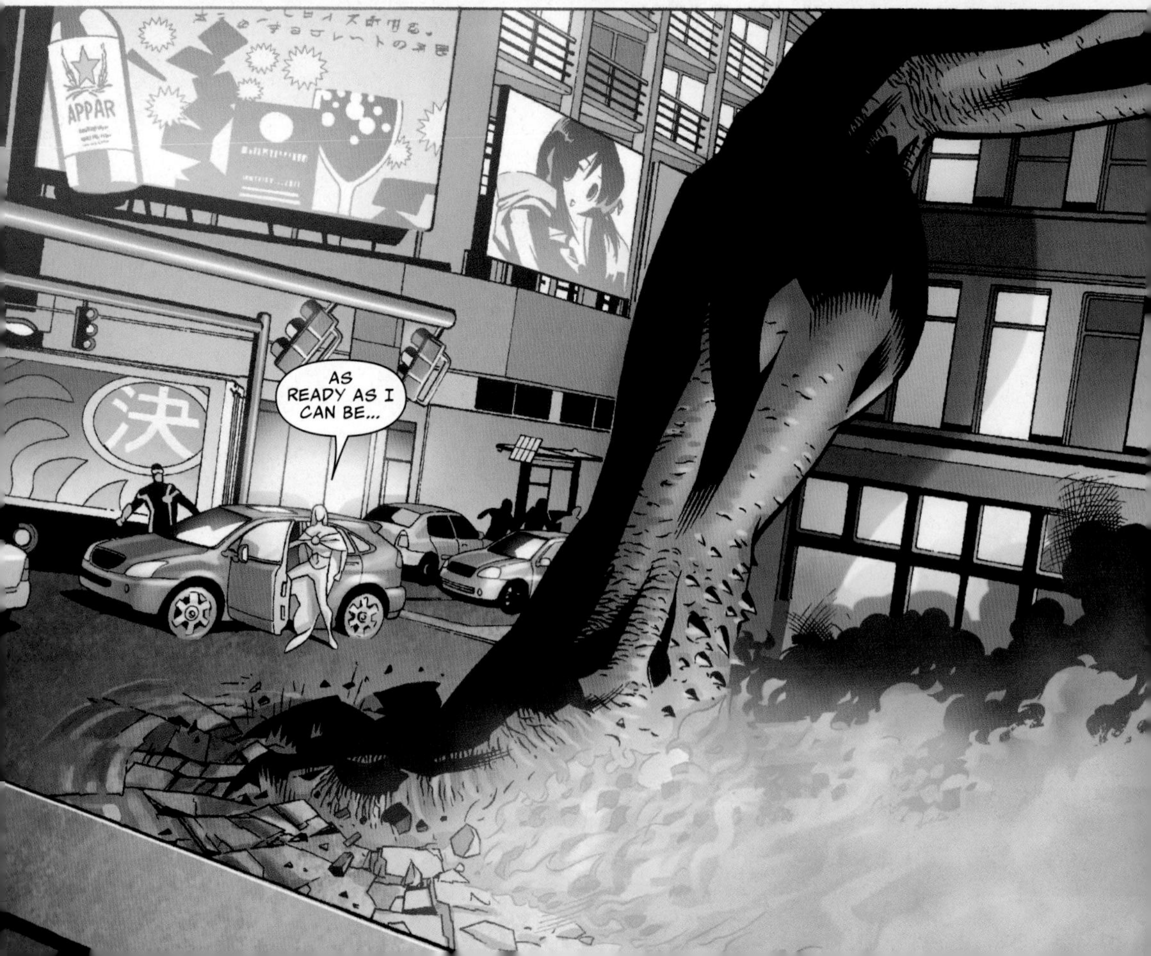
APPAR
決
AS READY AS I CAN BE...

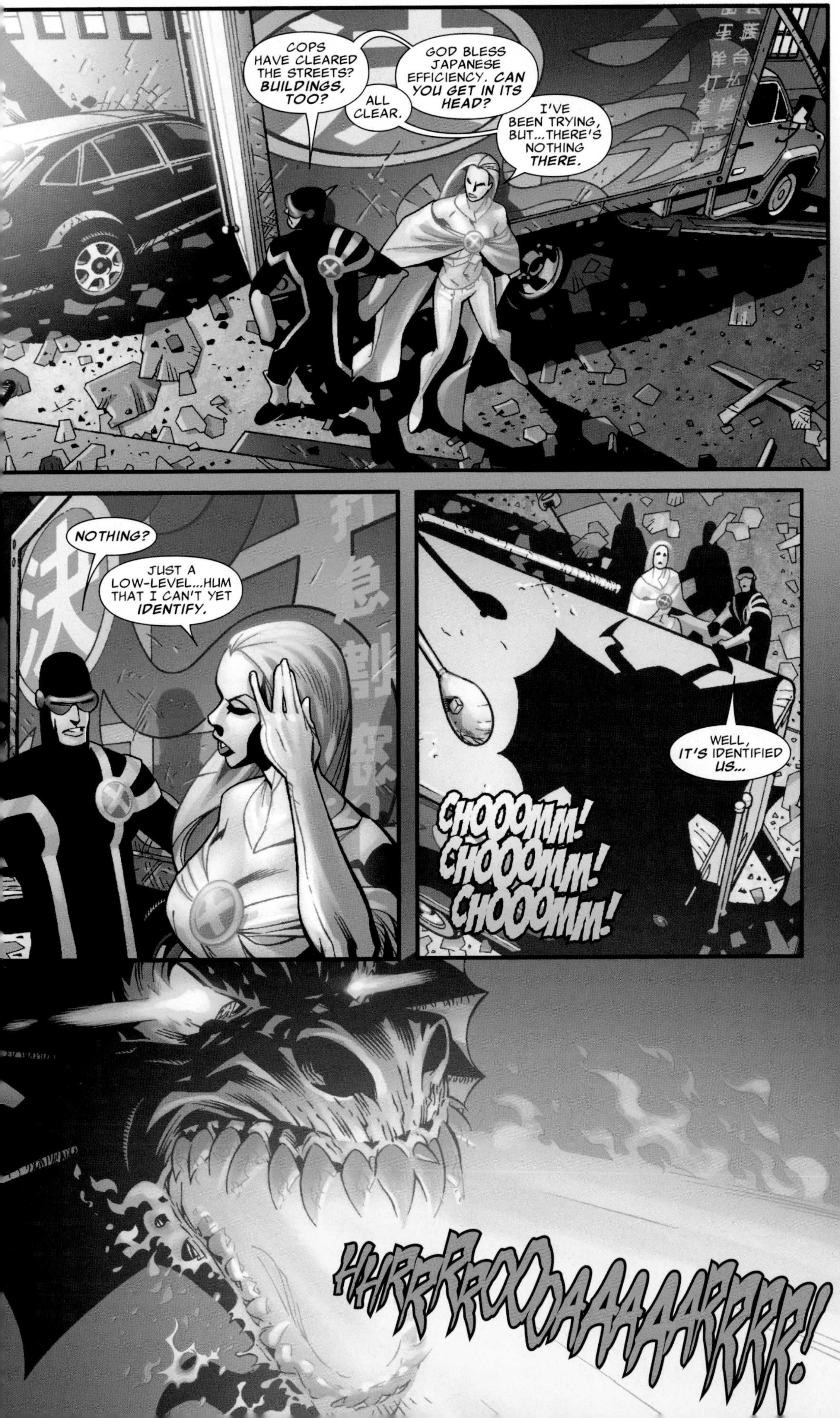

COPS HAVE CLEARED THE STREETS? BUILDINGS, TOO?
ALL CLEAR.
GOD BLESS JAPANESE EFFICIENCY. CAN YOU GET IN ITS HEAD?
I'VE BEEN TRYING, BUT...THERE'S NOTHING THERE.
NOTHING?
JUST A LOW-LEVEL...HUM THAT I CAN'T YET IDENTIFY.
WELL, IT'S IDENTIFIED US...
CHOOOMM! CHOOOMM! CHOOOMM!
HHRRRROOOAAAAARRRR!

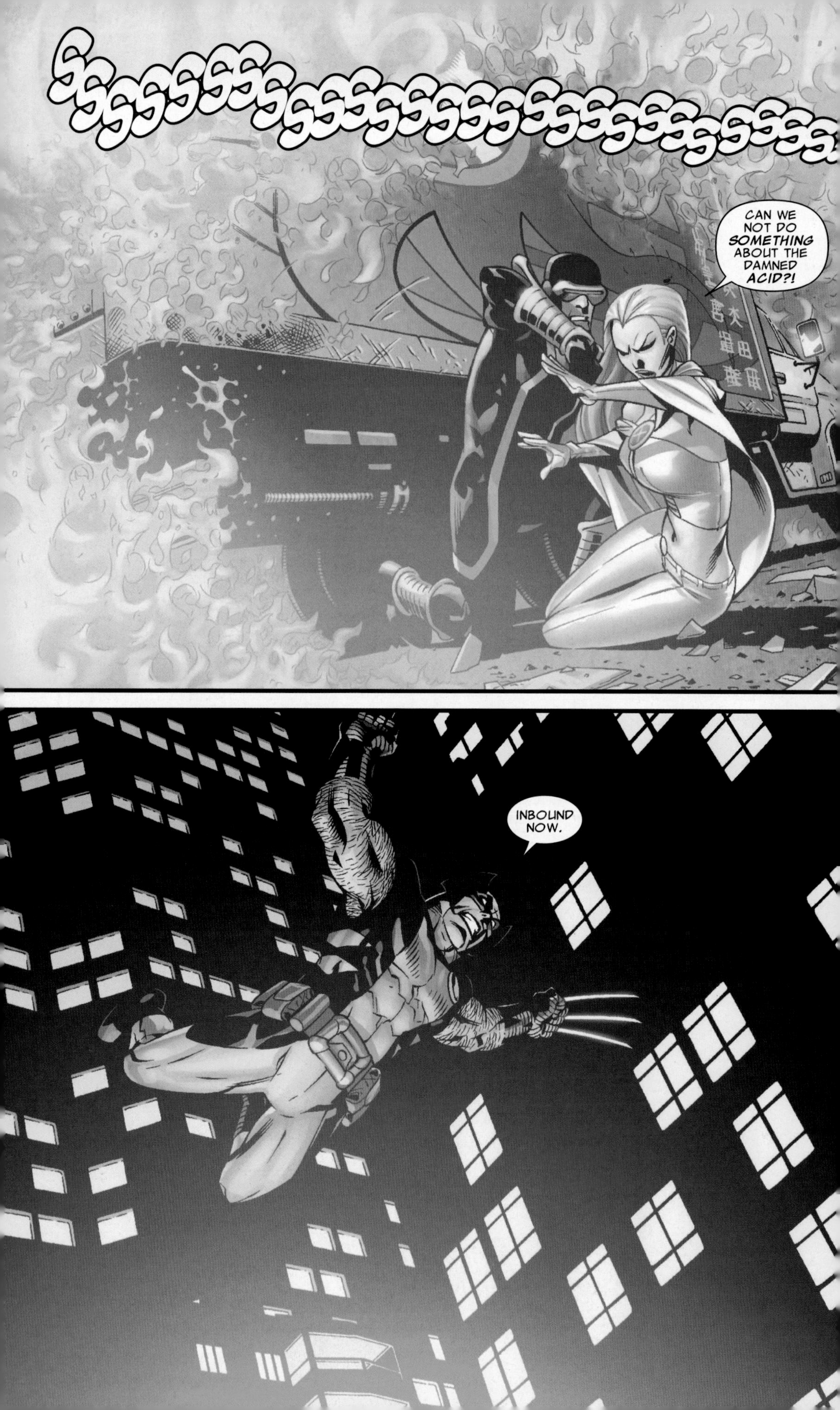
SSSSSSSSSSSSSSSSSSSSSSSSSSSSSS
CAN WE NOT DO SOMETHING ABOUT THE DAMNED ACID?!
INBOUND NOW.

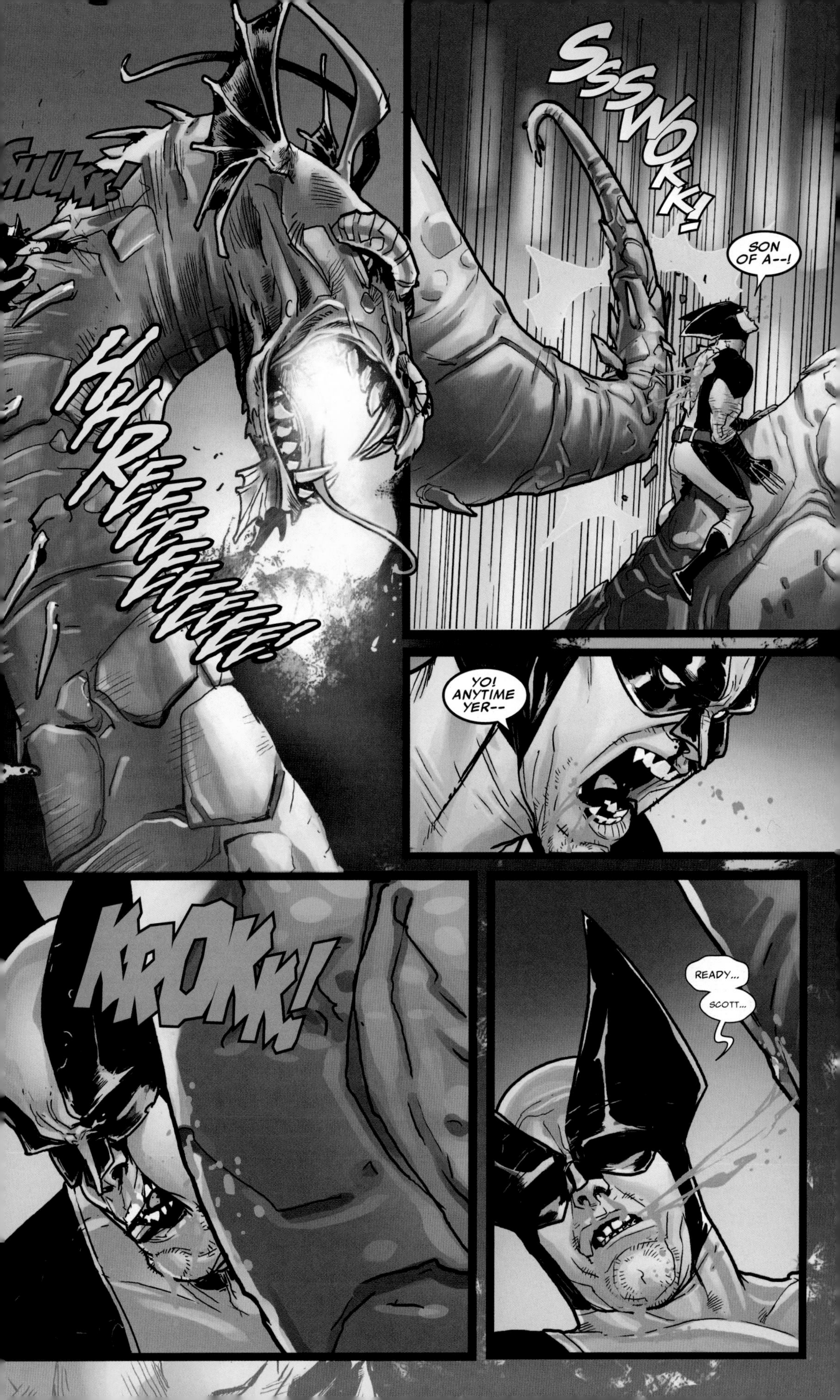

SHUNK!
HHREEEEEEEEEEEE!
SSSWOKK!
SON OF A--!
YO! ANYTIME YER--
KROKK!
READY...
SCOTT...

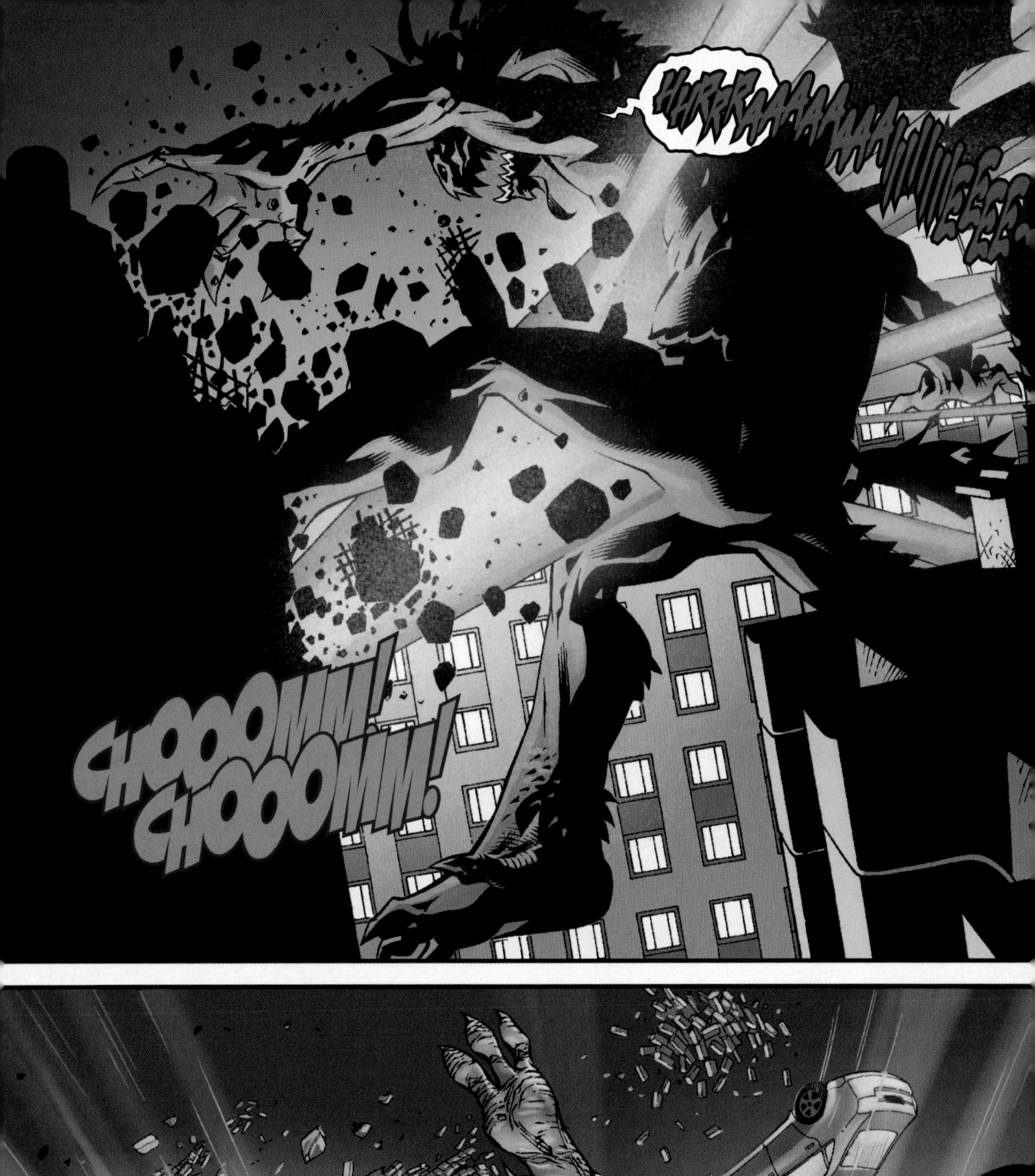
HURRRAAAAAAAIIIIIIEEEE...
CHOOOMM!
CHOOOMM!

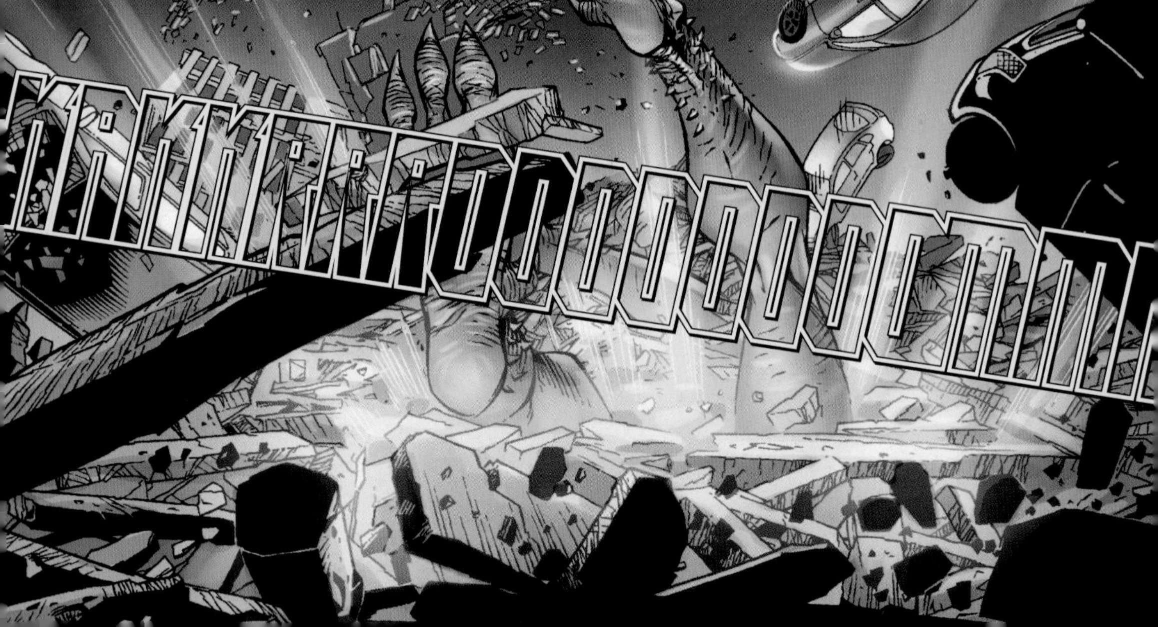

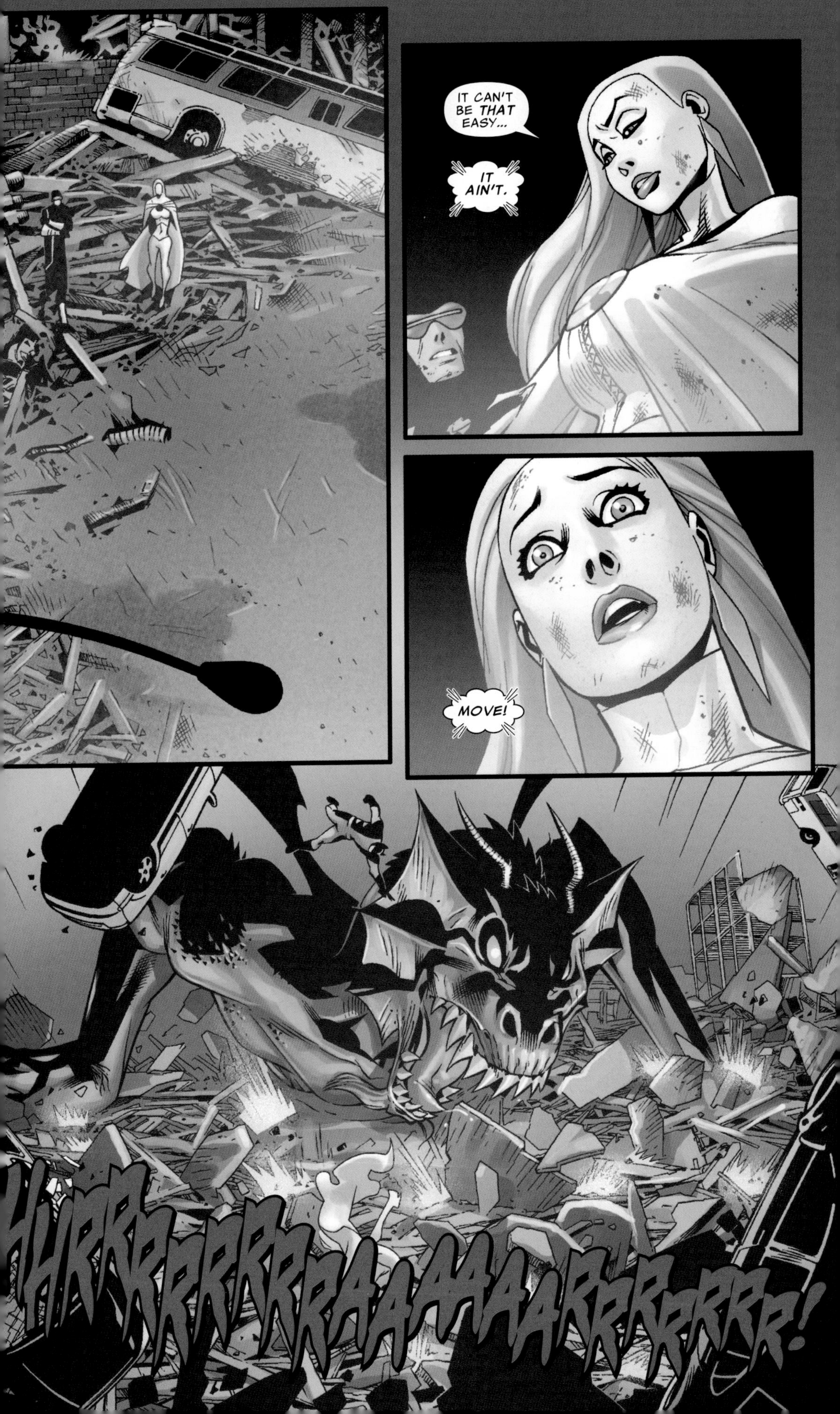
IT CAN'T BE THAT EASY...
IT AIN'T.
MOVE!
HURRRRRRRRAAAAAARRRRRRR!

OH, SH--!

WHERE'S BREWER?!

WHERE THE HELL IS OUR SHIP?!

STILL NO RADIO CONTACT WITH THE CREW, DIRECTOR BREWER--

I DON'T CARE ABOUT THE CREW! I CARE ABOUT THE DAMN SHIP!

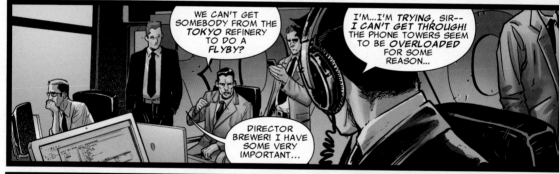

WE CAN'T GET SOMEBODY FROM THE TOKYO REFINERY TO DO A FLYBY?

I'M...I'M TRYING, SIR-- I CAN'T GET THROUGH! THE PHONE TOWERS SEEM TO BE OVERLOADED FOR SOME REASON...

DIRECTOR BREWER! I HAVE SOME VERY IMPORTANT...

THAT YOU NEED TO...

WHO THE HELL ARE YOU?

I'M...I'M DUNCAN CLARK, SIR. I'M A JUNIOR EXECUTIVE DOWN IN--

I HAVE RADIO CONTACT WITH THE CREW!

HELLO, BREWER...

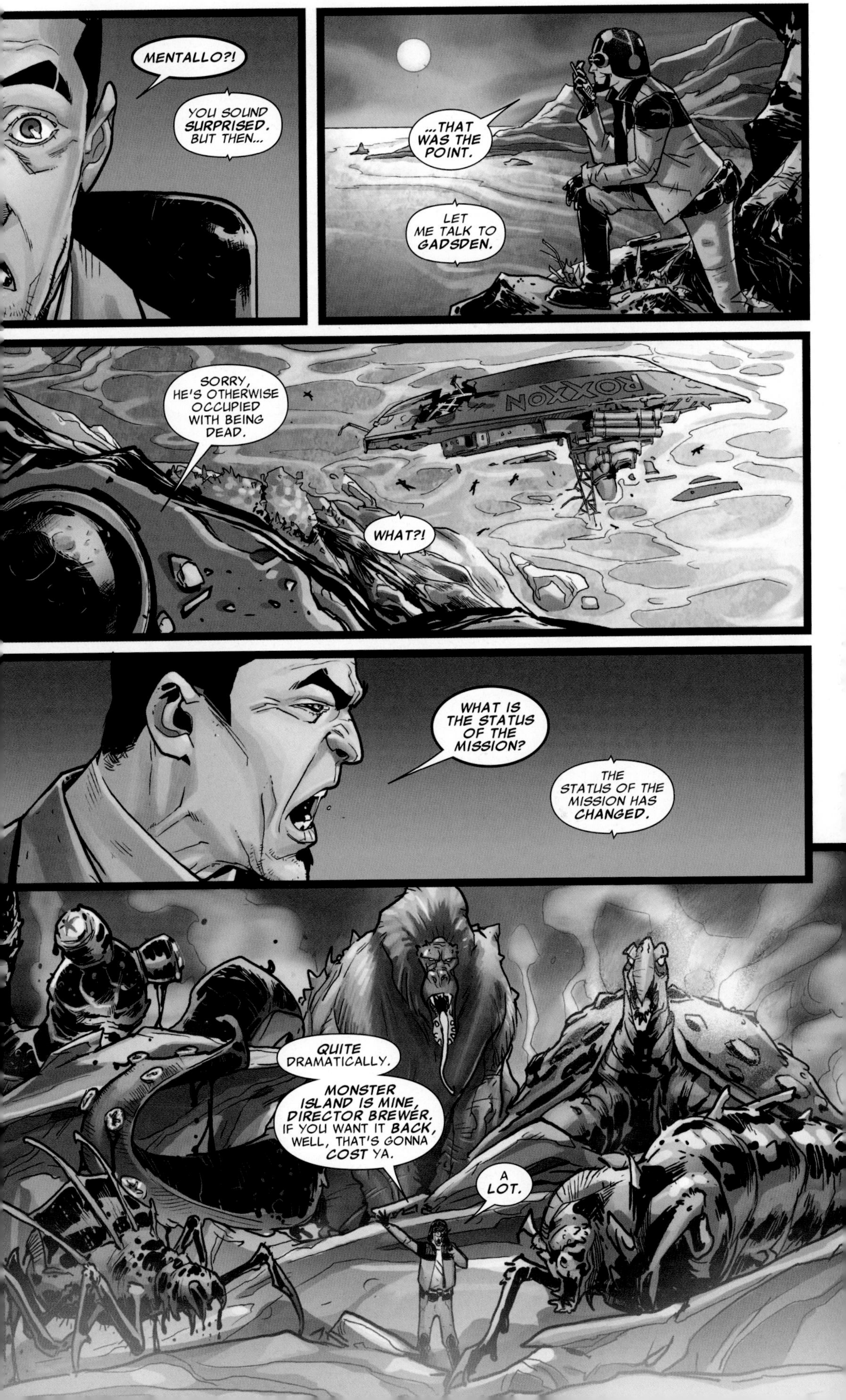
MENTALLO?!
YOU SOUND SURPRISED. BUT THEN...
...THAT WAS THE POINT.
LET ME TALK TO GADSDEN.
SORRY, HE'S OTHERWISE OCCUPIED WITH BEING DEAD.
ROXXON
WHAT?!
WHAT IS THE STATUS OF THE MISSION?
THE STATUS OF THE MISSION HAS CHANGED.
QUITE DRAMATICALLY.
MONSTER ISLAND IS MINE, DIRECTOR BREWER. IF YOU WANT IT BACK, WELL, THAT'S GONNA COST YA.
A LOT.

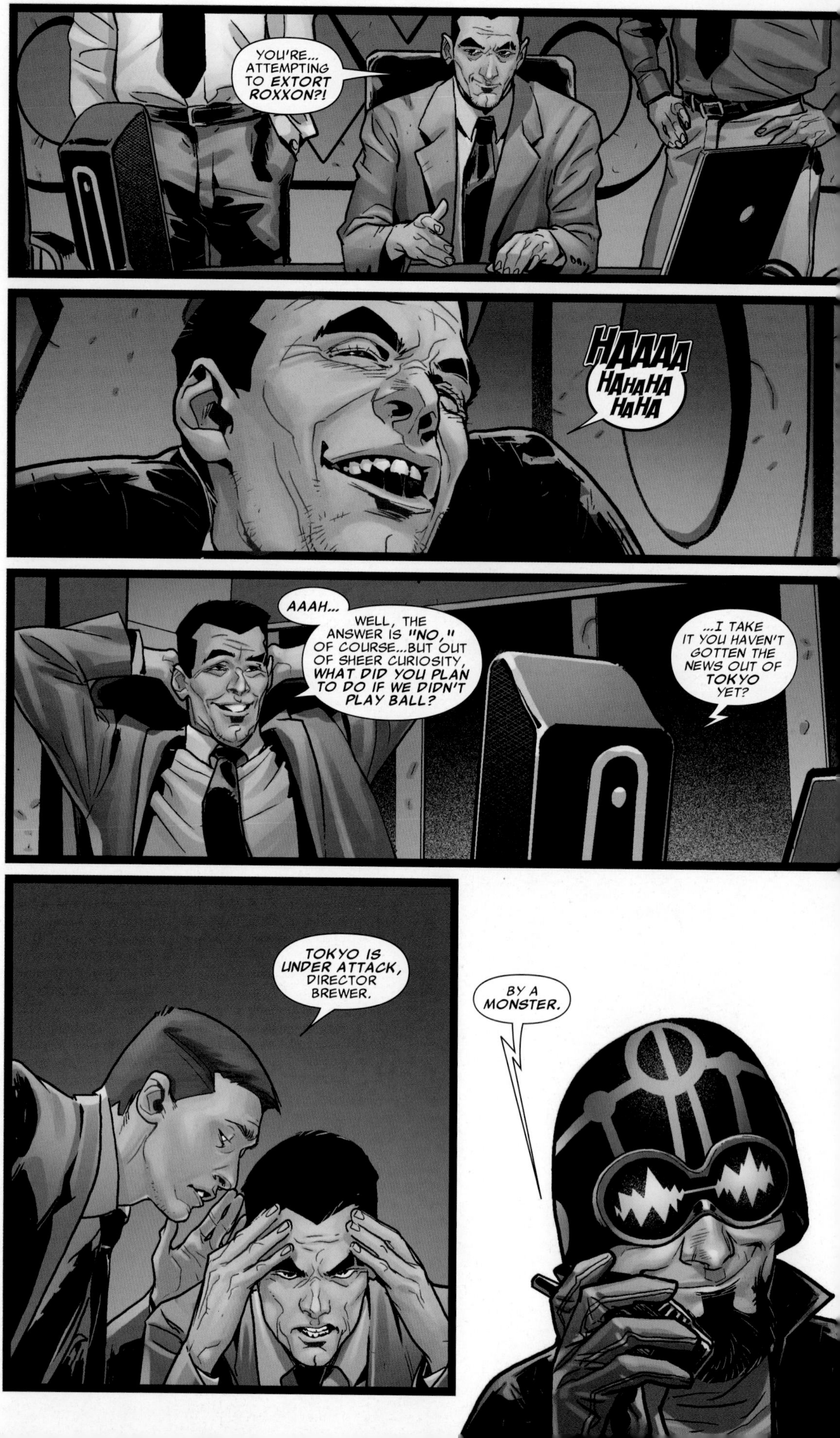
YOU'RE... ATTEMPTING TO EXTORT ROXXON?!
HAAAA HAHAHA HAHA
AAAH...
WELL, THE ANSWER IS "NO," OF COURSE...BUT OUT OF SHEER CURIOSITY, WHAT DID YOU PLAN TO DO IF WE DIDN'T PLAY BALL?
...I TAKE IT YOU HAVEN'T GOTTEN THE NEWS OUT OF TOKYO YET?
TOKYO IS UNDER ATTACK, DIRECTOR BREWER.
BY A MONSTER.

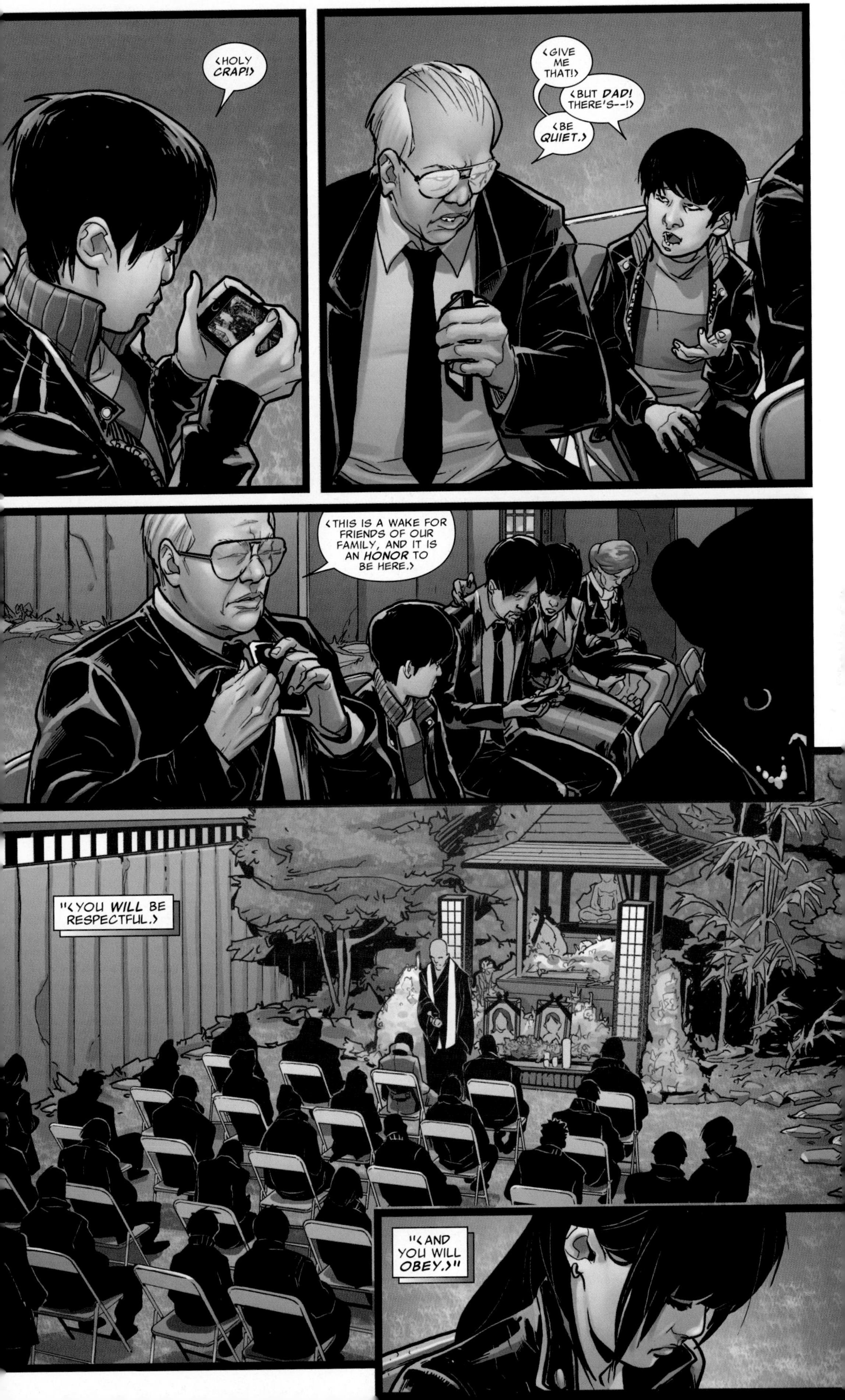
‹HOLY CRAP!›
‹GIVE ME THAT!›
‹BUT DAD! THERE'S--!›
‹BE QUIET.›
‹THIS IS A WAKE FOR FRIENDS OF OUR FAMILY, AND IT IS AN HONOR TO BE HERE.›
"‹YOU WILL BE RESPECTFUL.›
"‹AND YOU WILL OBEY.›"

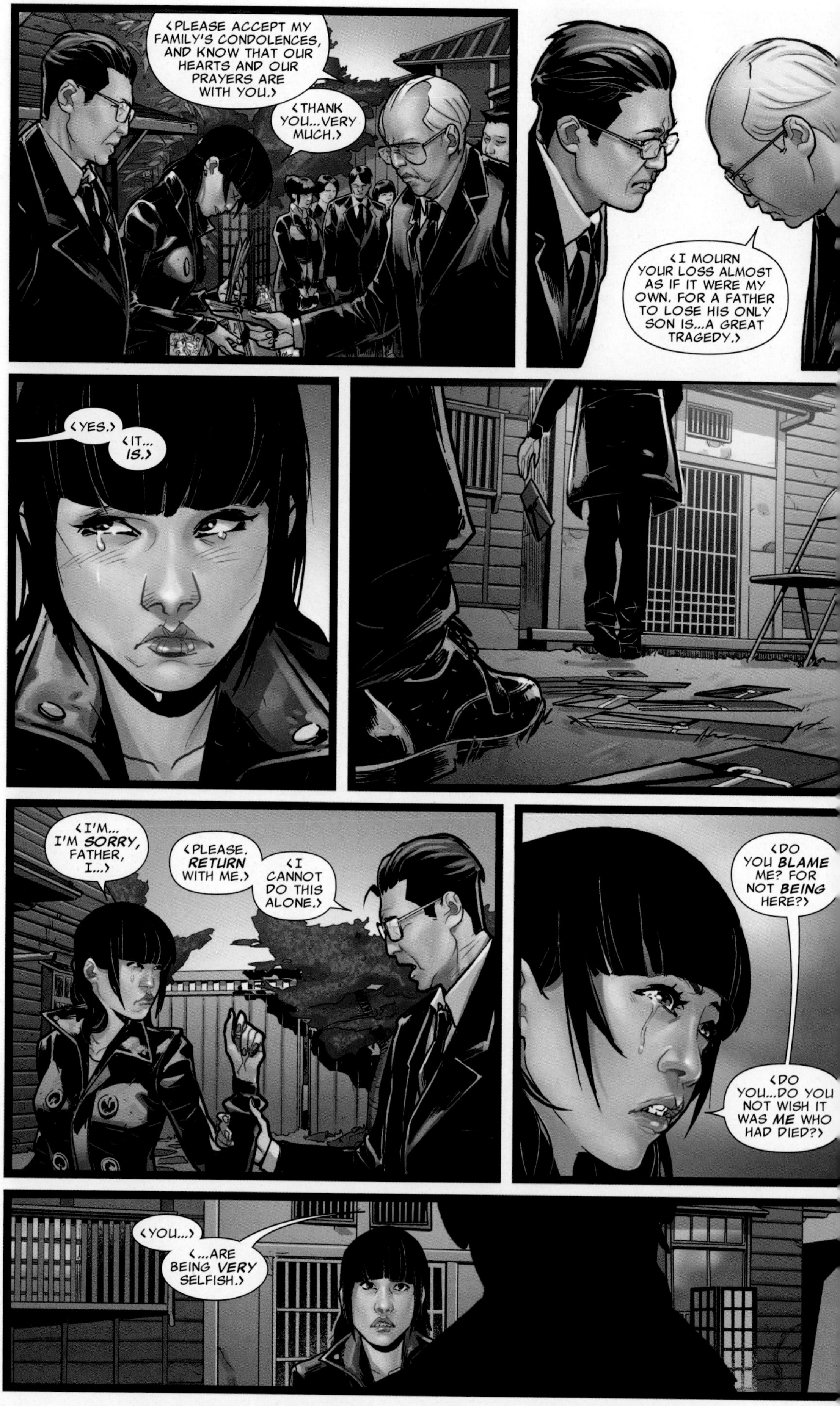
‹PLEASE ACCEPT MY FAMILY'S CONDOLENCES, AND KNOW THAT OUR HEARTS AND OUR PRAYERS ARE WITH YOU.›
‹THANK YOU...VERY MUCH.›
‹I MOURN YOUR LOSS ALMOST AS IF IT WERE MY OWN. FOR A FATHER TO LOSE HIS ONLY SON IS...A GREAT TRAGEDY.›
‹YES.›
‹IT... IS.›
‹I'M... I'M SORRY, FATHER, I...›
‹PLEASE. RETURN WITH ME.›
‹I CANNOT DO THIS ALONE.›
‹DO YOU BLAME ME? FOR NOT BEING HERE?›
‹DO YOU...DO YOU NOT WISH IT WAS ME WHO HAD DIED?›
‹YOU...›
‹...ARE BEING VERY SELFISH.›

÷GASP!÷

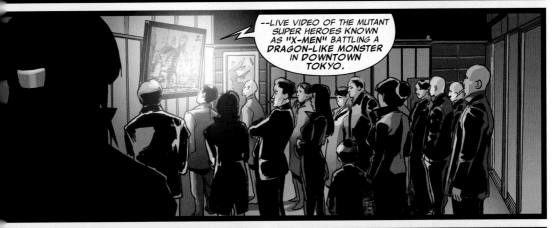

--LIVE VIDEO OF THE MUTANT SUPER HEROES KNOWN AS "X-MEN" BATTLING A DRAGON-LIKE MONSTER IN DOWNTOWN TOKYO.

HISAKO...?

‹NOW IS THE TIME TO STAND WITH YOUR FAMILY.›

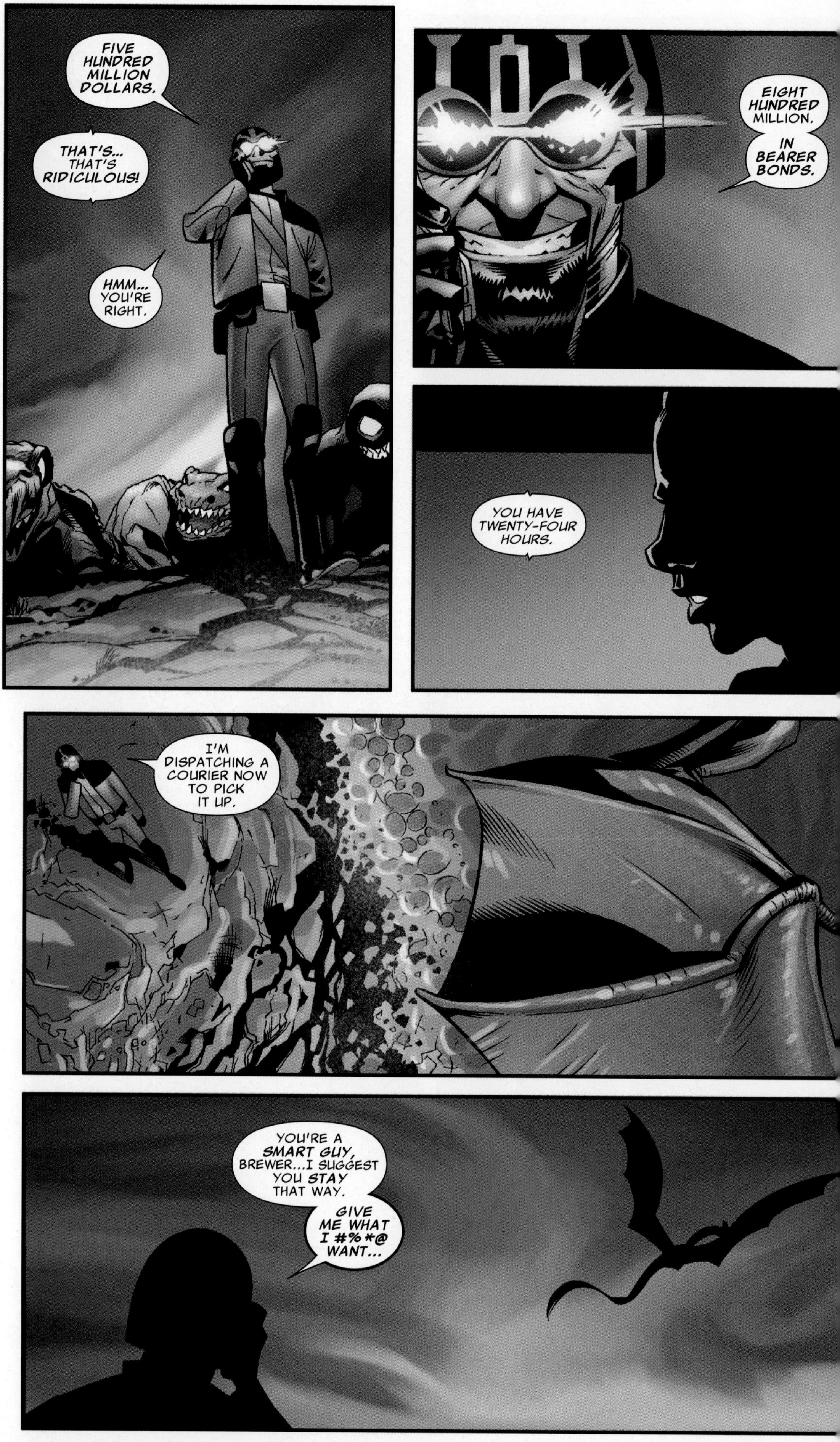
FIVE HUNDRED MILLION DOLLARS.
THAT'S... THAT'S RIDICULOUS!
HMM... YOU'RE RIGHT.
EIGHT HUNDRED MILLION.
IN BEARER BONDS.
YOU HAVE TWENTY-FOUR HOURS.
I'M DISPATCHING A COURIER NOW TO PICK IT UP.
YOU'RE A SMART GUY, BREWER...I SUGGEST YOU STAY THAT WAY.
GIVE ME WHAT I #%*@ WANT...

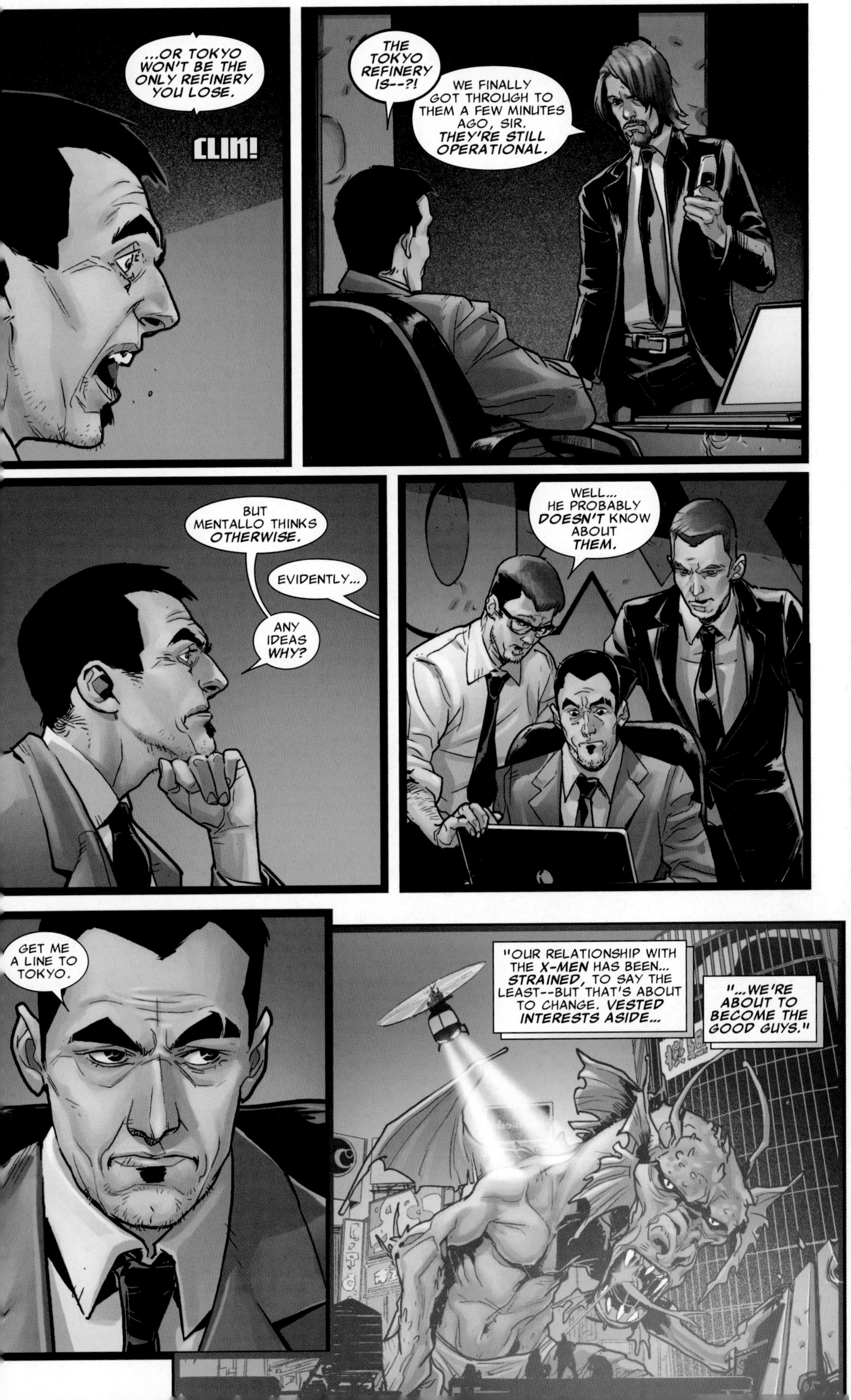

...OR TOKYO WON'T BE THE ONLY REFINERY YOU LOSE.
CLIK!
THE TOKYO REFINERY IS--?!
WE FINALLY GOT THROUGH TO THEM A FEW MINUTES AGO, SIR. THEY'RE STILL OPERATIONAL.
BUT MENTALLO THINKS OTHERWISE.
EVIDENTLY...
ANY IDEAS WHY?
WELL... HE PROBABLY DOESN'T KNOW ABOUT THEM.
GET ME A LINE TO TOKYO.
"OUR RELATIONSHIP WITH THE X-MEN HAS BEEN... STRAINED, TO SAY THE LEAST--BUT THAT'S ABOUT TO CHANGE. VESTED INTERESTS ASIDE...
"...WE'RE ABOUT TO BECOME THE GOOD GUYS."

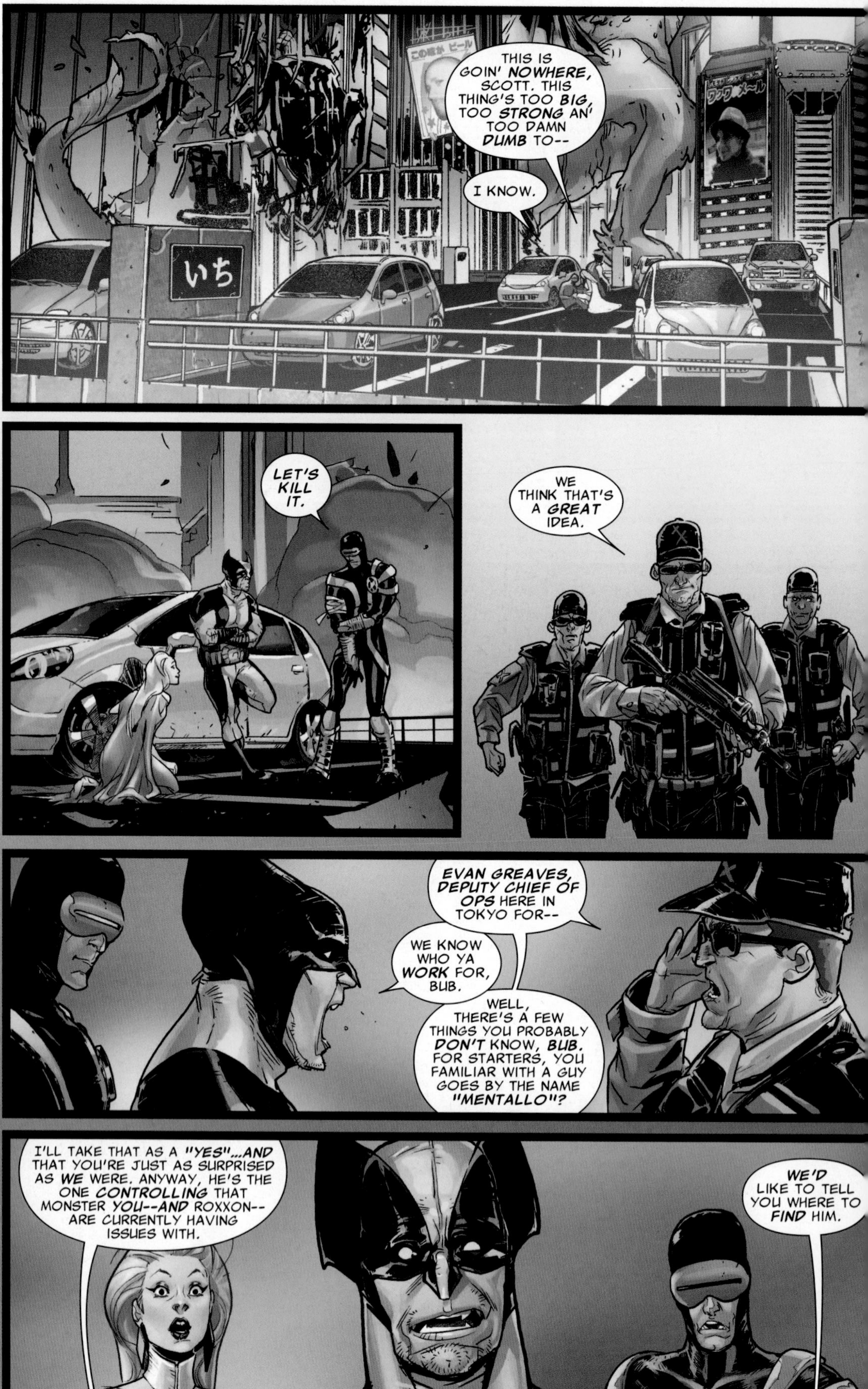
THIS IS GOIN' NOWHERE, SCOTT. THIS THING'S TOO BIG, TOO STRONG AN' TOO DAMN DUMB TO--
I KNOW.
LET'S KILL IT.
WE THINK THAT'S A GREAT IDEA.
EVAN GREAVES, DEPUTY CHIEF OF OPS HERE IN TOKYO FOR--
WE KNOW WHO YA WORK FOR, BUB.
WELL, THERE'S A FEW THINGS YOU PROBABLY DON'T KNOW, BUB. FOR STARTERS, YOU FAMILIAR WITH A GUY GOES BY THE NAME "MENTALLO"?
I'LL TAKE THAT AS A "YES"...AND THAT YOU'RE JUST AS SURPRISED AS WE WERE. ANYWAY, HE'S THE ONE CONTROLLING THAT MONSTER YOU--AND ROXXON--ARE CURRENTLY HAVING ISSUES WITH.
WE'D LIKE TO TELL YOU WHERE TO FIND HIM.

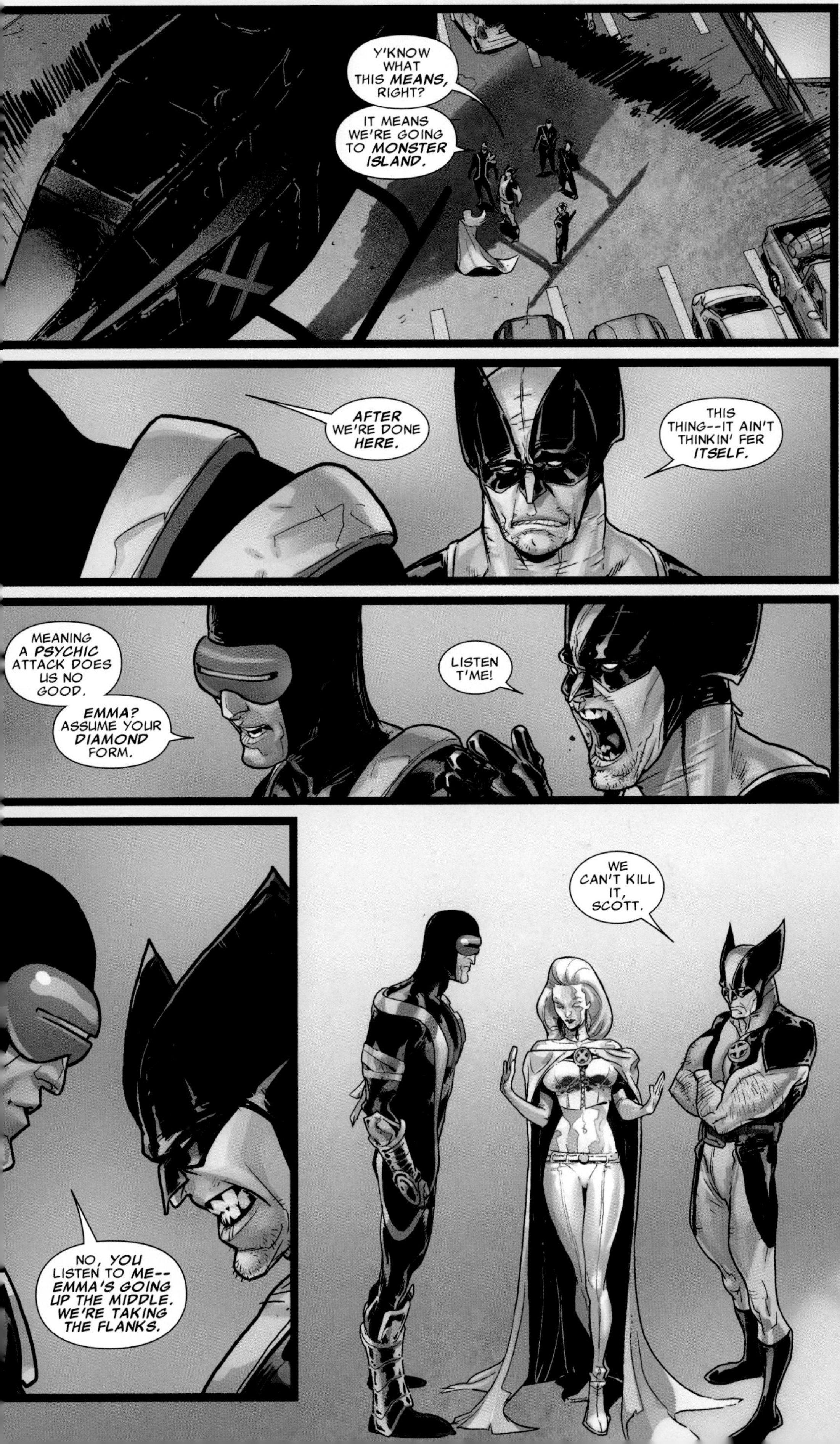
Y'KNOW WHAT THIS MEANS, RIGHT?
IT MEANS WE'RE GOING TO MONSTER ISLAND.
AFTER WE'RE DONE HERE.
THIS THING--IT AIN'T THINKIN' FER ITSELF.
MEANING A PSYCHIC ATTACK DOES US NO GOOD.
EMMA? ASSUME YOUR DIAMOND FORM.
LISTEN T'ME!
NO, YOU LISTEN TO ME--EMMA'S GOING UP THE MIDDLE. WE'RE TAKING THE FLANKS.
WE CAN'T KILL IT, SCOTT.

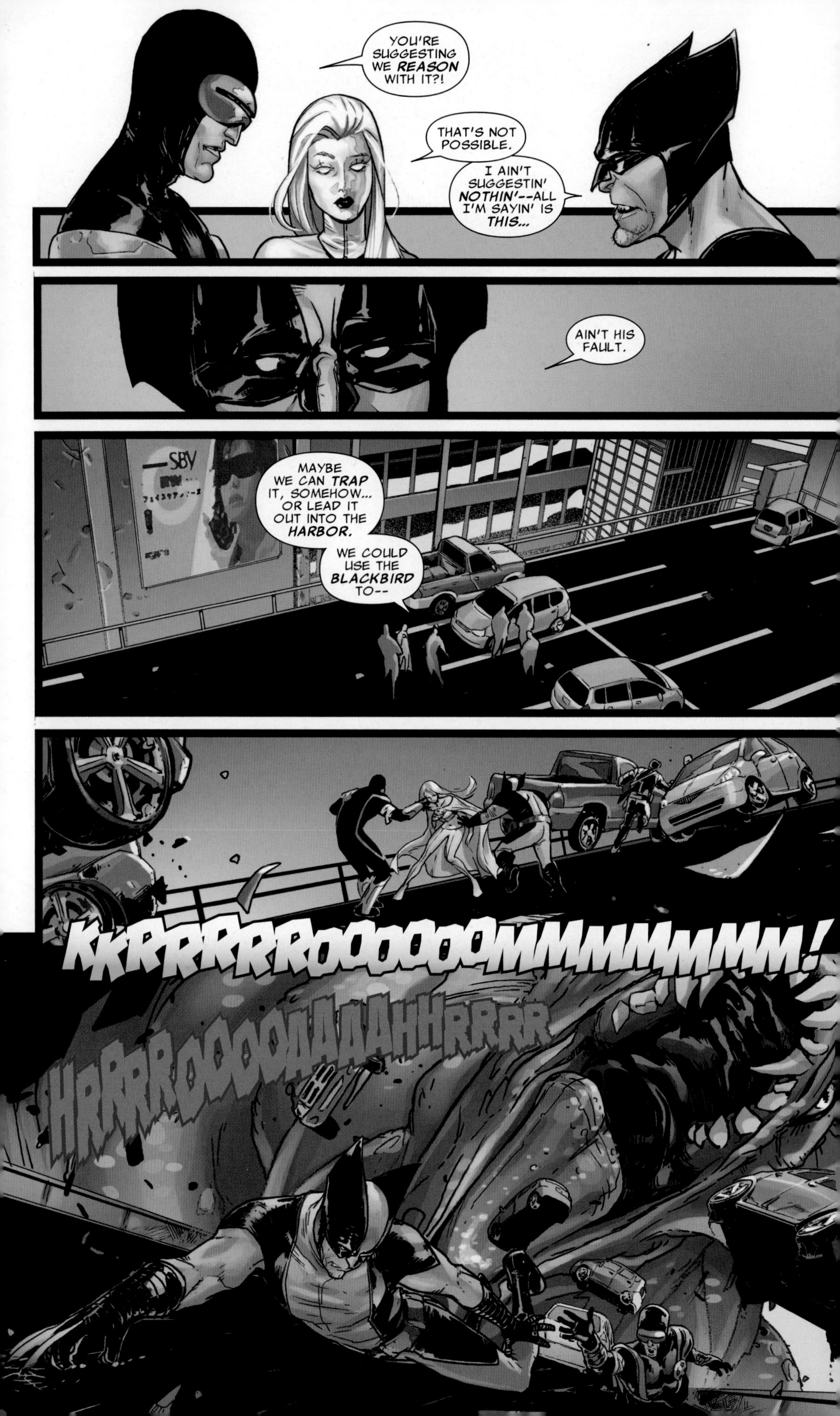
YOU'RE SUGGESTING WE REASON WITH IT?!
THAT'S NOT POSSIBLE.
I AIN'T SUGGESTIN' NOTHIN'--ALL I'M SAYIN' IS THIS...
AIN'T HIS FAULT.
SBY
MAYBE WE CAN TRAP IT, SOMEHOW... OR LEAD IT OUT INTO THE HARBOR.
WE COULD USE THE BLACKBIRD TO--
KKRRRRROOOOOOMMMMMMMM!
HRRRROOOOAAAAHHRRRR

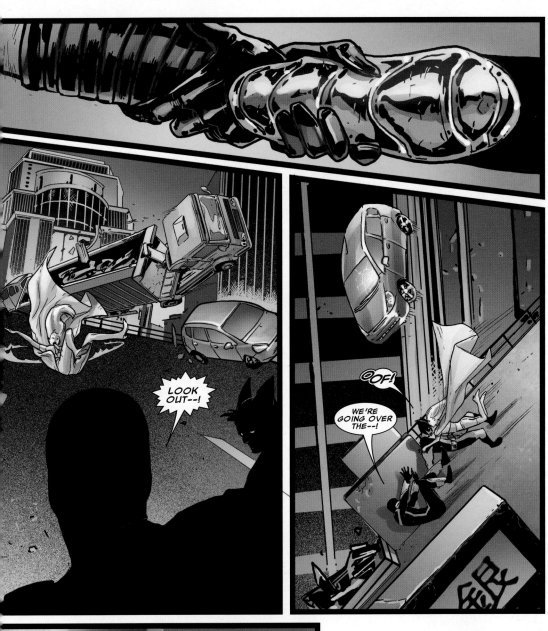

LOOK OUT--!

OOF!

WE'RE GOING OVER THE--!

EDGE...?

WHAT'RE YOU DOIN' HERE?

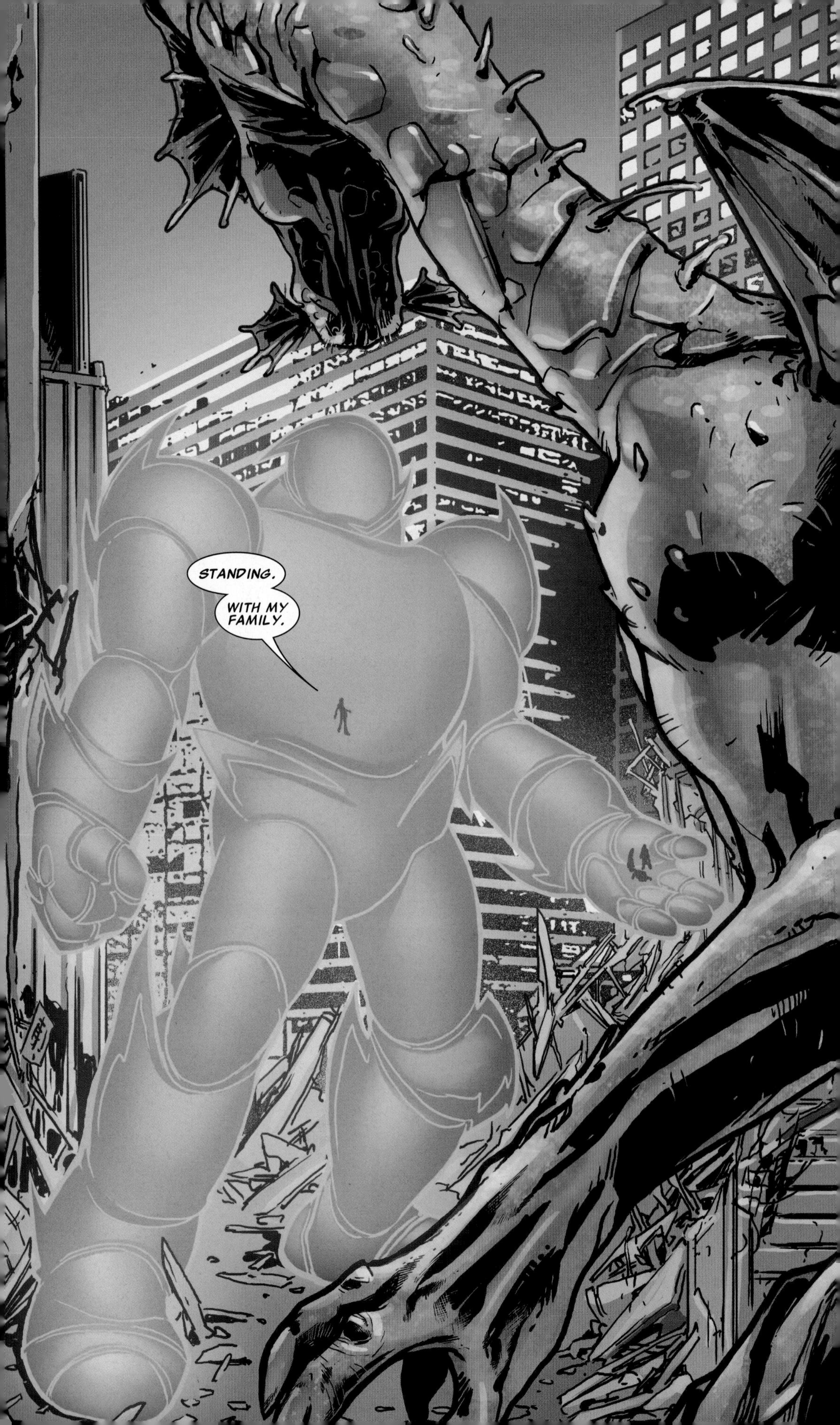
STANDING.
WITH MY FAMILY.

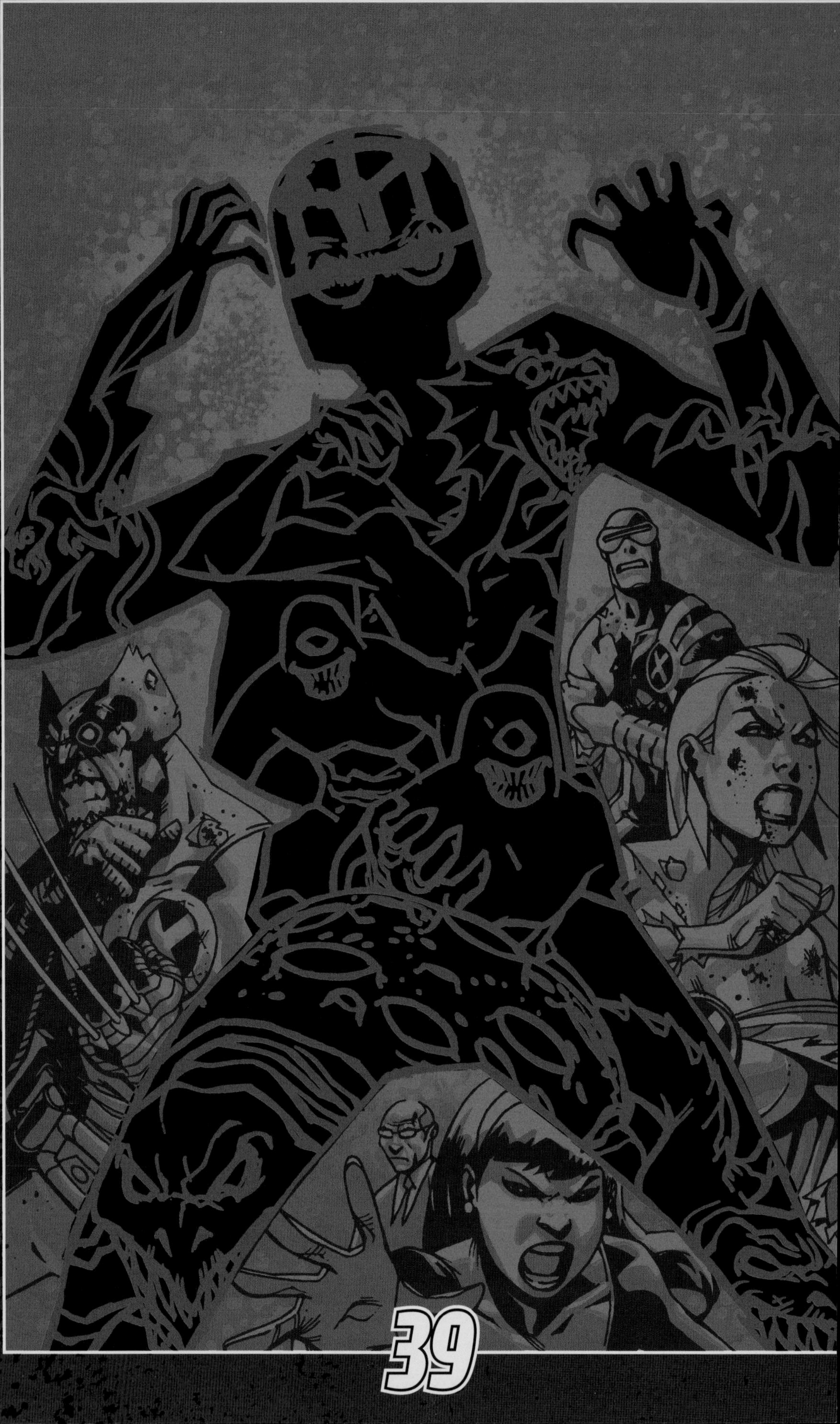
39

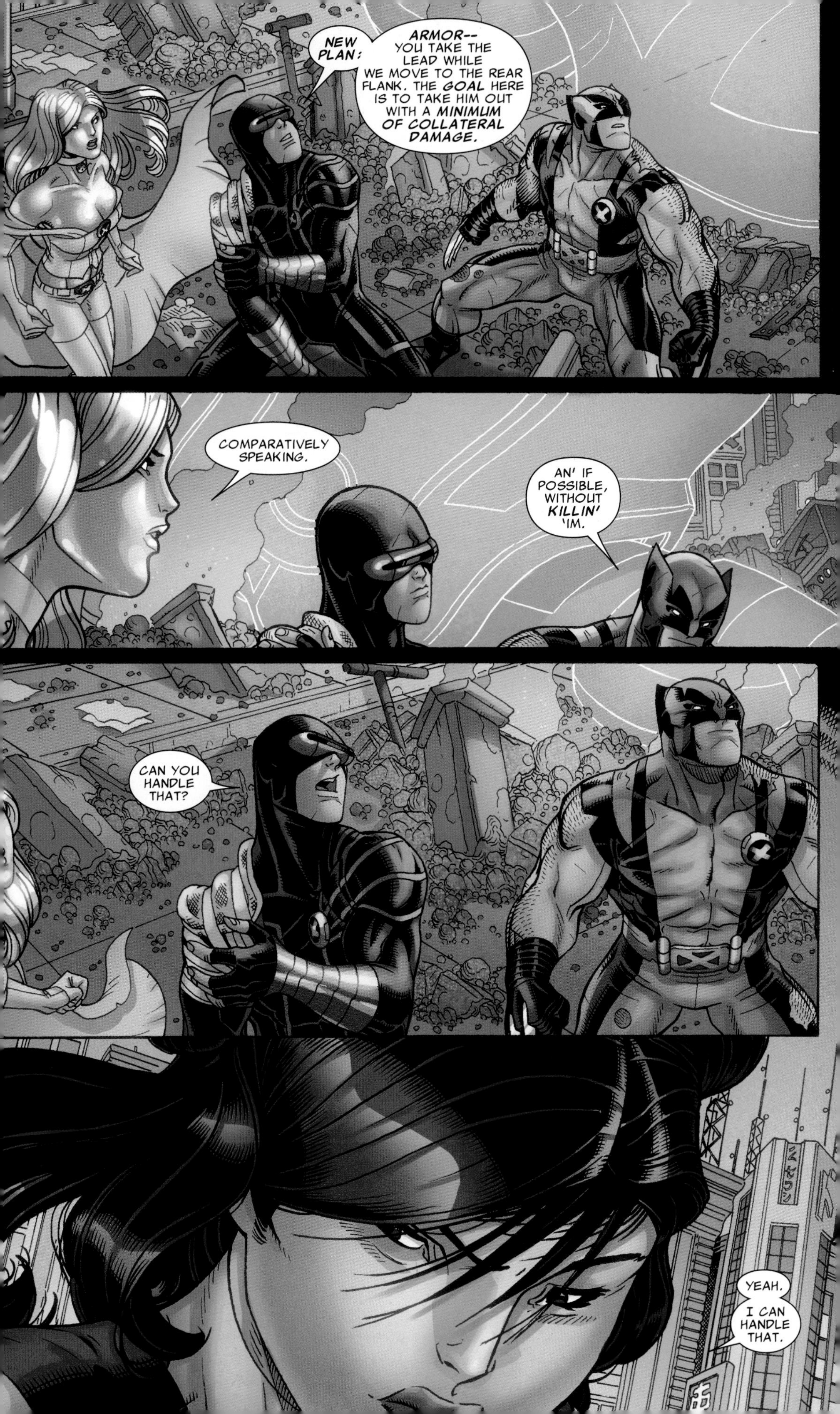
NEW PLAN:
ARMOR-- YOU TAKE THE LEAD WHILE WE MOVE TO THE REAR FLANK. THE GOAL HERE IS TO TAKE HIM OUT WITH A MINIMUM OF COLLATERAL DAMAGE.
COMPARATIVELY SPEAKING.
AN' IF POSSIBLE, WITHOUT KILLIN' 'IM.
CAN YOU HANDLE THAT?
YEAH.
I CAN HANDLE THAT.

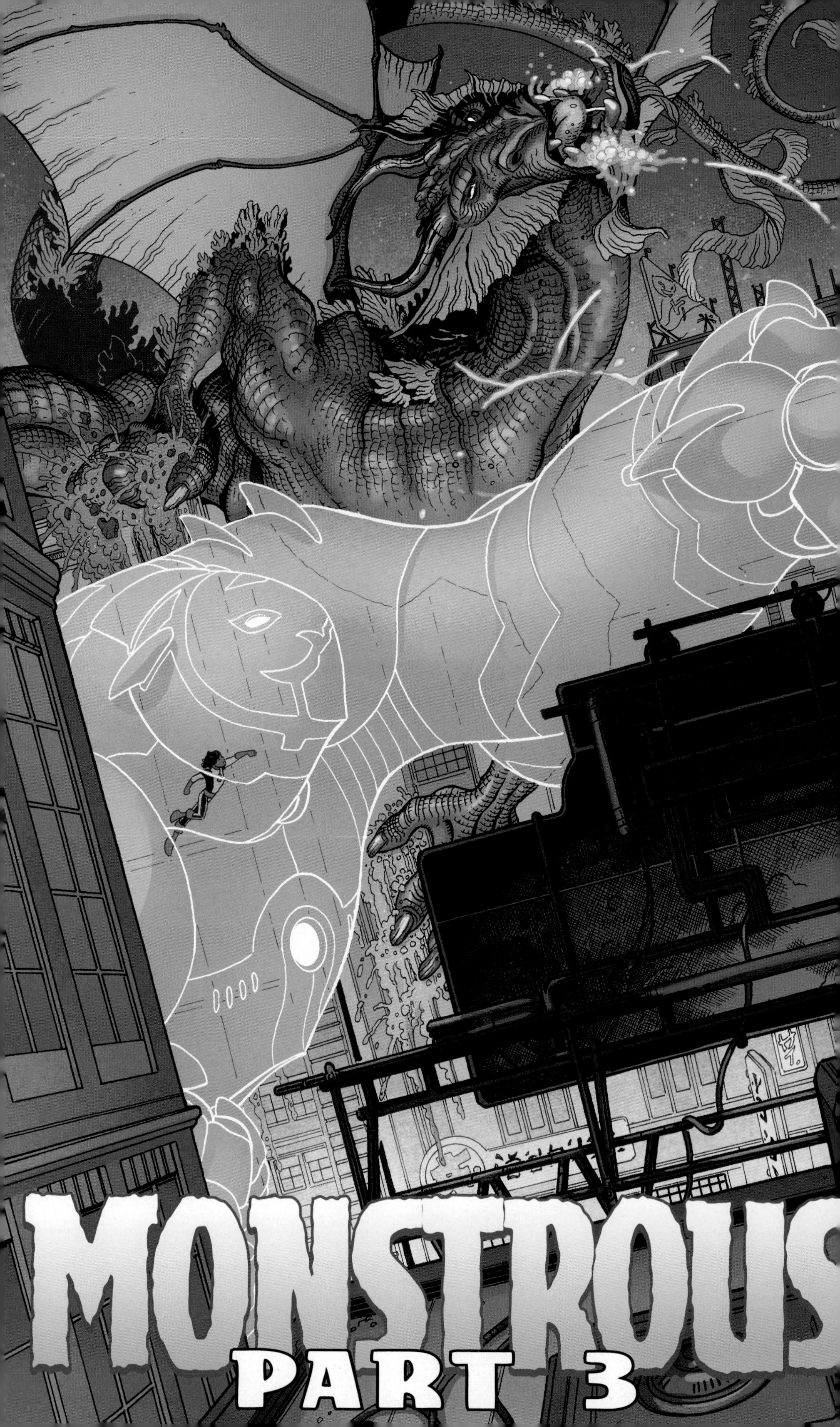
MONSTROUS
PART 3

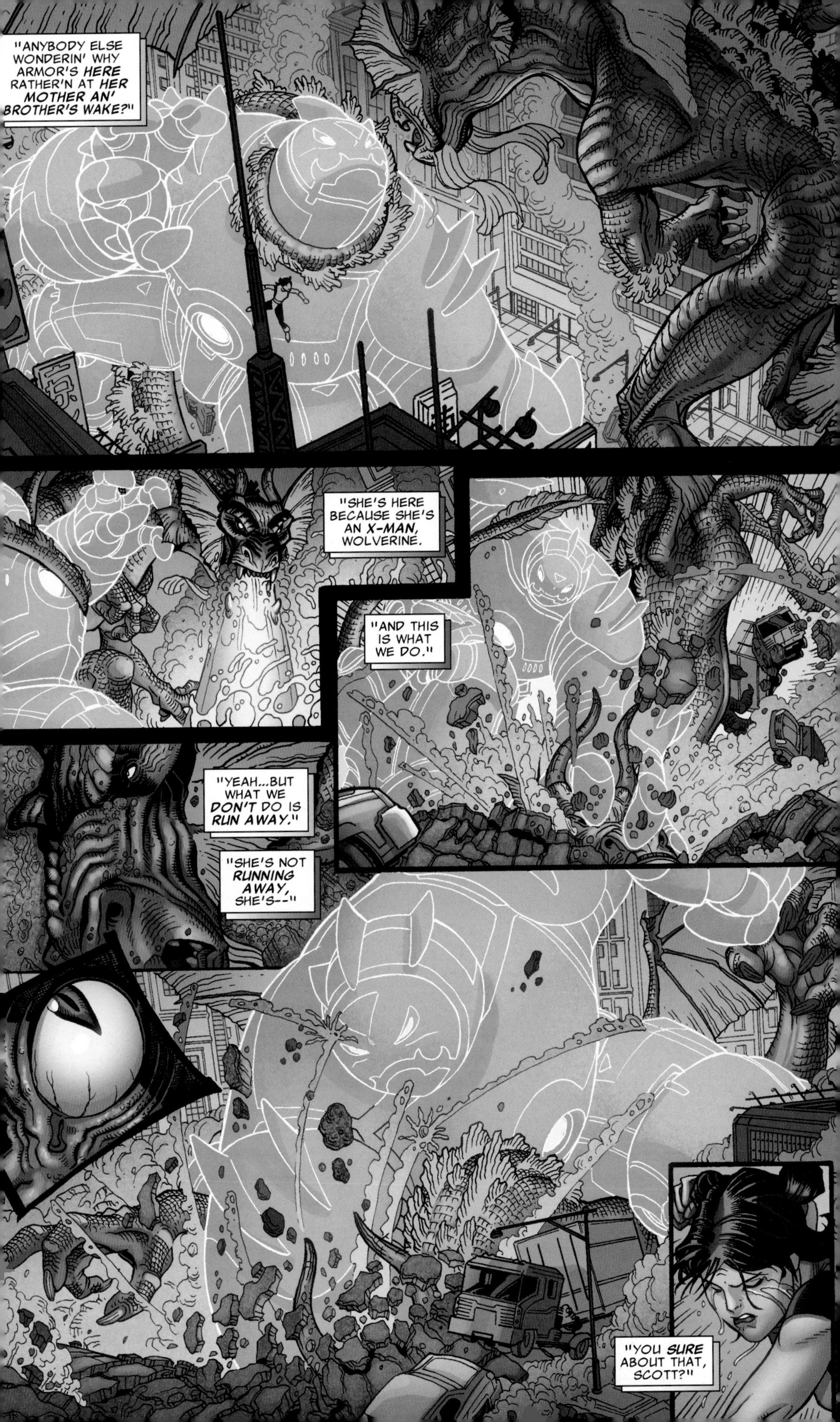
"ANYBODY ELSE WONDERIN' WHY ARMOR'S HERE RATHER'N AT HER MOTHER AN' BROTHER'S WAKE?"
"SHE'S HERE BECAUSE SHE'S AN X-MAN, WOLVERINE.
"AND THIS IS WHAT WE DO."
"YEAH...BUT WHAT WE DON'T DO IS RUN AWAY."
"SHE'S NOT RUNNING AWAY, SHE'S--"
"YOU SURE ABOUT THAT, SCOTT?"

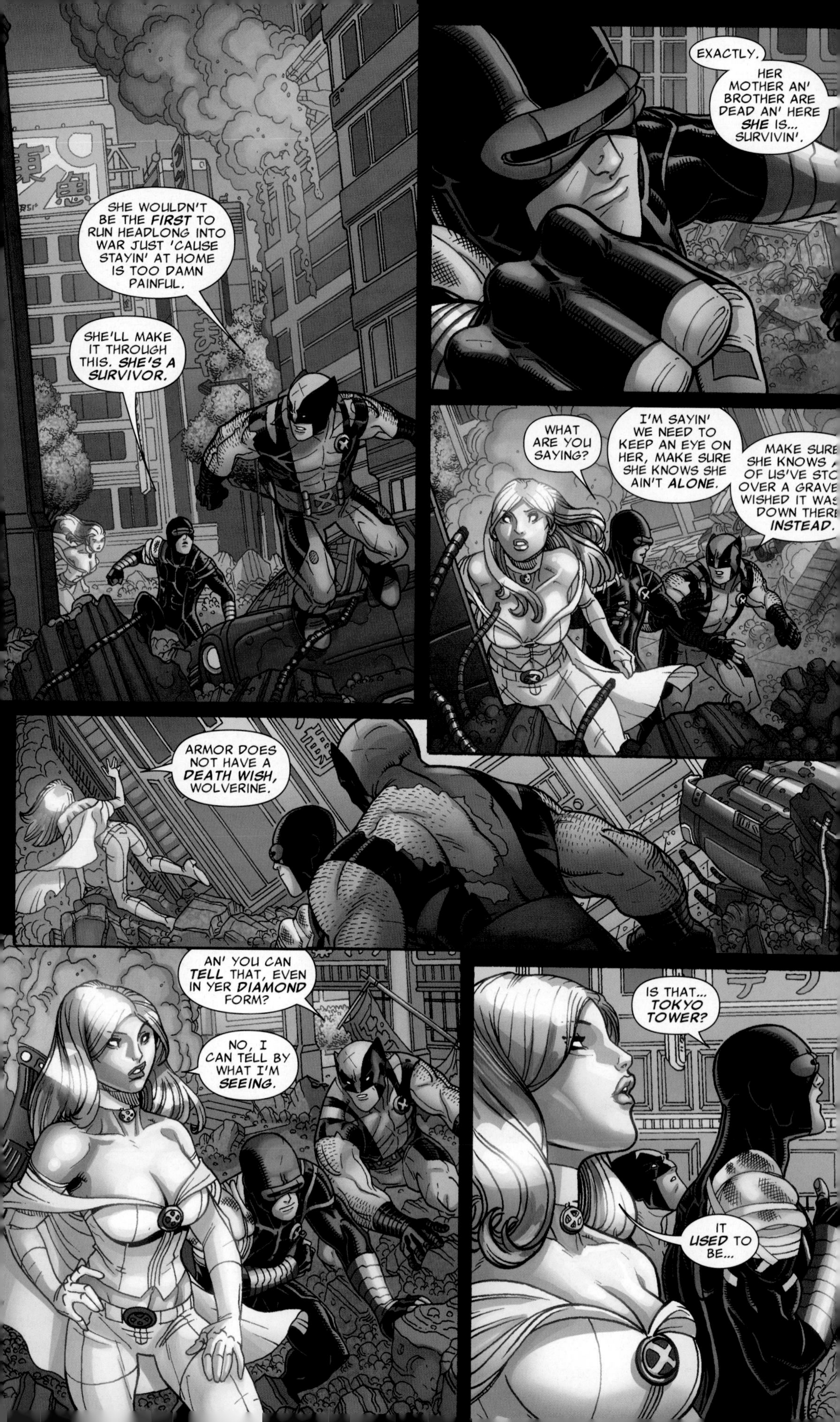
SHE WOULDN'T BE THE FIRST TO RUN HEADLONG INTO WAR JUST 'CAUSE STAYIN' AT HOME IS TOO DAMN PAINFUL.
SHE'LL MAKE IT THROUGH THIS. SHE'S A SURVIVOR.
EXACTLY.
HER MOTHER AN' BROTHER ARE DEAD AN' HERE SHE IS... SURVIVIN'.
WHAT ARE YOU SAYING?
I'M SAYIN' WE NEED TO KEEP AN EYE ON HER, MAKE SURE SHE KNOWS SHE AIN'T ALONE.
ARMOR DOES NOT HAVE A DEATH WISH, WOLVERINE.
AN' YOU CAN TELL THAT, EVEN IN YER DIAMOND FORM?
NO, I CAN TELL BY WHAT I'M SEEING.
IS THAT... TOKYO TOWER?
IT USED TO BE...

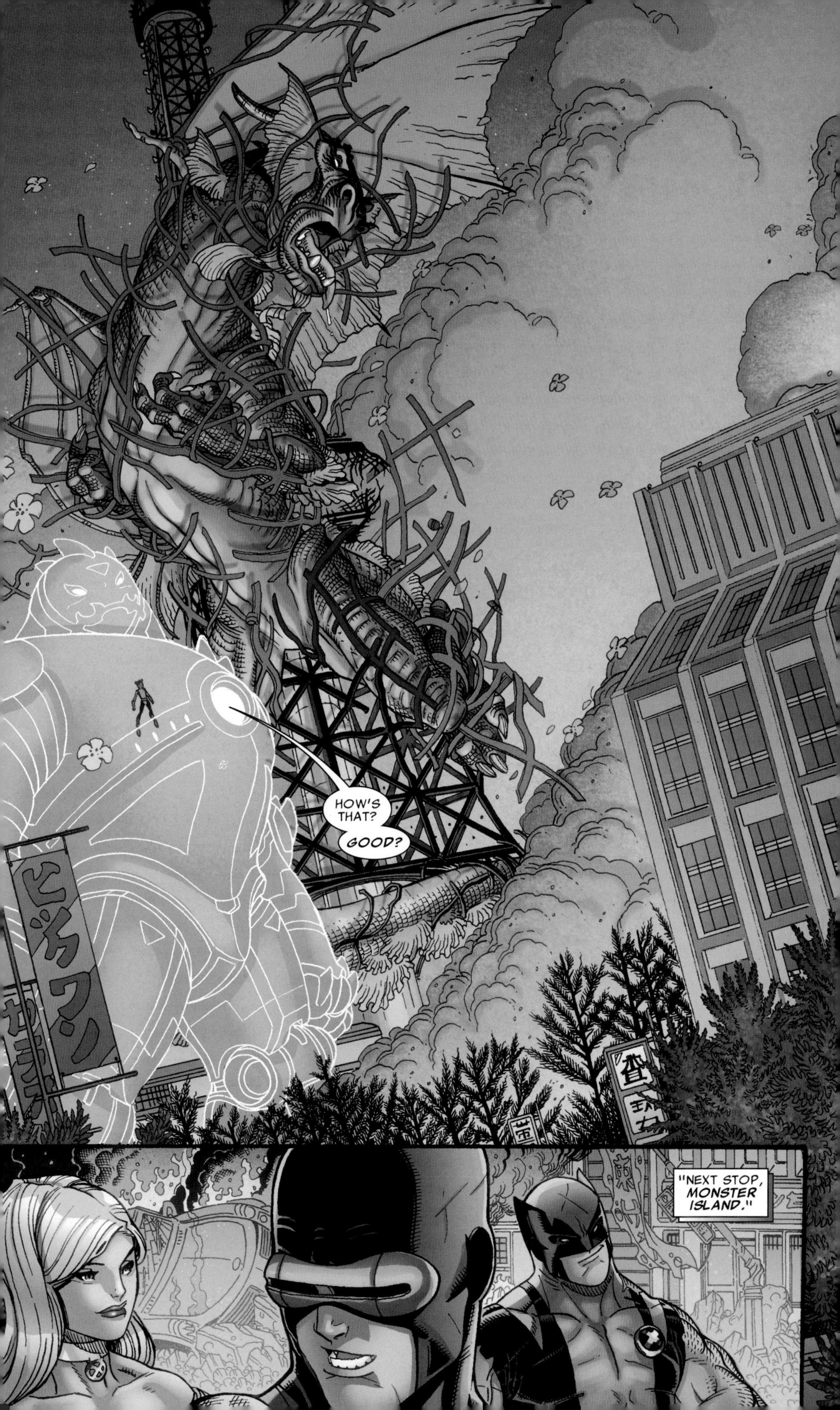
HOW'S THAT? GOOD?
"NEXT STOP, MONSTER ISLAND."

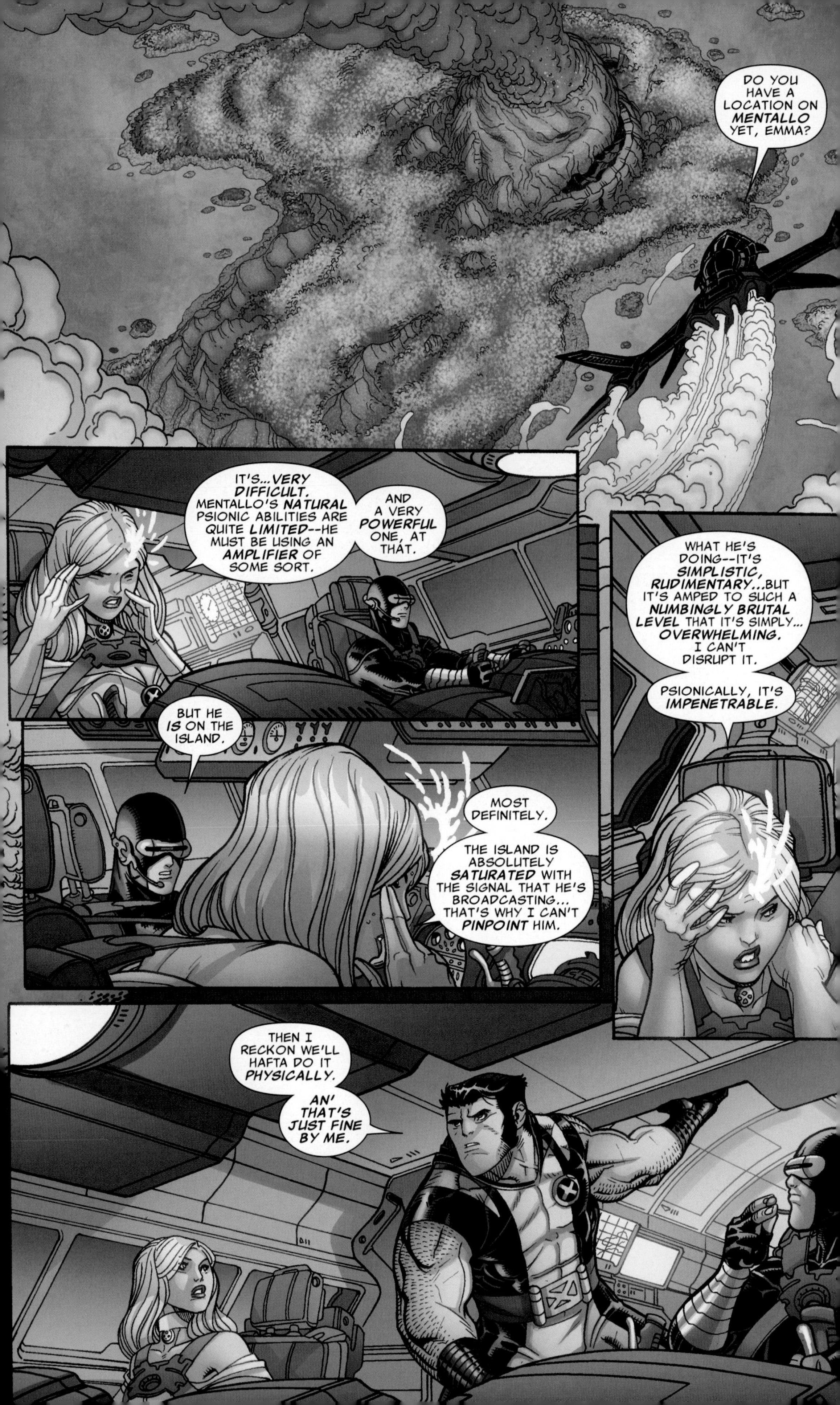

DO YOU HAVE A LOCATION ON MENTALLO YET, EMMA?
IT'S...VERY DIFFICULT. MENTALLO'S NATURAL PSIONIC ABILITIES ARE QUITE LIMITED--HE MUST BE USING AN AMPLIFIER OF SOME SORT.
AND A VERY POWERFUL ONE, AT THAT.
WHAT HE'S DOING--IT'S SIMPLISTIC, RUDIMENTARY...BUT IT'S AMPED TO SUCH A NUMBINGLY BRUTAL LEVEL THAT IT'S SIMPLY... OVERWHELMING. I CAN'T DISRUPT IT.
PSIONICALLY, IT'S IMPENETRABLE.
BUT HE IS ON THE ISLAND.
MOST DEFINITELY.
THE ISLAND IS ABSOLUTELY SATURATED WITH THE SIGNAL THAT HE'S BROADCASTING... THAT'S WHY I CAN'T PINPOINT HIM.
THEN I RECKON WE'LL HAFTA DO IT PHYSICALLY.
AN' THAT'S JUST FINE BY ME.

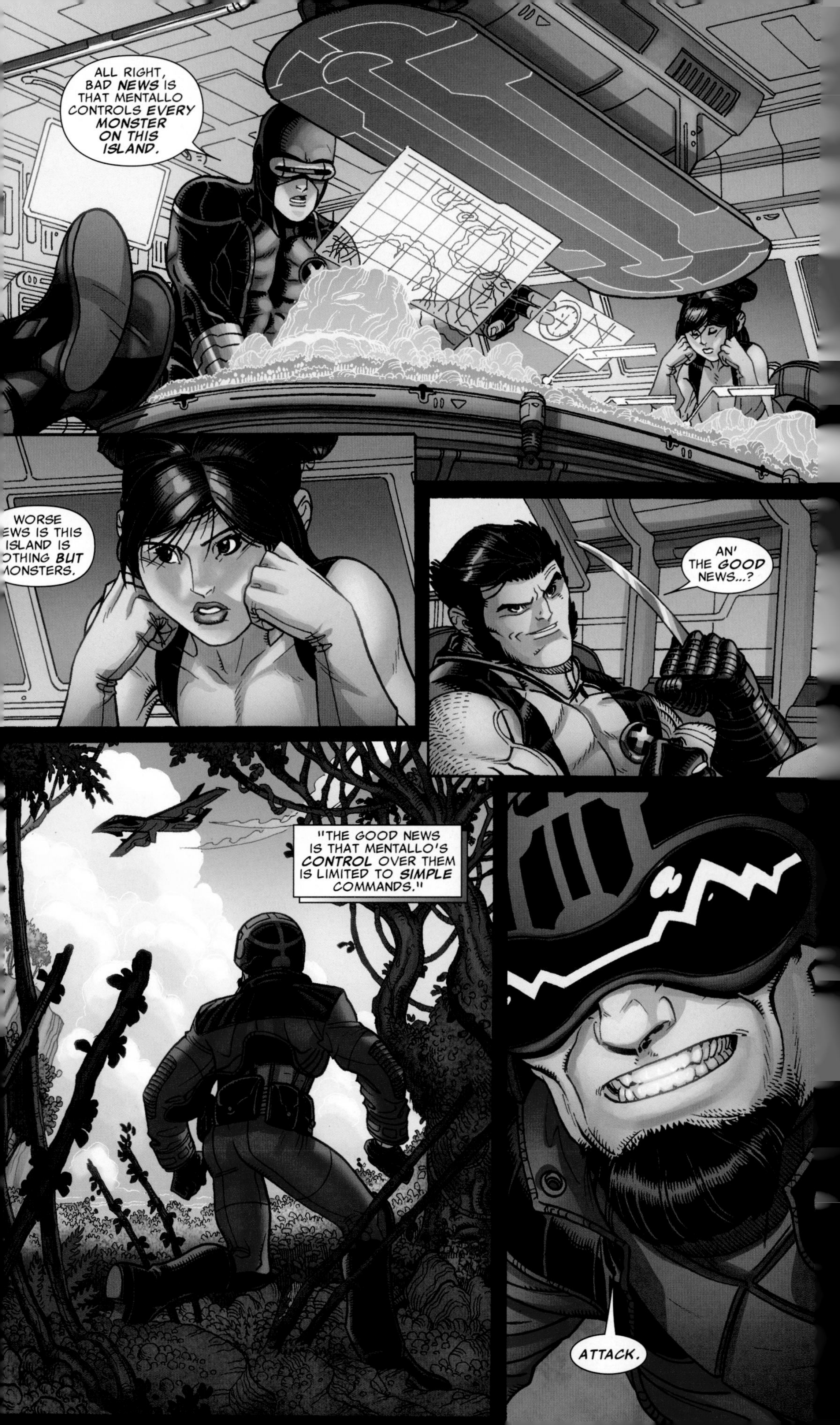
ALL RIGHT, BAD NEWS IS THAT MENTALLO CONTROLS EVERY MONSTER ON THIS ISLAND.
WORSE EWS IS THIS ISLAND IS OTHING BUT MONSTERS.
AN' THE GOOD NEWS...?
"THE GOOD NEWS IS THAT MENTALLO'S CONTROL OVER THEM IS LIMITED TO SIMPLE COMMANDS."
ATTACK.

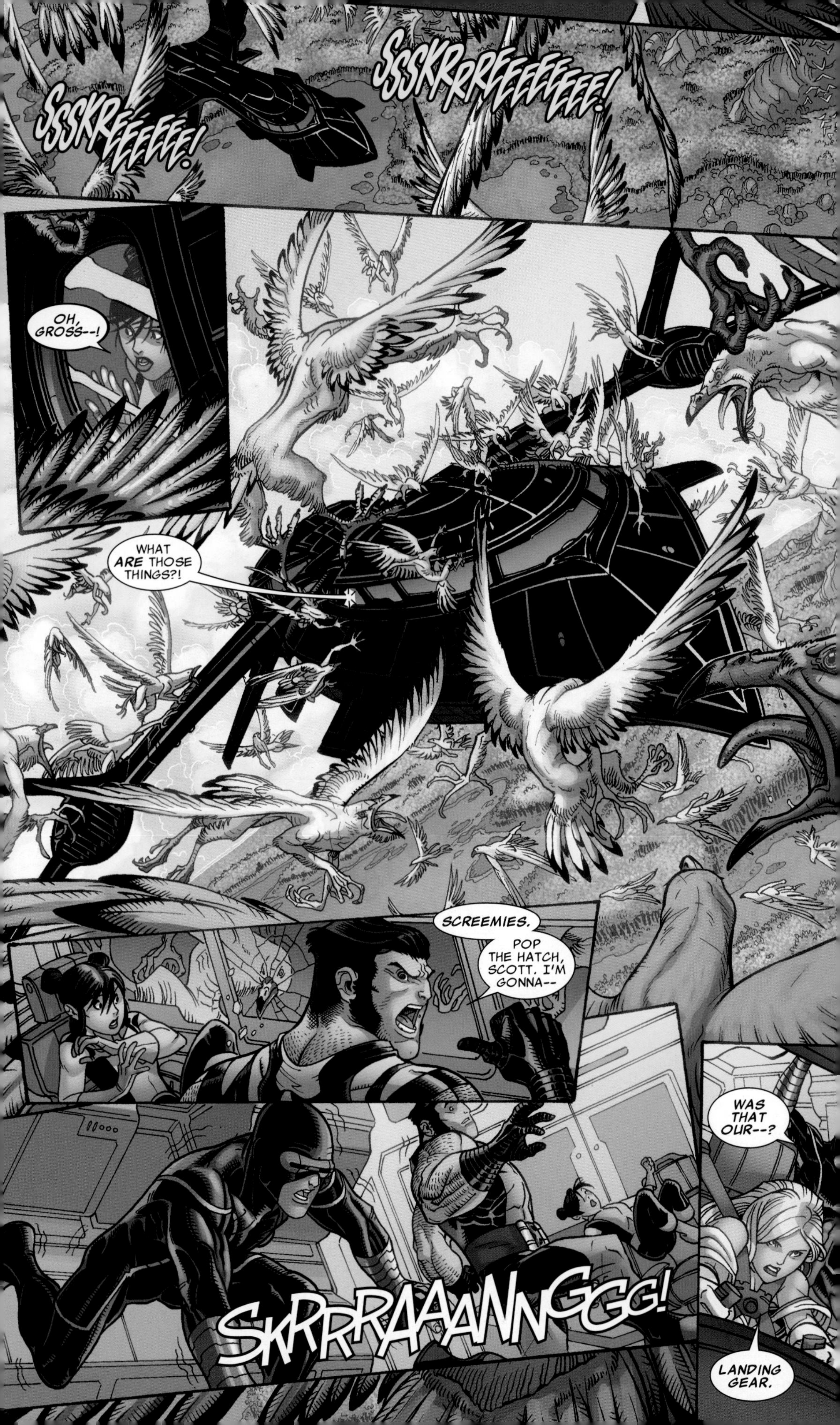
SSSKREEEEEEE!
SSSKRRRREEEEEEEEE!
OH, GROSS--!
WHAT ARE THOSE THINGS?!
SCREEMIES.
POP THE HATCH, SCOTT. I'M GONNA--
WAS THAT OUR--?
SKRRRAAANNGGG!
LANDING GEAR.

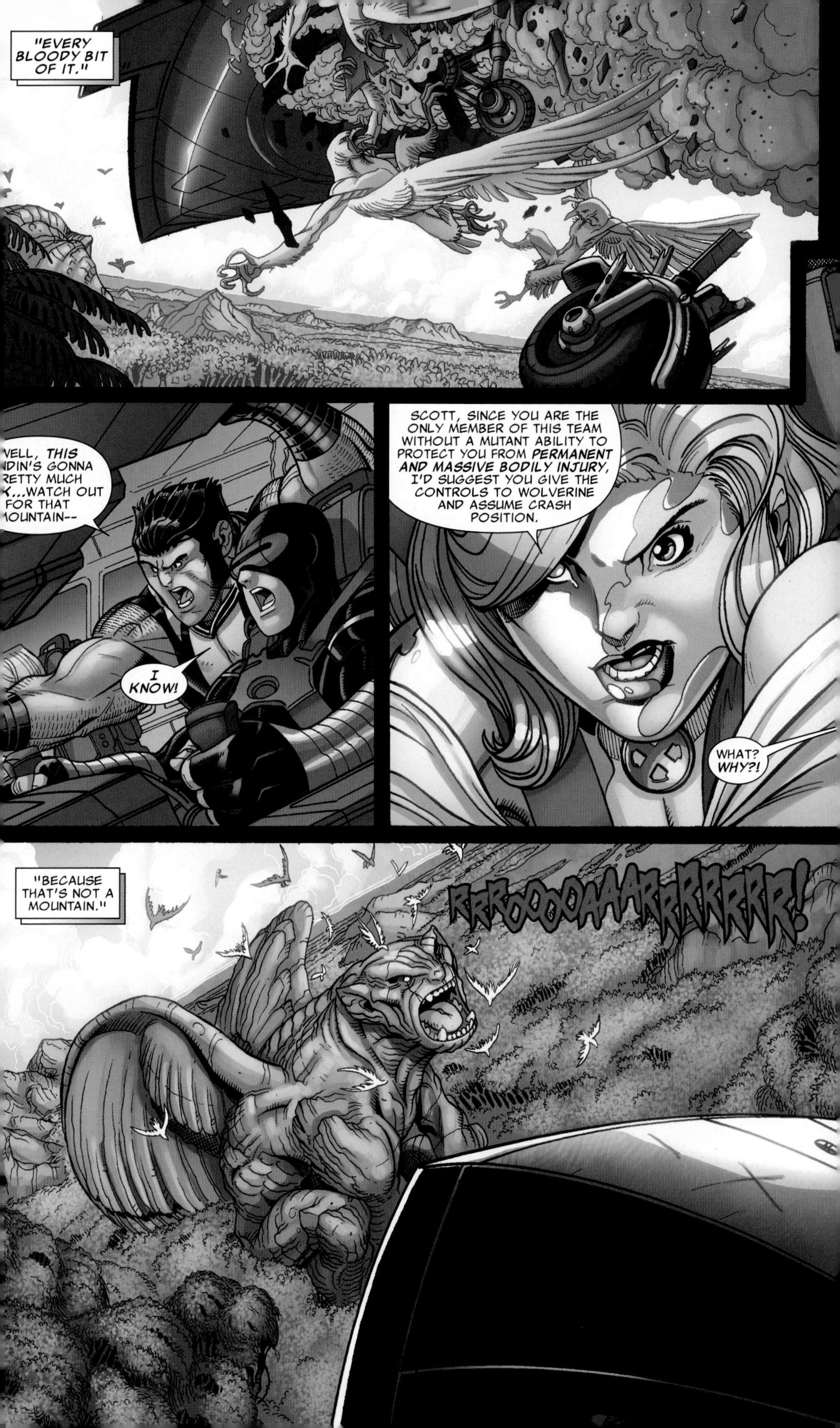
"EVERY BLOODY BIT OF IT."
VELL, THIS NDIN'S GONNA RETTY MUCH K...WATCH OUT FOR THAT OUNTAIN--
I KNOW!
SCOTT, SINCE YOU ARE THE ONLY MEMBER OF THIS TEAM WITHOUT A MUTANT ABILITY TO PROTECT YOU FROM PERMANENT AND MASSIVE BODILY INJURY, I'D SUGGEST YOU GIVE THE CONTROLS TO WOLVERINE AND ASSUME CRASH POSITION.
WHAT? WHY?!
"BECAUSE THAT'S NOT A MOUNTAIN."
RRROOOOAAARRRRRRR!

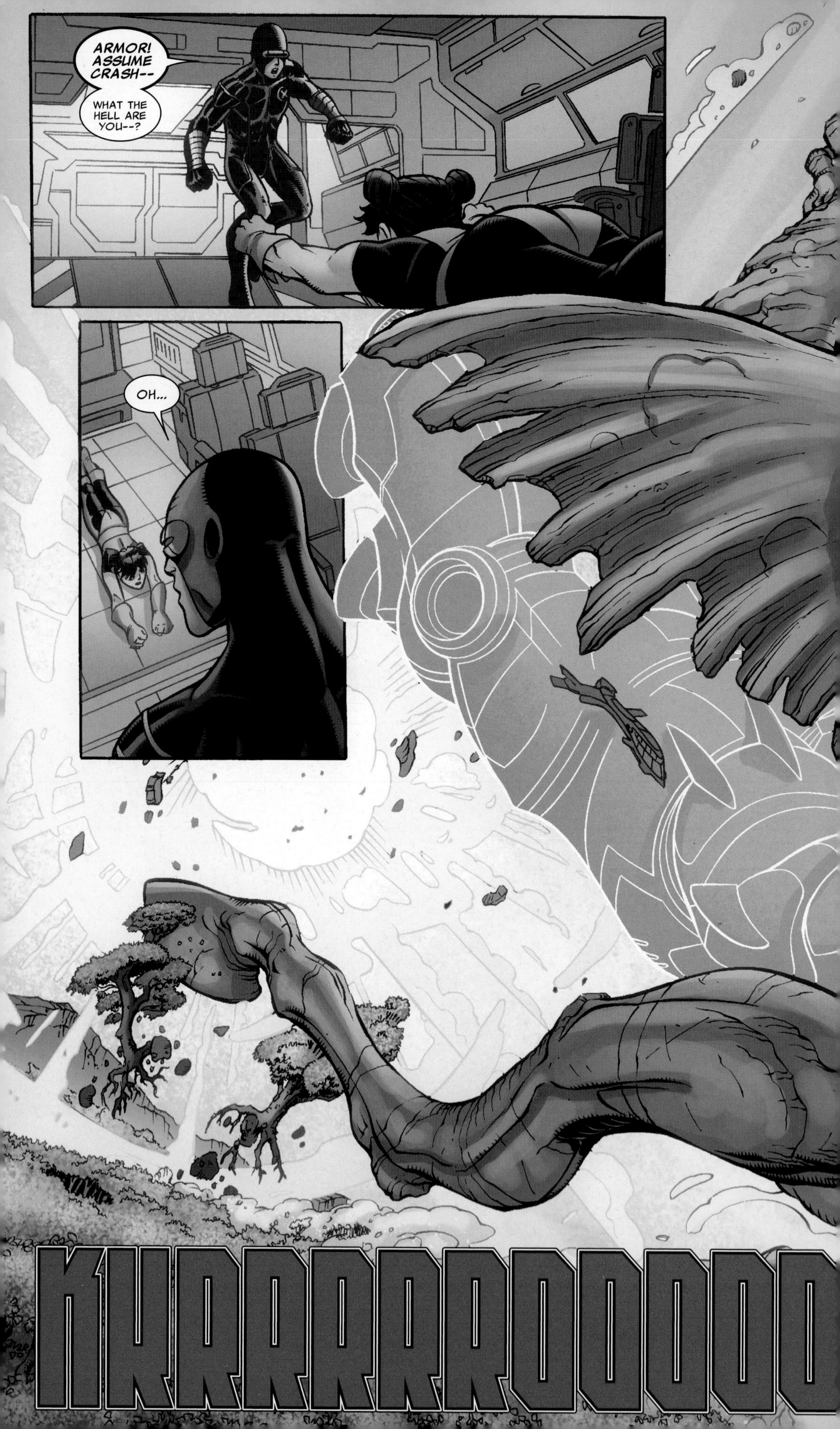
ARMOR! ASSUME CRASH--
WHAT THE HELL ARE YOU--?
OH...
KHRRRRRROOOOOO

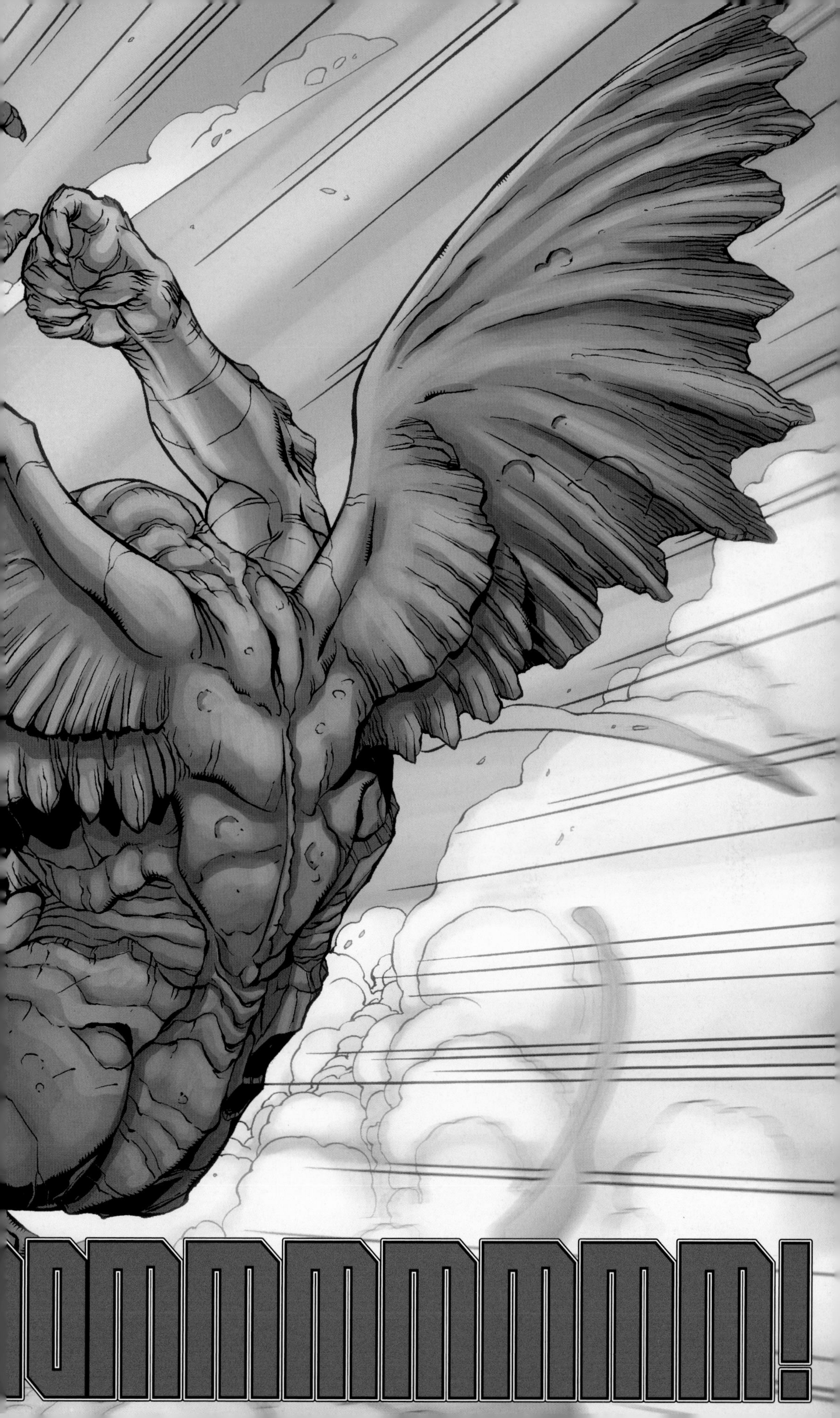
OMMMMMMMM!

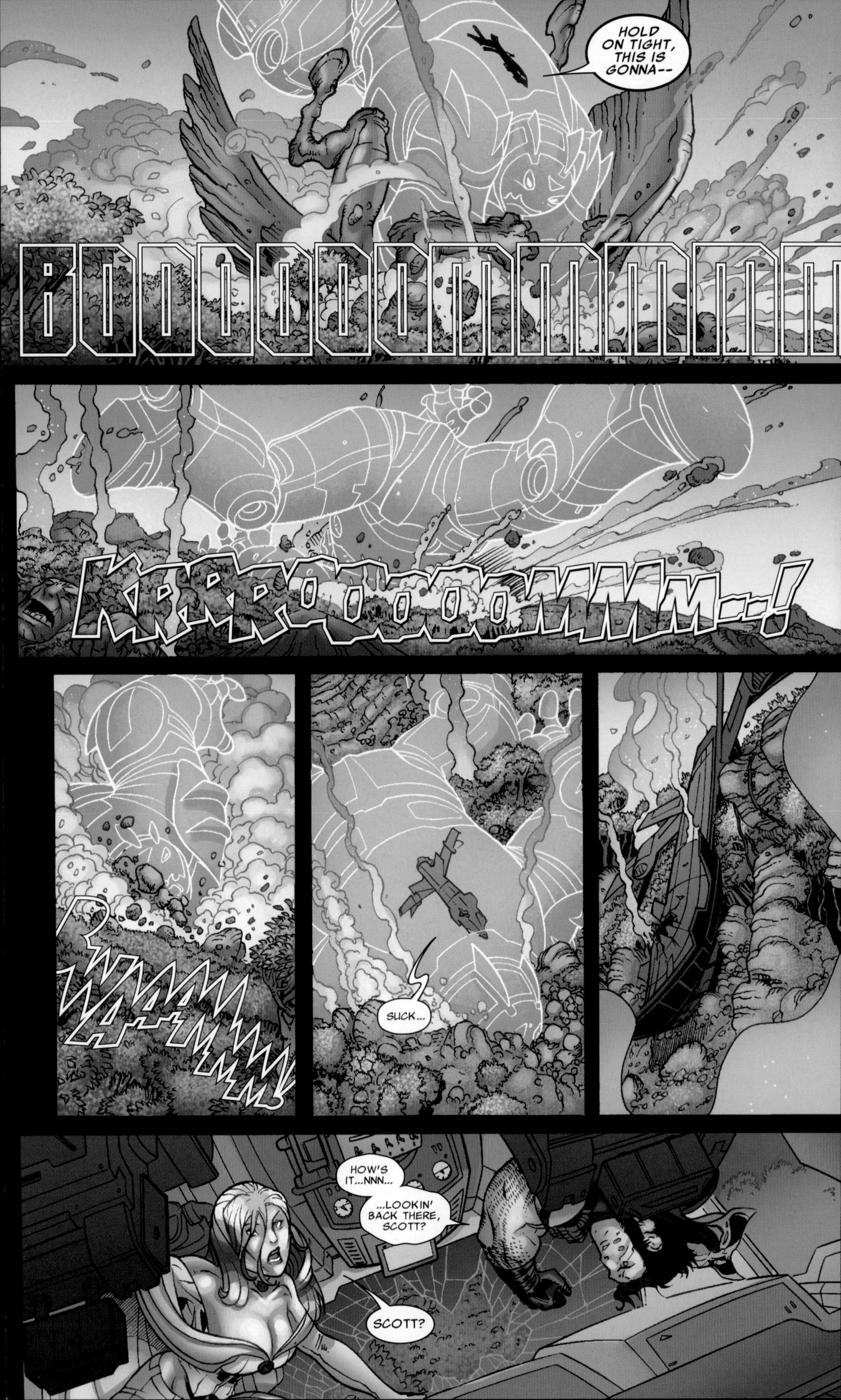

HOLD ON TIGHT, THIS IS GONNA--
BOOOOOOMMMMMM
KRRROOOOOOMMMM--!
SUCK...
HOW'S IT...NNN...
...LOOKIN' BACK THERE, SCOTT?
SCOTT?

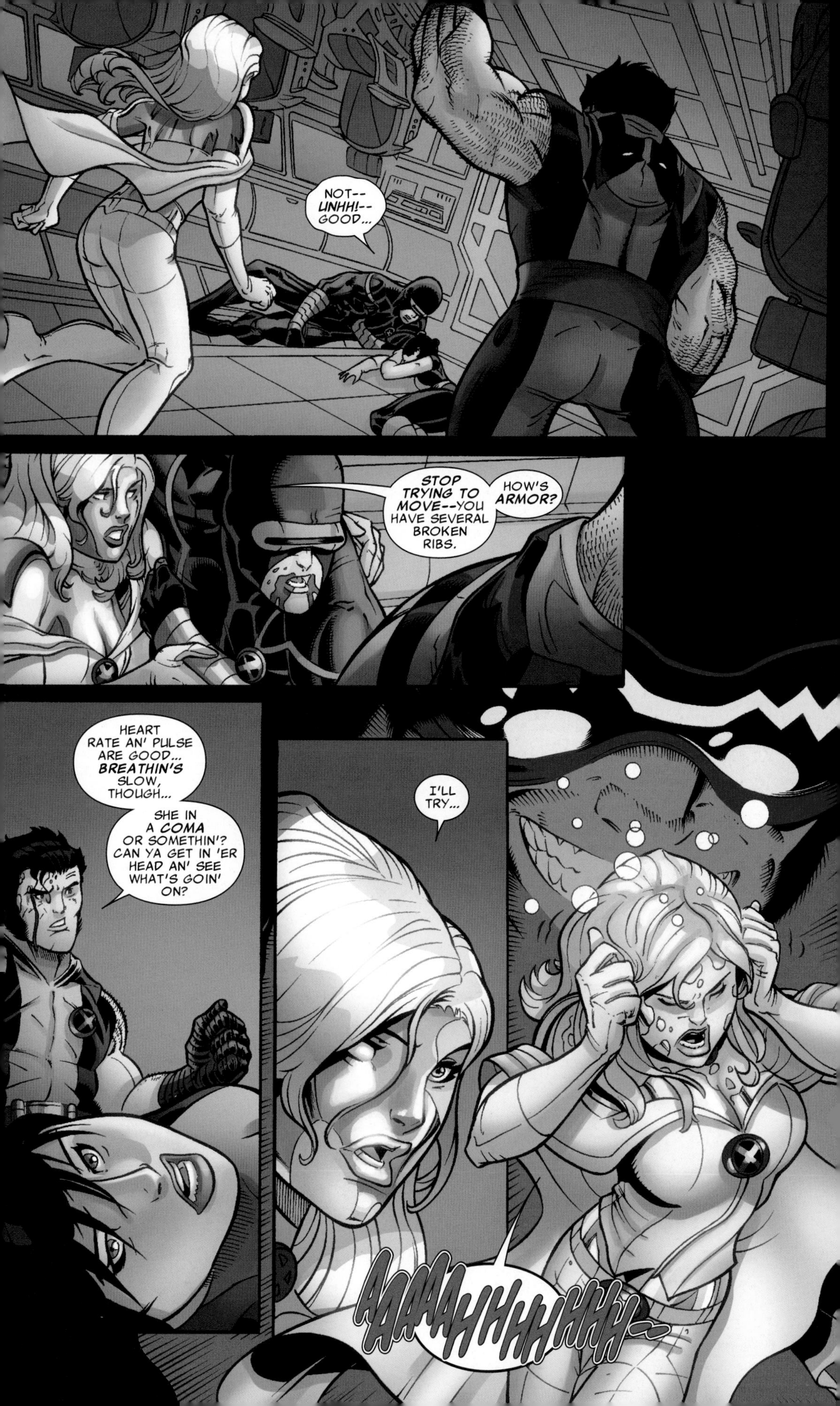
NOT-- UNHH!-- GOOD...
STOP TRYING TO MOVE--YOU HAVE SEVERAL BROKEN RIBS.
HOW'S ARMOR?
HEART RATE AN' PULSE ARE GOOD... BREATHIN'S SLOW, THOUGH...
SHE IN A COMA OR SOMETHIN'? CAN YA GET IN 'ER HEAD AN' SEE WHAT'S GOIN' ON?
I'LL TRY...
AAAAAHHHHHHH--

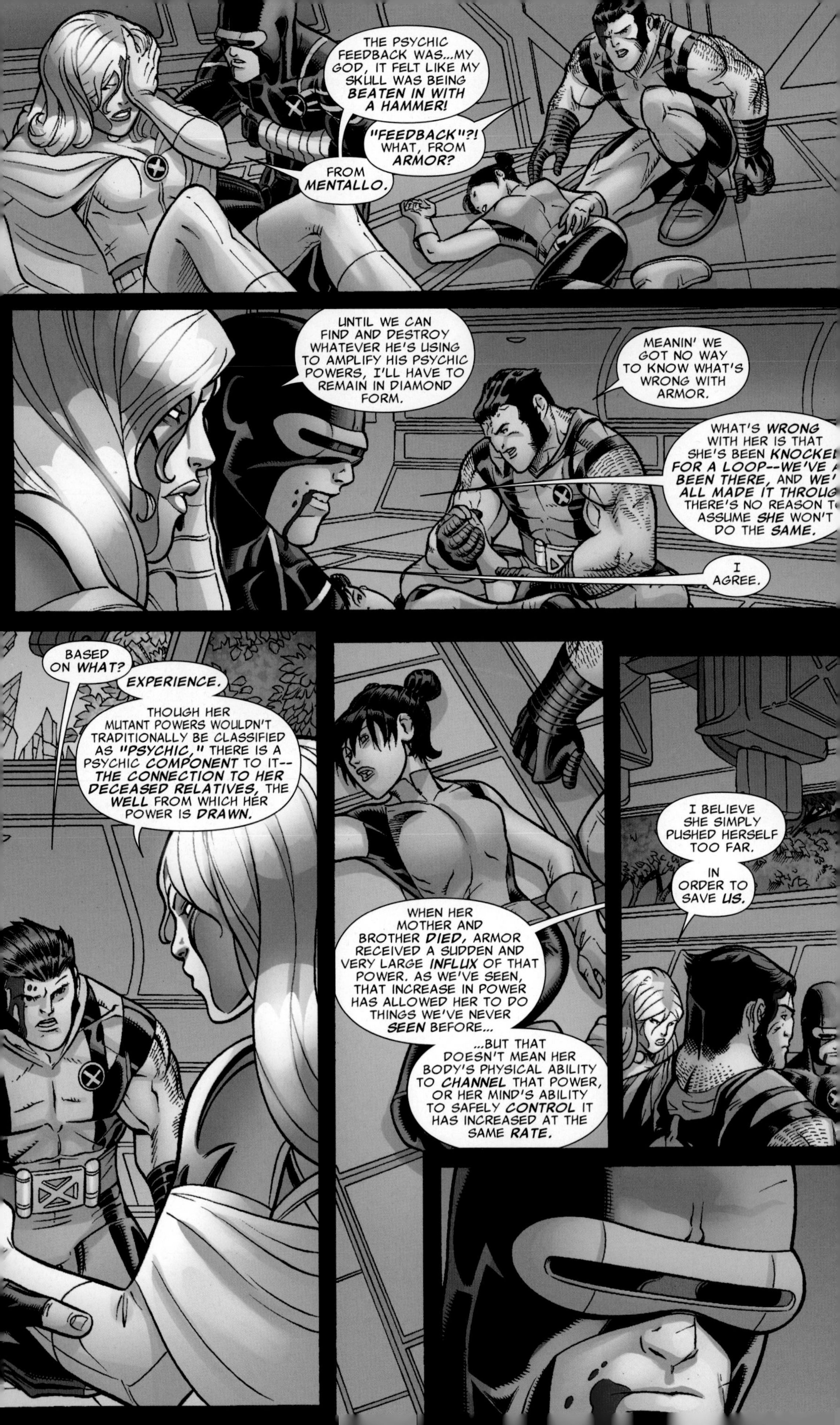
THE PSYCHIC FEEDBACK WAS...MY GOD, IT FELT LIKE MY SKULL WAS BEING BEATEN IN WITH A HAMMER!
"FEEDBACK"?! WHAT, FROM ARMOR?
FROM MENTALLO.
UNTIL WE CAN FIND AND DESTROY WHATEVER HE'S USING TO AMPLIFY HIS PSYCHIC POWERS, I'LL HAVE TO REMAIN IN DIAMOND FORM.
MEANIN' WE GOT NO WAY TO KNOW WHAT'S WRONG WITH ARMOR.
WHAT'S WRONG WITH HER IS THAT SHE'S BEEN KNOCKED FOR A LOOP--WE'VE BEEN THERE, AND WE'VE ALL MADE IT THROUGH. THERE'S NO REASON TO ASSUME SHE WON'T DO THE SAME.
I AGREE.
BASED ON WHAT?
EXPERIENCE.
THOUGH HER MUTANT POWERS WOULDN'T TRADITIONALLY BE CLASSIFIED AS "PSYCHIC," THERE IS A PSYCHIC COMPONENT TO IT-- THE CONNECTION TO HER DECEASED RELATIVES, THE WELL FROM WHICH HER POWER IS DRAWN.
WHEN HER MOTHER AND BROTHER DIED, ARMOR RECEIVED A SUDDEN AND VERY LARGE INFLUX OF THAT POWER. AS WE'VE SEEN, THAT INCREASE IN POWER HAS ALLOWED HER TO DO THINGS WE'VE NEVER SEEN BEFORE...
...BUT THAT DOESN'T MEAN HER BODY'S PHYSICAL ABILITY TO CHANNEL THAT POWER, OR HER MIND'S ABILITY TO SAFELY CONTROL IT HAS INCREASED AT THE SAME RATE.
I BELIEVE SHE SIMPLY PUSHED HERSELF TOO FAR.
IN ORDER TO SAVE US.

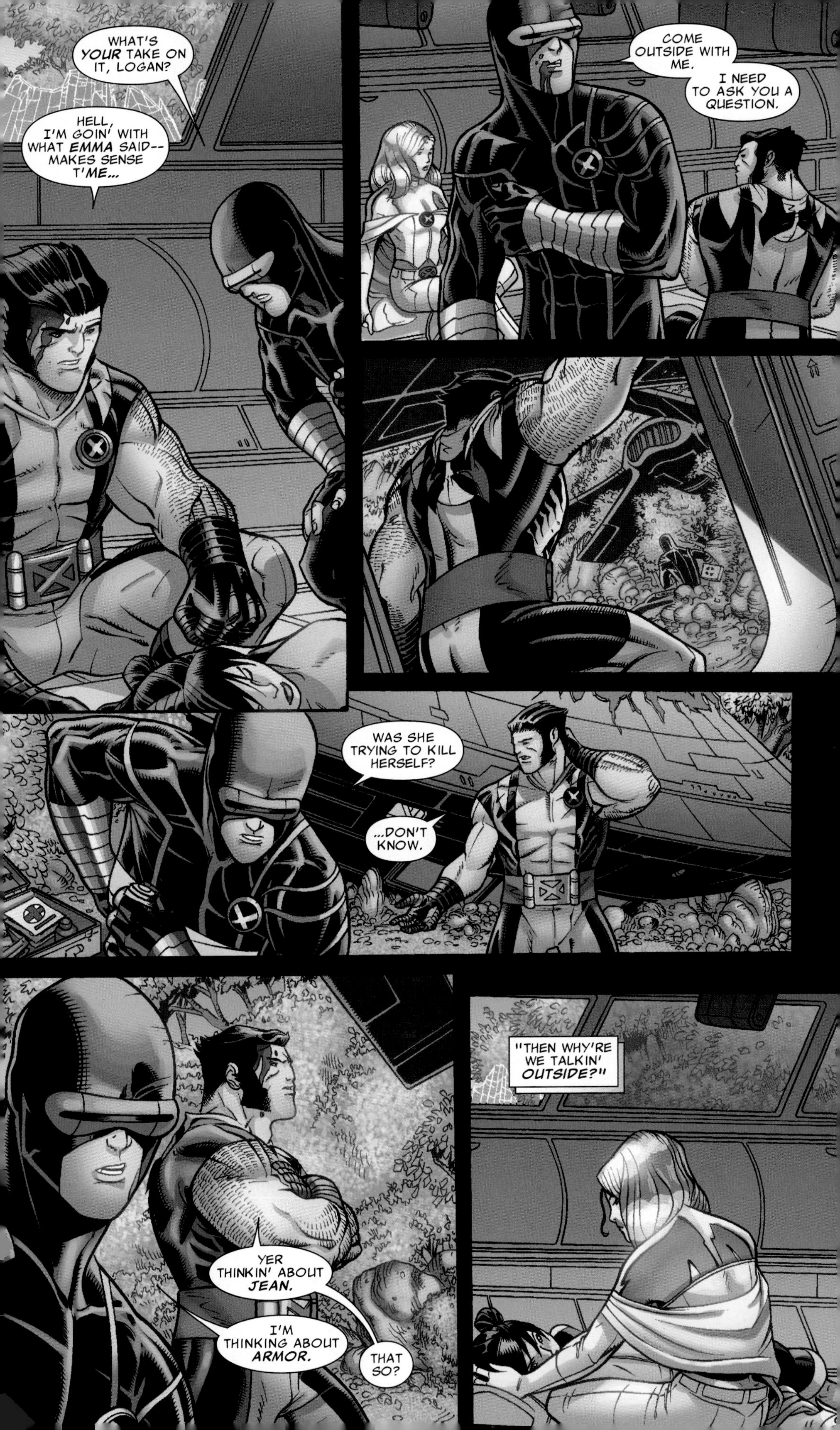
WHAT'S *YOUR* TAKE ON IT, LOGAN?
HELL, I'M GOIN' WITH WHAT *EMMA* SAID-- MAKES SENSE T'*ME...*
COME OUTSIDE WITH ME.
I NEED TO ASK YOU A QUESTION.
WAS SHE TRYING TO KILL HERSELF?
...DON'T KNOW.
"THEN WHY'RE WE TALKIN' *OUTSIDE?*"
YER THINKIN' ABOUT *JEAN.*
I'M THINKING ABOUT *ARMOR.*
THAT SO?

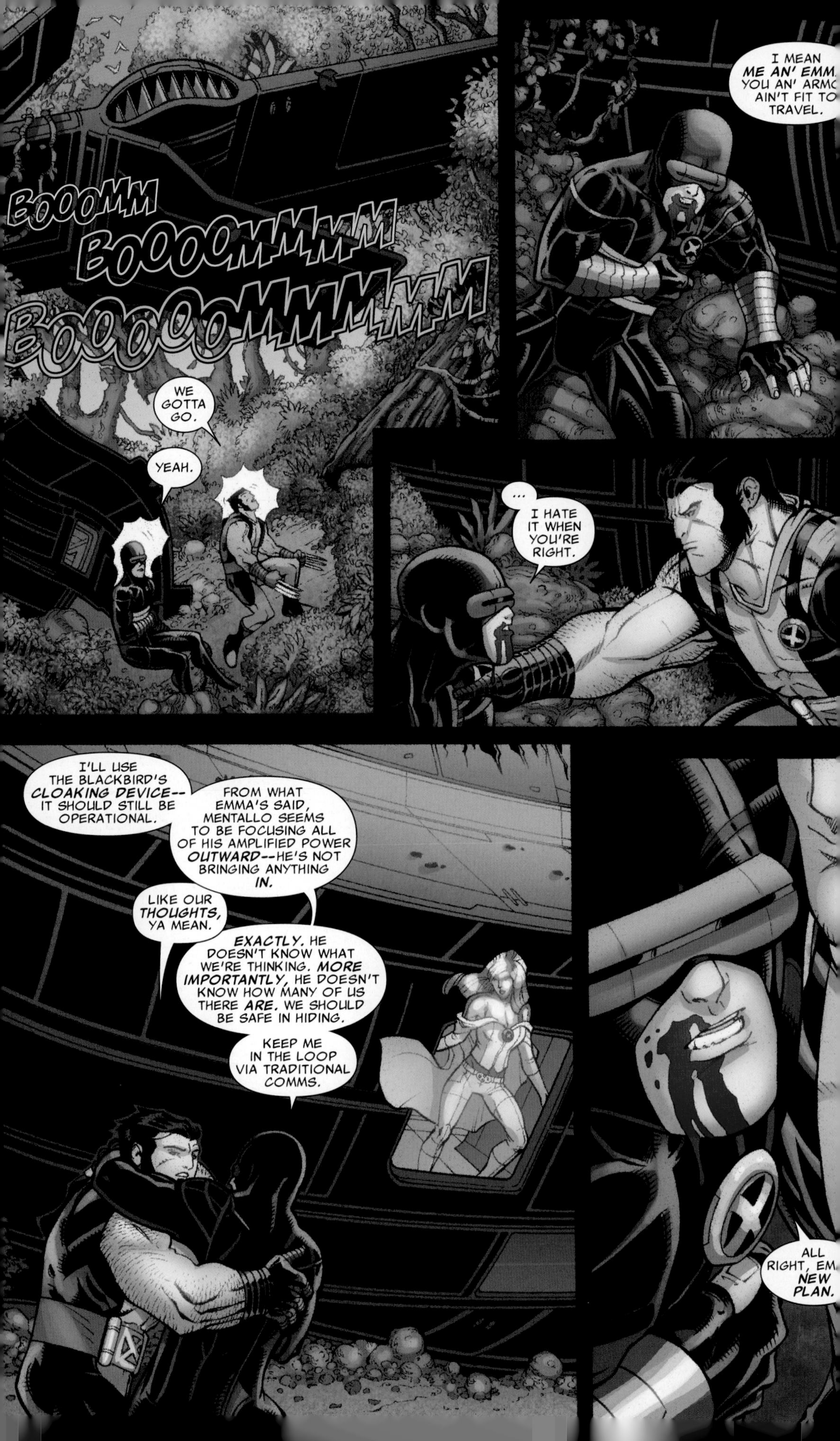
BOOOMM
BOOOOMMMMM
BOOOOOMMMMMM
I MEAN ME AN' EMM. YOU AN' ARMO AIN'T FIT TO TRAVEL.
WE GOTTA GO.
YEAH.
... I HATE IT WHEN YOU'RE RIGHT.
I'LL USE THE BLACKBIRD'S CLOAKING DEVICE-- IT SHOULD STILL BE OPERATIONAL.
FROM WHAT EMMA'S SAID, MENTALLO SEEMS TO BE FOCUSING ALL OF HIS AMPLIFIED POWER OUTWARD--HE'S NOT BRINGING ANYTHING IN.
LIKE OUR THOUGHTS, YA MEAN.
EXACTLY. HE DOESN'T KNOW WHAT WE'RE THINKING. MORE IMPORTANTLY, HE DOESN'T KNOW HOW MANY OF US THERE ARE. WE SHOULD BE SAFE IN HIDING.
KEEP ME IN THE LOOP VIA TRADITIONAL COMMS.
ALL RIGHT, EM NEW PLAN.

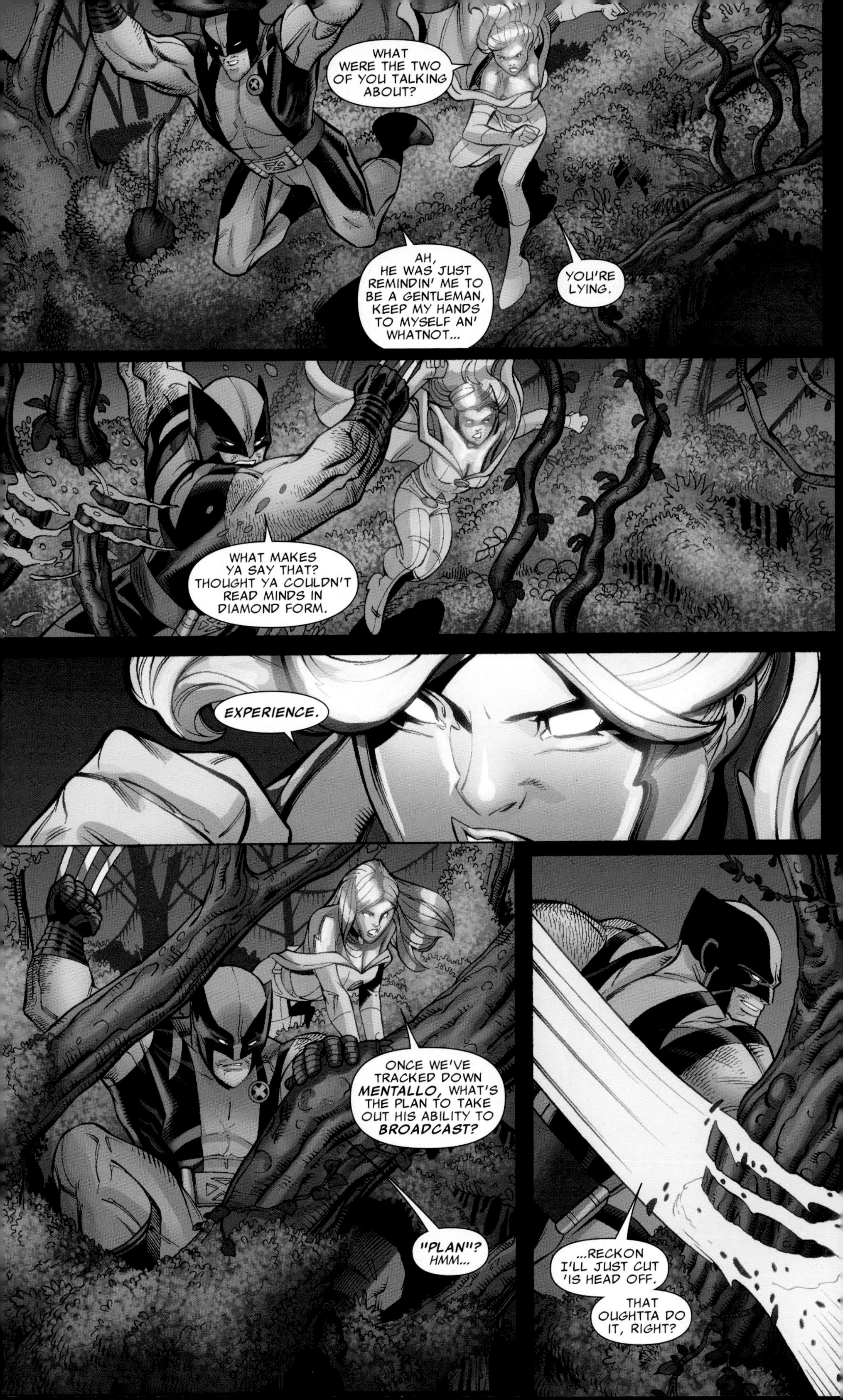
WHAT WERE THE TWO OF YOU TALKING ABOUT?
AH, HE WAS JUST REMINDIN' ME TO BE A GENTLEMAN, KEEP MY HANDS TO MYSELF AN' WHATNOT...
YOU'RE LYING.
WHAT MAKES YA SAY THAT? THOUGHT YA COULDN'T READ MINDS IN DIAMOND FORM.
EXPERIENCE.
ONCE WE'VE TRACKED DOWN MENTALLO, WHAT'S THE PLAN TO TAKE OUT HIS ABILITY TO BROADCAST?
"PLAN"? HMM...
...RECKON I'LL JUST CUT 'IS HEAD OFF.
THAT OUGHTTA DO IT, RIGHT?

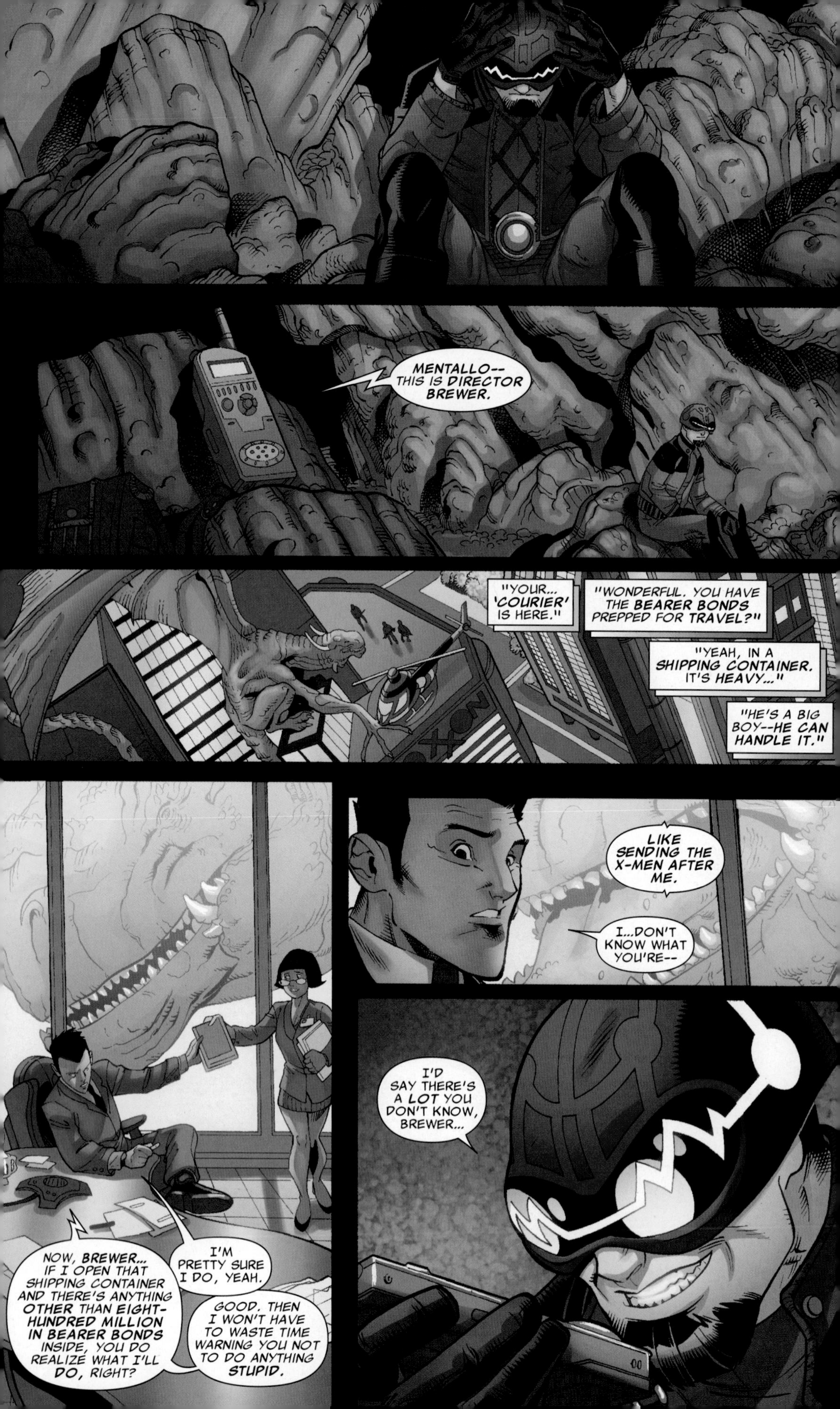

MENTALLO-- THIS IS DIRECTOR BREWER.
"YOUR... 'COURIER' IS HERE."
"WONDERFUL. YOU HAVE THE BEARER BONDS PREPPED FOR TRAVEL?"
"YEAH, IN A SHIPPING CONTAINER. IT'S HEAVY..."
"HE'S A BIG BOY--HE CAN HANDLE IT."
NOW, BREWER... IF I OPEN THAT SHIPPING CONTAINER AND THERE'S ANYTHING OTHER THAN EIGHT-HUNDRED MILLION IN BEARER BONDS INSIDE, YOU DO REALIZE WHAT I'LL DO, RIGHT?
I'M PRETTY SURE I DO, YEAH.
GOOD. THEN I WON'T HAVE TO WASTE TIME WARNING YOU NOT TO DO ANYTHING STUPID.
LIKE SENDING THE X-MEN AFTER ME.
I...DON'T KNOW WHAT YOU'RE--
I'D SAY THERE'S A LOT YOU DON'T KNOW, BREWER...

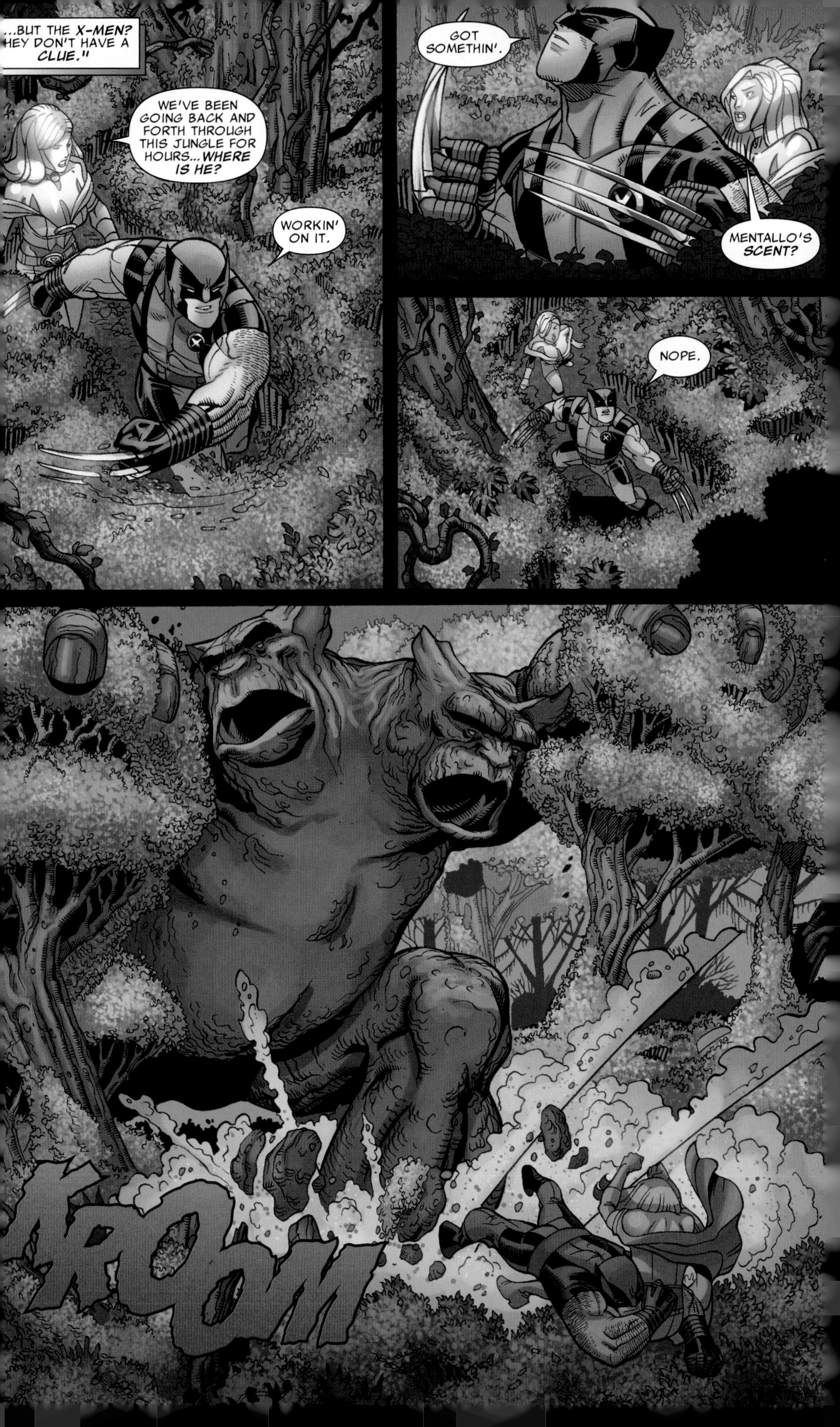

...BUT THE X-MEN? HEY DON'T HAVE A CLUE."
WE'VE BEEN GOING BACK AND FORTH THROUGH THIS JUNGLE FOR HOURS... WHERE IS HE?
WORKIN' ON IT.
GOT SOMETHIN'.
MENTALLO'S SCENT?
NOPE.
KROOM

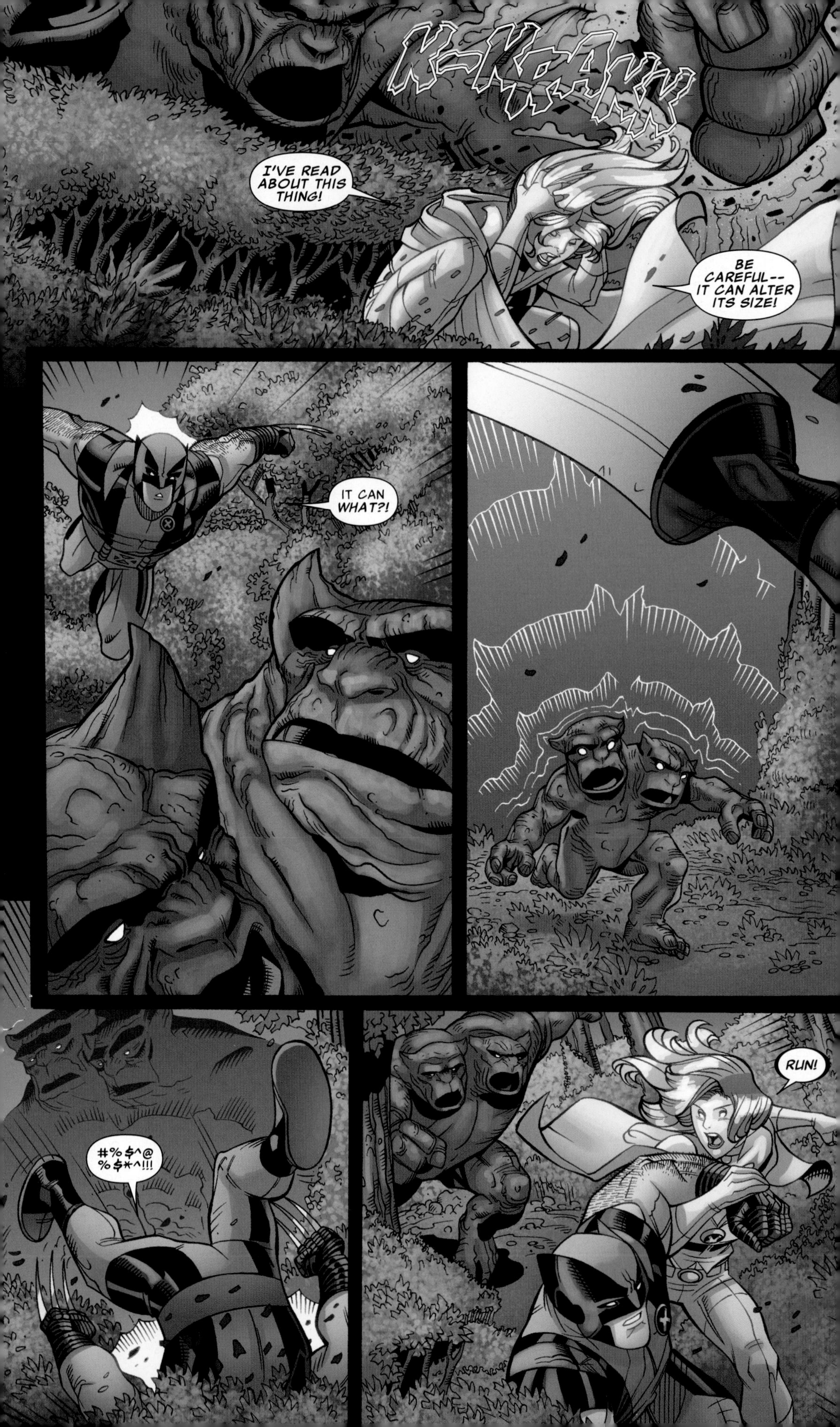
K-KRAKK!
I'VE READ ABOUT THIS THING!
BE CAREFUL-- IT CAN ALTER ITS SIZE!
IT CAN WHAT?!
#% $^@ % $*^!!!
RUN!

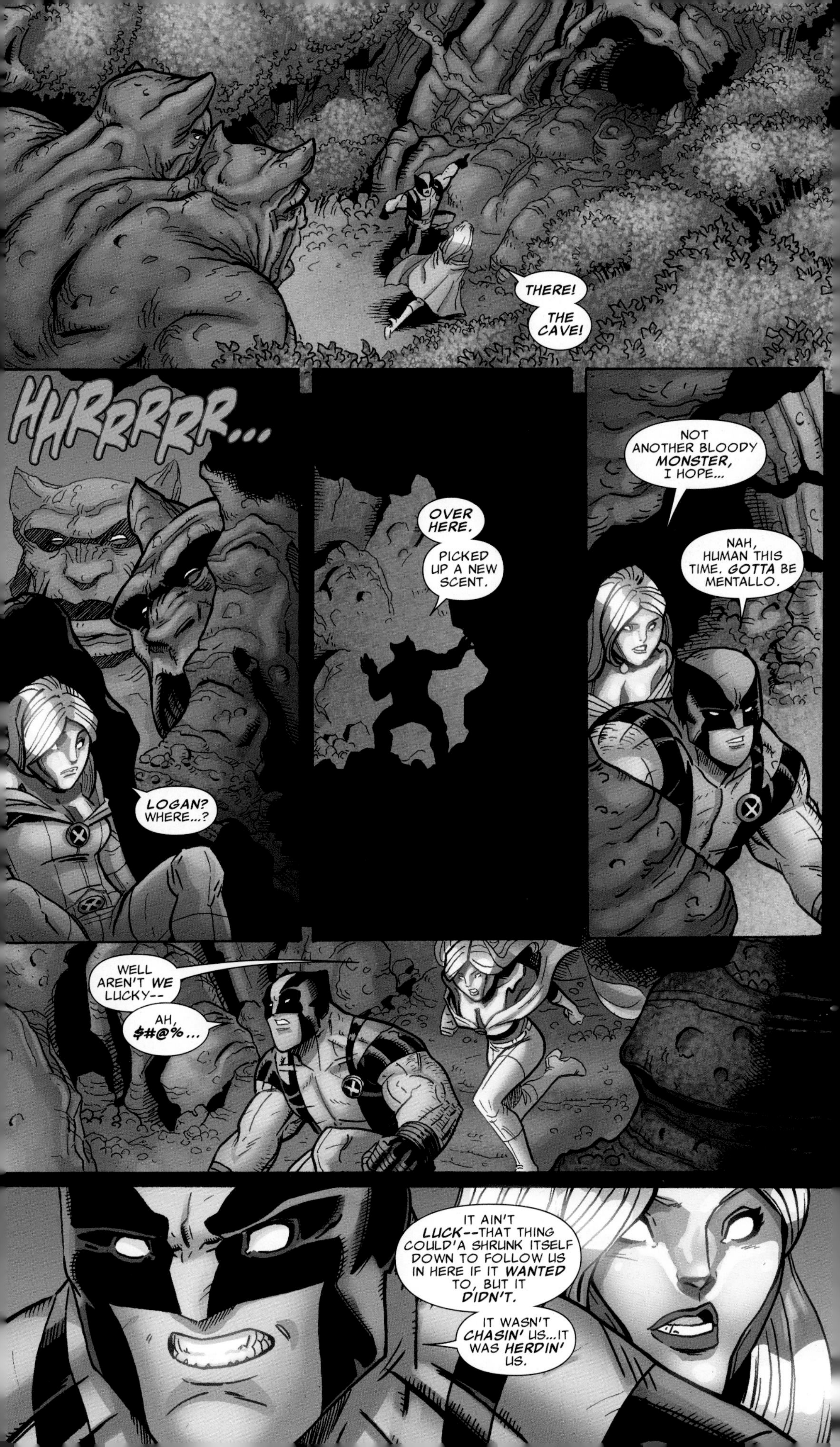
THERE!
THE CAVE!
HURRRRR...
LOGAN? WHERE...?
OVER HERE.
PICKED UP A NEW SCENT.
NOT ANOTHER BLOODY MONSTER, I HOPE...
NAH, HUMAN THIS TIME. GOTTA BE MENTALLO.
WELL AREN'T WE LUCKY--
AH, $#@%...
IT AIN'T LUCK--THAT THING COULD'A SHRUNK ITSELF DOWN TO FOLLOW US IN HERE IF IT WANTED TO, BUT IT DIDN'T.
IT WASN'T CHASIN' US...IT WAS HERDIN' US.

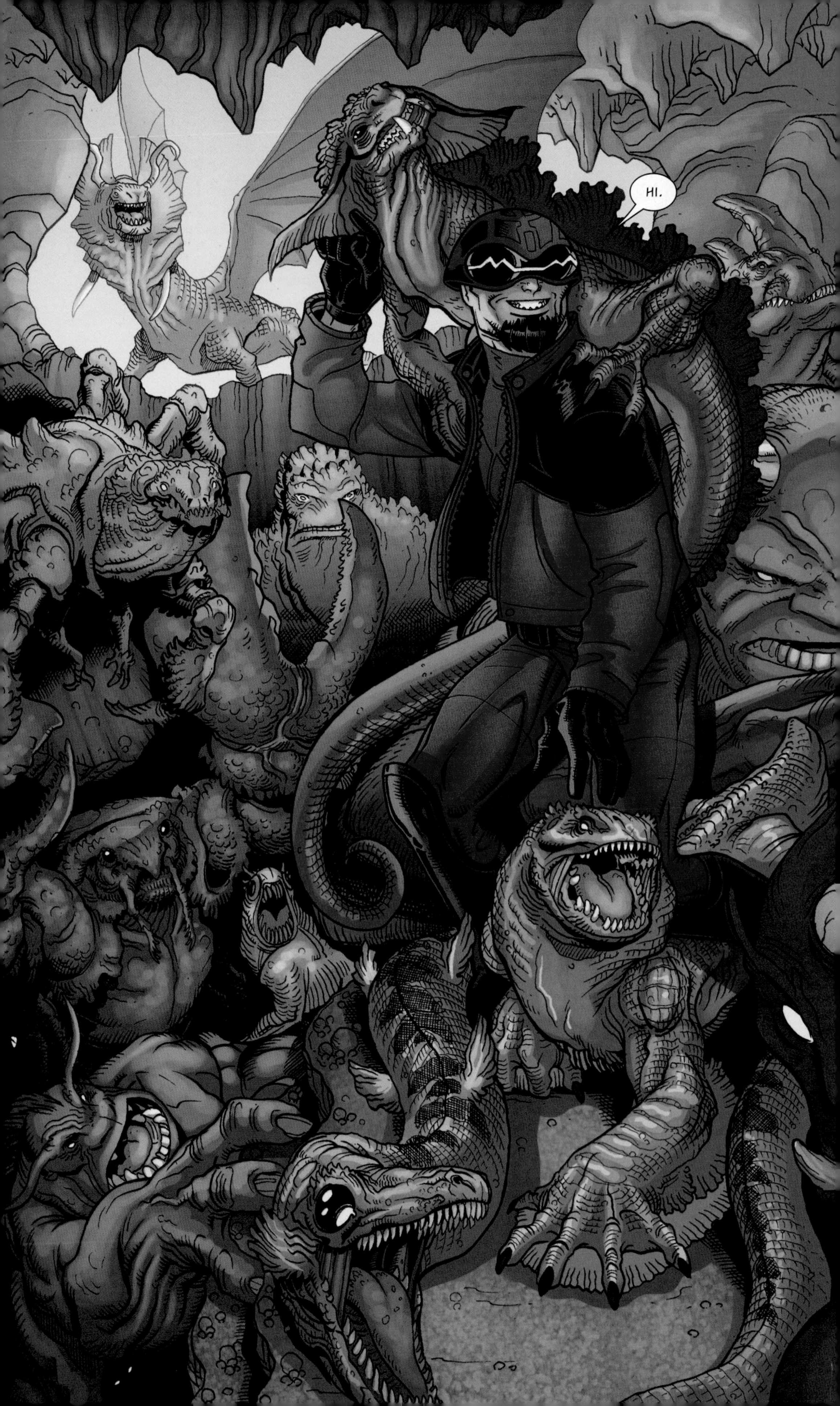
HI.

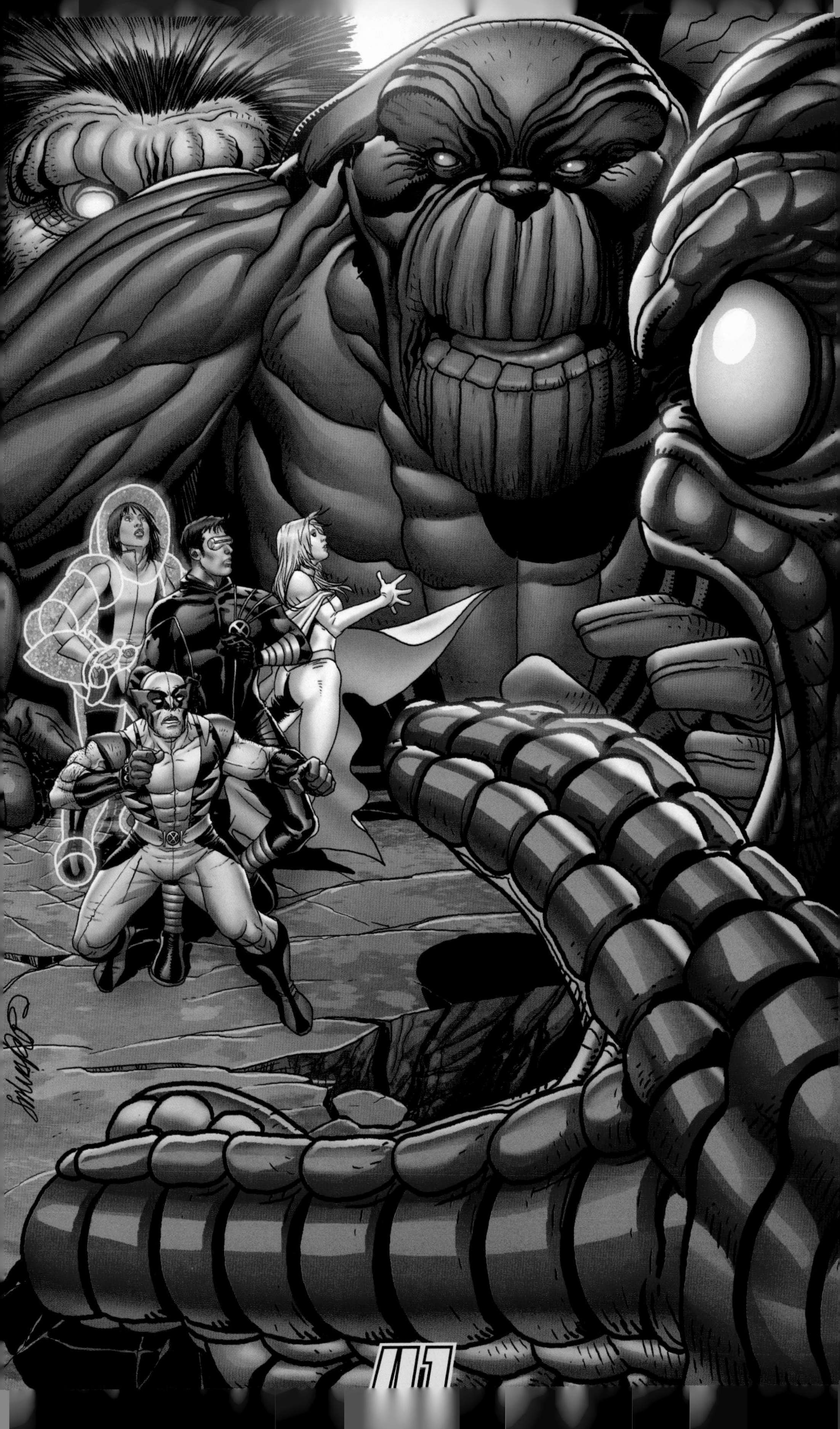

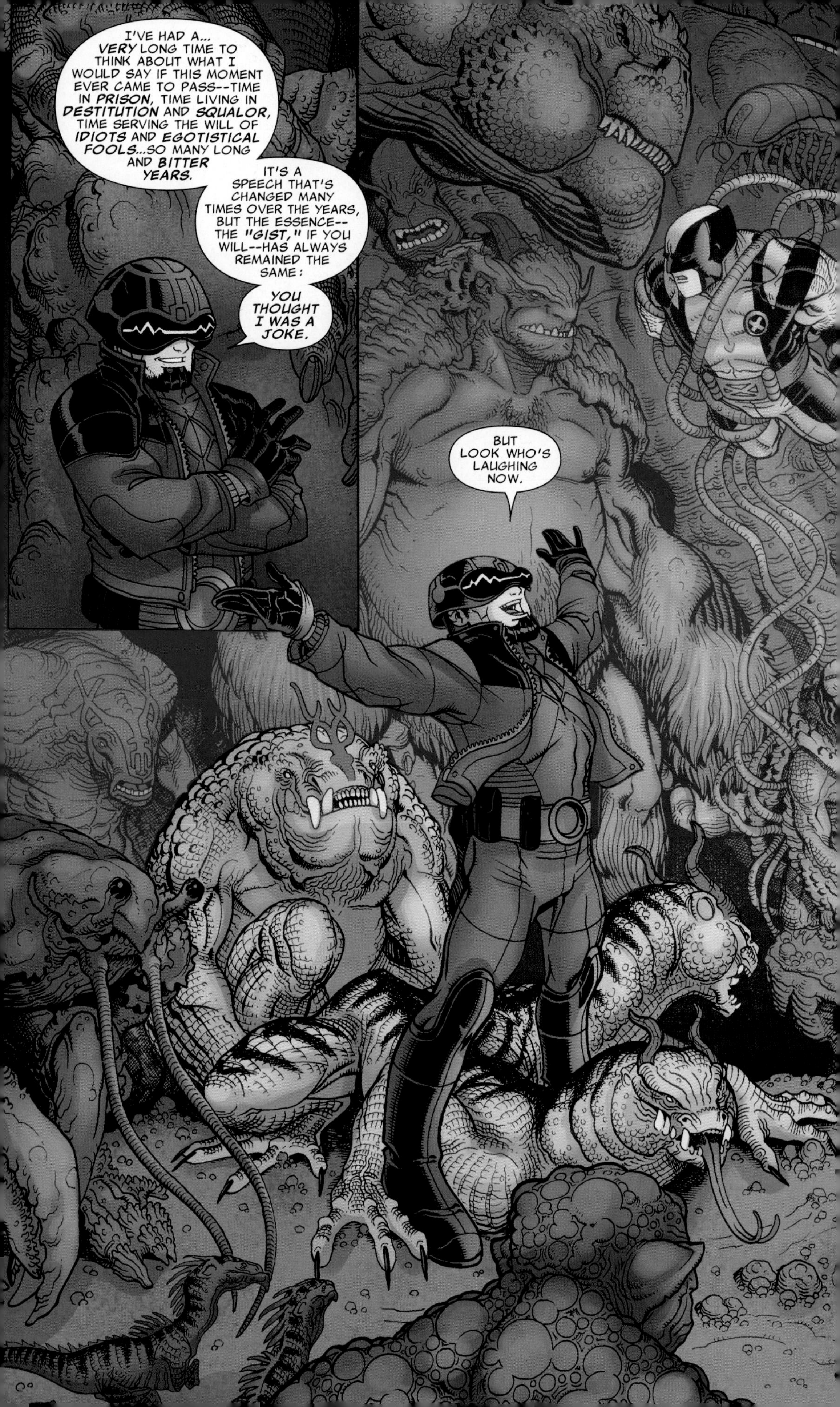

I'VE HAD A... **VERY** LONG TIME TO THINK ABOUT WHAT I WOULD SAY IF THIS MOMENT EVER CAME TO PASS--TIME IN **PRISON**, TIME LIVING IN **DESTITUTION** AND **SQUALOR**, TIME SERVING THE WILL OF **IDIOTS** AND **EGOTISTICAL FOOLS**...SO MANY LONG AND **BITTER YEARS**.
IT'S A SPEECH THAT'S CHANGED MANY TIMES OVER THE YEARS, BUT THE ESSENCE--THE **"GIST,"** IF YOU WILL--HAS ALWAYS REMAINED THE SAME:
YOU THOUGHT I WAS A JOKE.
BUT LOOK WHO'S LAUGHING NOW.

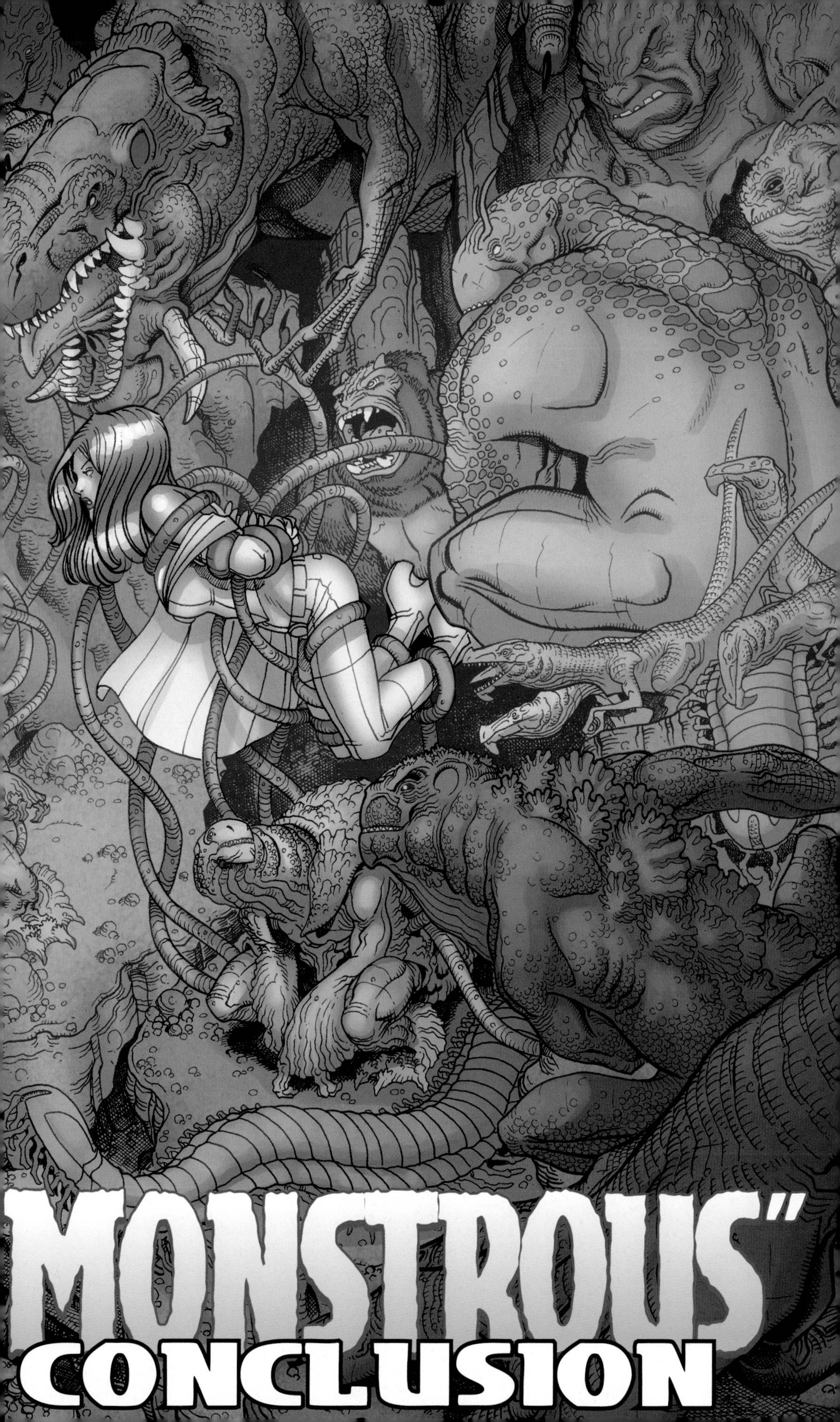

MONSTROUS"
CONCLUSION

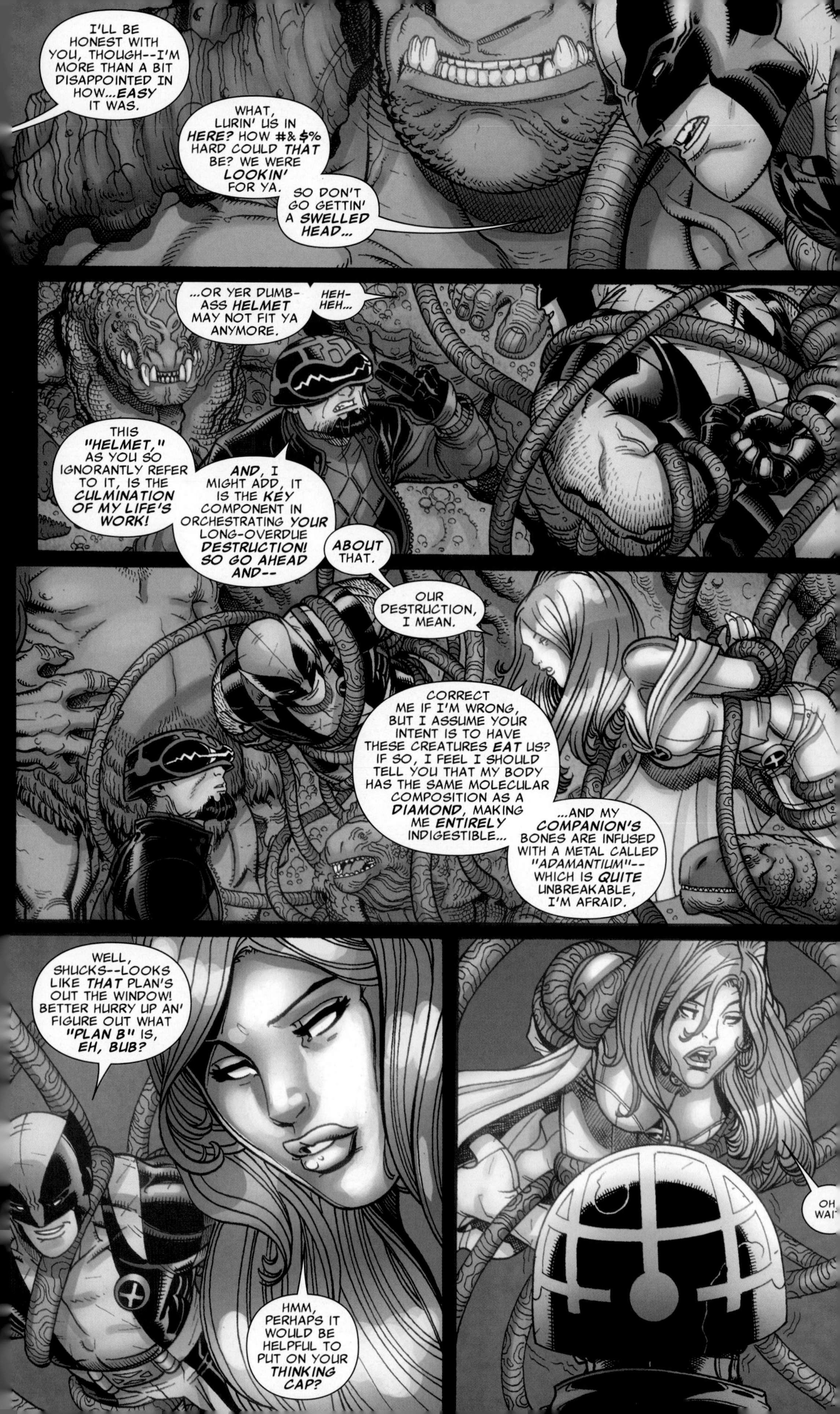
I'LL BE HONEST WITH YOU, THOUGH--I'M MORE THAN A BIT DISAPPOINTED IN HOW...EASY IT WAS.
WHAT, LURIN' US IN HERE? HOW #& $% HARD COULD THAT BE? WE WERE LOOKIN' FOR YA.
SO DON'T GO GETTIN' A SWELLED HEAD...
...OR YER DUMB-ASS HELMET MAY NOT FIT YA ANYMORE.
HEH-HEH...
THIS "HELMET," AS YOU SO IGNORANTLY REFER TO IT, IS THE CULMINATION OF MY LIFE'S WORK!
AND, I MIGHT ADD, IT IS THE KEY COMPONENT IN ORCHESTRATING YOUR LONG-OVERDUE DESTRUCTION! SO GO AHEAD AND--
ABOUT THAT.
OUR DESTRUCTION, I MEAN.
CORRECT ME IF I'M WRONG, BUT I ASSUME YOUR INTENT IS TO HAVE THESE CREATURES EAT US? IF SO, I FEEL I SHOULD TELL YOU THAT MY BODY HAS THE SAME MOLECULAR COMPOSITION AS A DIAMOND, MAKING ME ENTIRELY INDIGESTIBLE...
...AND MY COMPANION'S BONES ARE INFUSED WITH A METAL CALLED "ADAMANTIUM"--WHICH IS QUITE UNBREAKABLE, I'M AFRAID.
WELL, SHUCKS--LOOKS LIKE THAT PLAN'S OUT THE WINDOW! BETTER HURRY UP AN' FIGURE OUT WHAT "PLAN B" IS, EH, BUB?
HMM, PERHAPS IT WOULD BE HELPFUL TO PUT ON YOUR THINKING CAP?
OH, WAI'

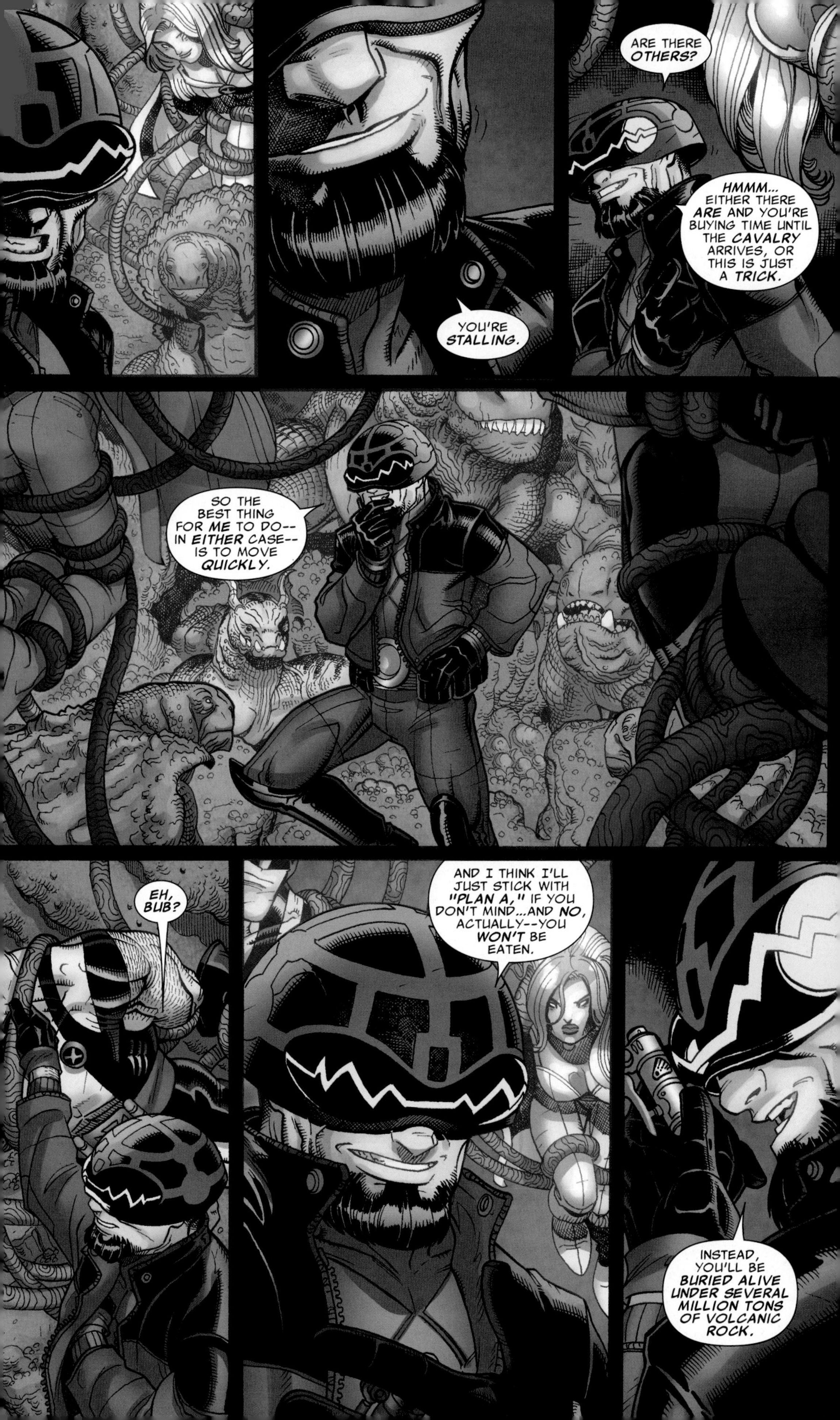
YOU'RE STALLING.
ARE THERE OTHERS?
HMMM... EITHER THERE ARE AND YOU'RE BUYING TIME UNTIL THE CAVALRY ARRIVES, OR THIS IS JUST A TRICK.
SO THE BEST THING FOR ME TO DO-- IN EITHER CASE-- IS TO MOVE QUICKLY.
EH, BUB?
AND I THINK I'LL JUST STICK WITH "PLAN A," IF YOU DON'T MIND...AND NO, ACTUALLY--YOU WON'T BE EATEN.
INSTEAD, YOU'LL BE BURIED ALIVE UNDER SEVERAL MILLION TONS OF VOLCANIC ROCK.

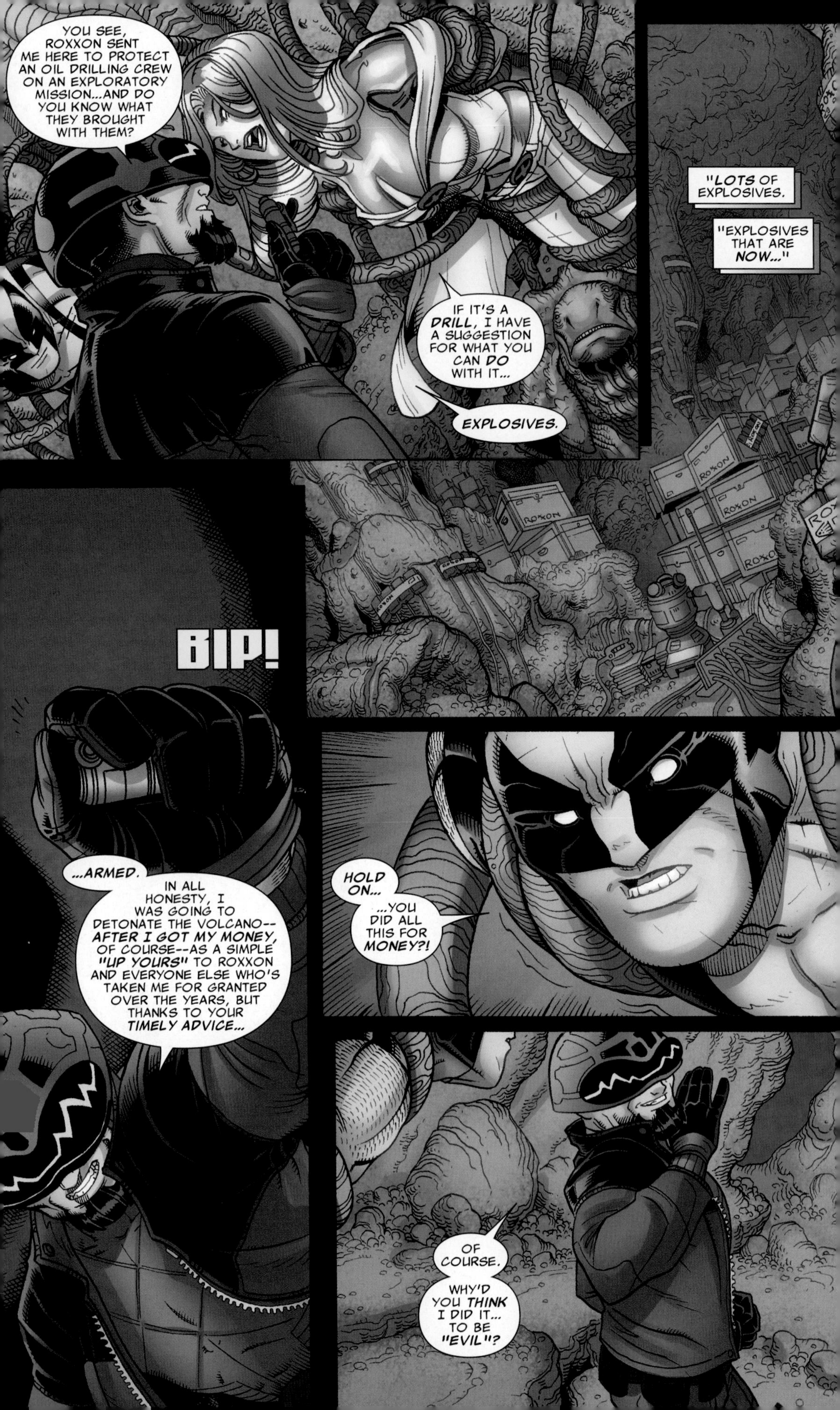
YOU SEE, ROXXON SENT ME HERE TO PROTECT AN OIL DRILLING CREW ON AN EXPLORATORY MISSION...AND DO YOU KNOW WHAT THEY BROUGHT WITH THEM?
IF IT'S A DRILL, I HAVE A SUGGESTION FOR WHAT YOU CAN DO WITH IT...
EXPLOSIVES.
"LOTS OF EXPLOSIVES.
"EXPLOSIVES THAT ARE NOW..."
ROXON
BIP!
...ARMED.
IN ALL HONESTY, I WAS GOING TO DETONATE THE VOLCANO--AFTER I GOT MY MONEY, OF COURSE--AS A SIMPLE "UP YOURS" TO ROXXON AND EVERYONE ELSE WHO'S TAKEN ME FOR GRANTED OVER THE YEARS, BUT THANKS TO YOUR TIMELY ADVICE...
HOLD ON...
...YOU DID ALL THIS FOR MONEY?!
OF COURSE.
WHY'D YOU THINK I DID IT... TO BE "EVIL"?

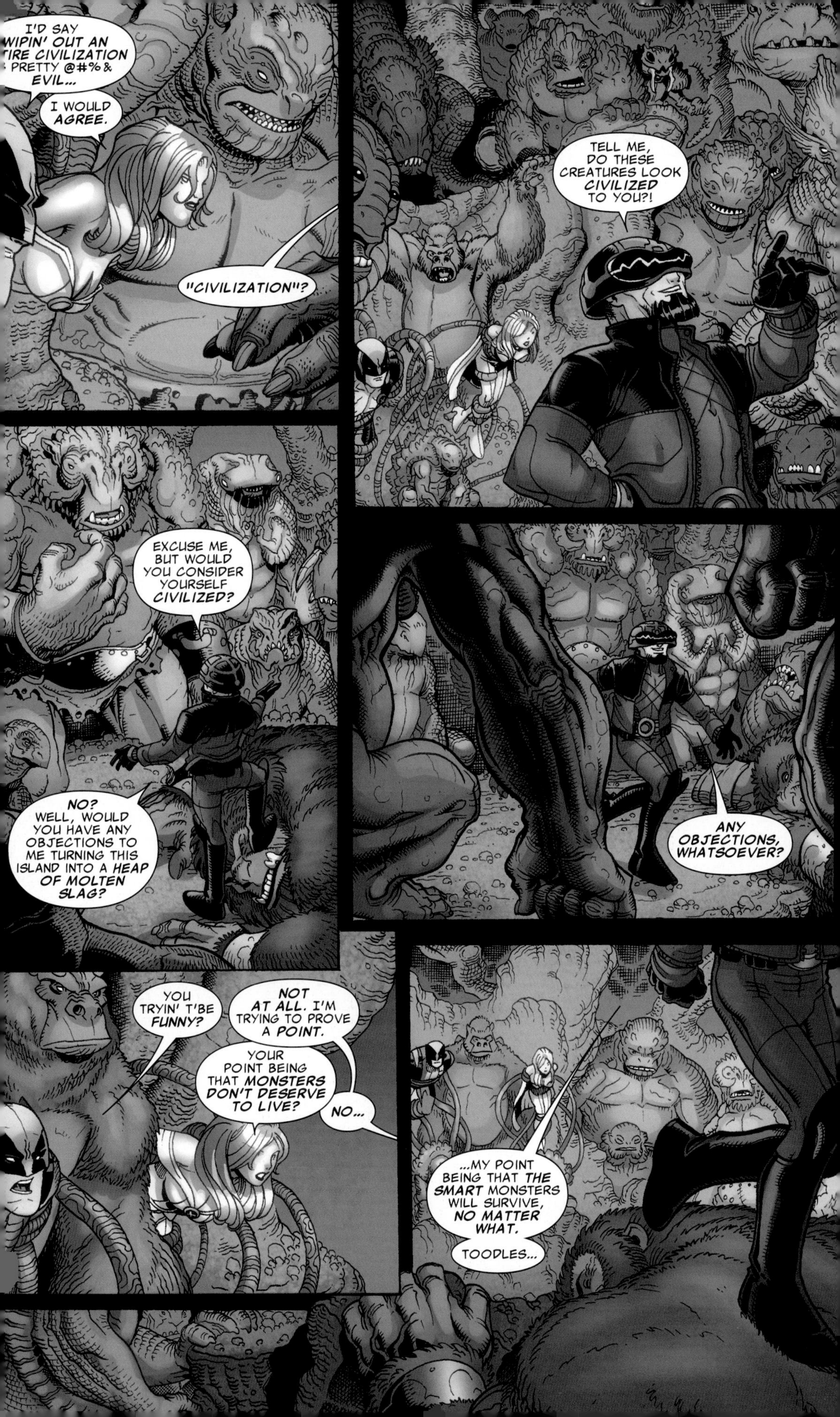
I'D SAY WIPIN' OUT AN TIRE CIVILIZATION PRETTY @#%& EVIL...
I WOULD AGREE.
"CIVILIZATION"?
TELL ME, DO THESE CREATURES LOOK CIVILIZED TO YOU?!
EXCUSE ME, BUT WOULD YOU CONSIDER YOURSELF CIVILIZED?
NO? WELL, WOULD YOU HAVE ANY OBJECTIONS TO ME TURNING THIS ISLAND INTO A HEAP OF MOLTEN SLAG?
ANY OBJECTIONS, WHATSOEVER?
YOU TRYIN' T'BE FUNNY?
NOT AT ALL. I'M TRYING TO PROVE A POINT.
YOUR POINT BEING THAT MONSTERS DON'T DESERVE TO LIVE?
NO...
...MY POINT BEING THAT THE SMART MONSTERS WILL SURVIVE, NO MATTER WHAT.
TOODLES...

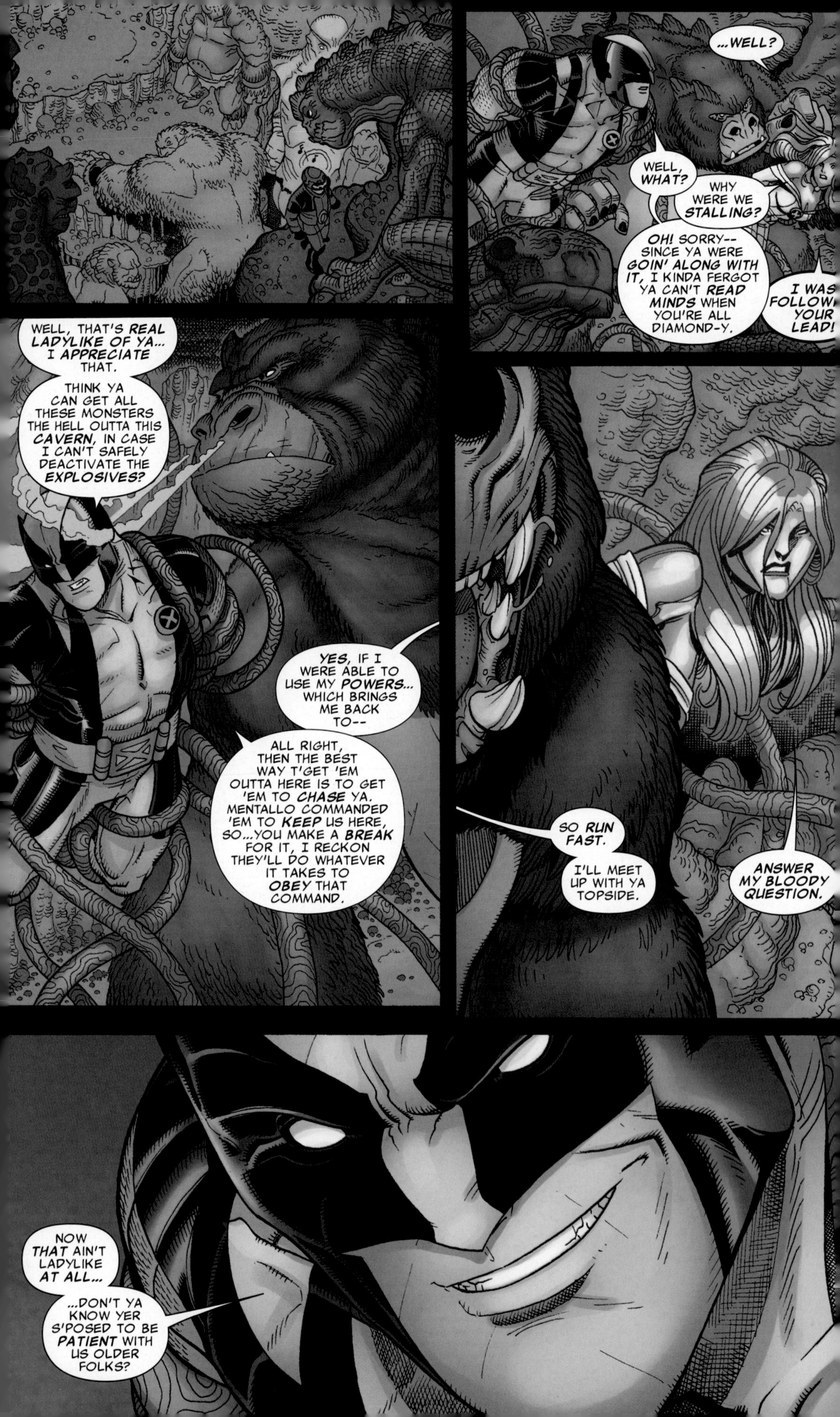
...WELL?
WELL, WHAT?
WHY WERE WE STALLING?
OH! SORRY-- SINCE YA WERE GOIN' ALONG WITH IT, I KINDA FERGOT YA CAN'T READ MINDS WHEN YOU'RE ALL DIAMOND-Y.
I WAS FOLLOW YOUR LEAD!
WELL, THAT'S REAL LADYLIKE OF YA... I APPRECIATE THAT.
THINK YA CAN GET ALL THESE MONSTERS THE HELL OUTTA THIS CAVERN, IN CASE I CAN'T SAFELY DEACTIVATE THE EXPLOSIVES?
YES, IF I WERE ABLE TO USE MY POWERS... WHICH BRINGS ME BACK TO--
ALL RIGHT, THEN THE BEST WAY T'GET 'EM OUTTA HERE IS TO GET 'EM TO CHASE YA. MENTALLO COMMANDED 'EM TO KEEP US HERE, SO...YOU MAKE A BREAK FOR IT, I RECKON THEY'LL DO WHATEVER IT TAKES TO OBEY THAT COMMAND.
SO RUN FAST.
I'LL MEET UP WITH YA TOPSIDE.
ANSWER MY BLOODY QUESTION.
NOW THAT AIN'T LADYLIKE AT ALL...
...DON'T YA KNOW YER S'POSED TO BE PATIENT WITH US OLDER FOLKS?

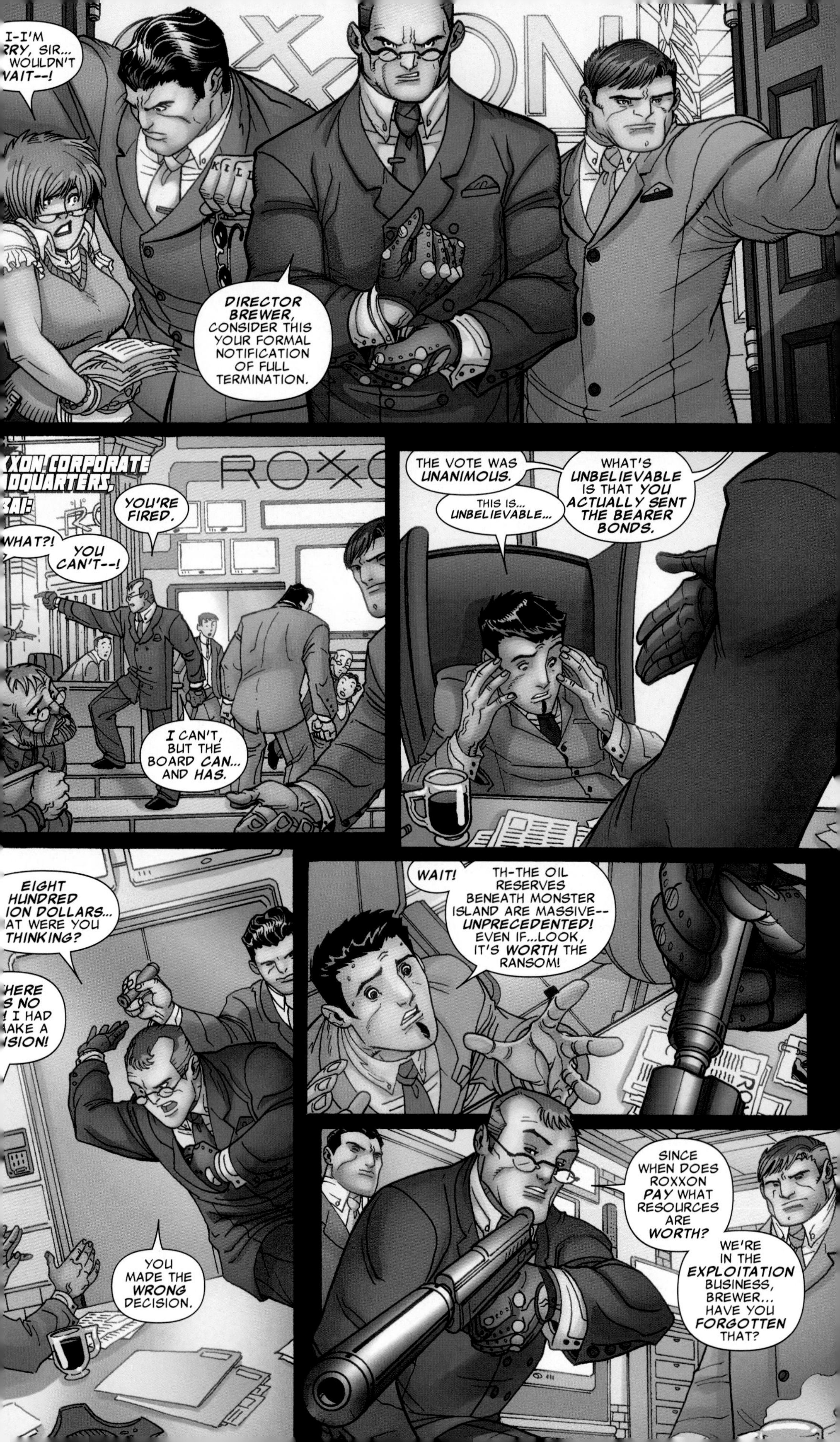
I-I'M
RRY, SIR... WOULDN'T WAIT--!
DIRECTOR BREWER, CONSIDER THIS YOUR FORMAL NOTIFICATION OF FULL TERMINATION.
XON CORPORATE DQUARTERS, BAI:
YOU'RE FIRED.
WHAT?!
YOU CAN'T--!
I CAN'T, BUT THE BOARD CAN... AND HAS.
THE VOTE WAS UNANIMOUS.
THIS IS... UNBELIEVABLE...
WHAT'S UNBELIEVABLE IS THAT YOU ACTUALLY SENT THE BEARER BONDS.
EIGHT HUNDRED ION DOLLARS... AT WERE YOU THINKING?
HERE S NO ! I HAD AKE A SION!
YOU MADE THE WRONG DECISION.
WAIT!
TH-THE OIL RESERVES BENEATH MONSTER ISLAND ARE MASSIVE-- UNPRECEDENTED! EVEN IF...LOOK, IT'S WORTH THE RANSOM!
SINCE WHEN DOES ROXXON PAY WHAT RESOURCES ARE WORTH?
WE'RE IN THE EXPLOITATION BUSINESS, BREWER... HAVE YOU FORGOTTEN THAT?

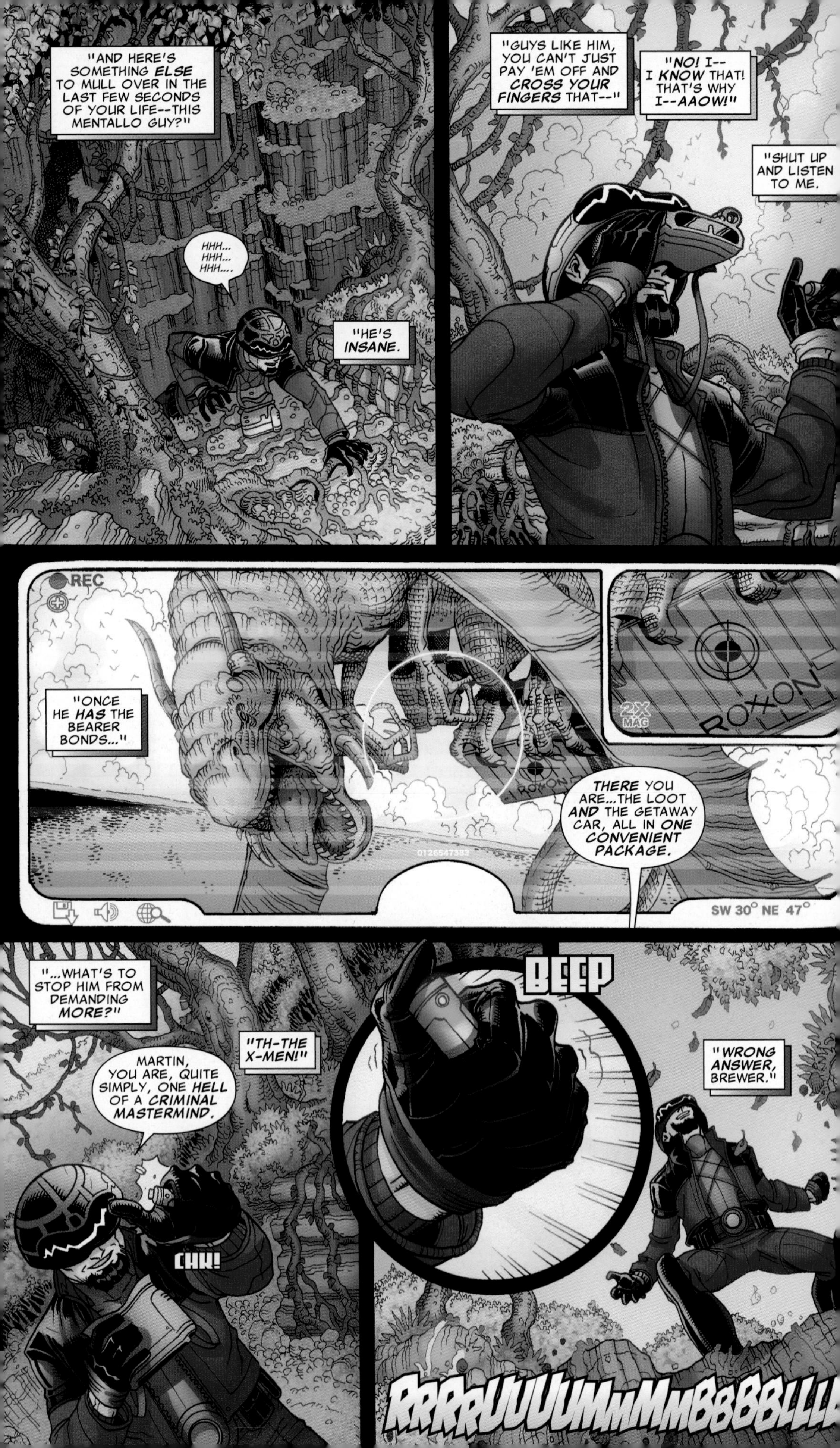
"AND HERE'S SOMETHING ELSE TO MULL OVER IN THE LAST FEW SECONDS OF YOUR LIFE--THIS MENTALLO GUY?"
HHH... HHH... HHH....
"HE'S INSANE.
"GUYS LIKE HIM, YOU CAN'T JUST PAY 'EM OFF AND CROSS YOUR FINGERS THAT--"
"NO! I-- I KNOW THAT! THAT'S WHY I--AAOW!"
"SHUT UP AND LISTEN TO ME.
REC
"ONCE HE HAS THE BEARER BONDS..."
2X MAG
ROXON
THERE YOU ARE...THE LOOT AND THE GETAWAY CAR, ALL IN ONE CONVENIENT PACKAGE.
0126547383
SW 30° NE 47°
"...WHAT'S TO STOP HIM FROM DEMANDING MORE?"
"TH-THE X-MEN!"
MARTIN, YOU ARE, QUITE SIMPLY, ONE HELL OF A CRIMINAL MASTERMIND.
CHK!
BEEP
"WRONG ANSWER, BREWER."
RRRRUUUUMMMMMBBBBLLLL

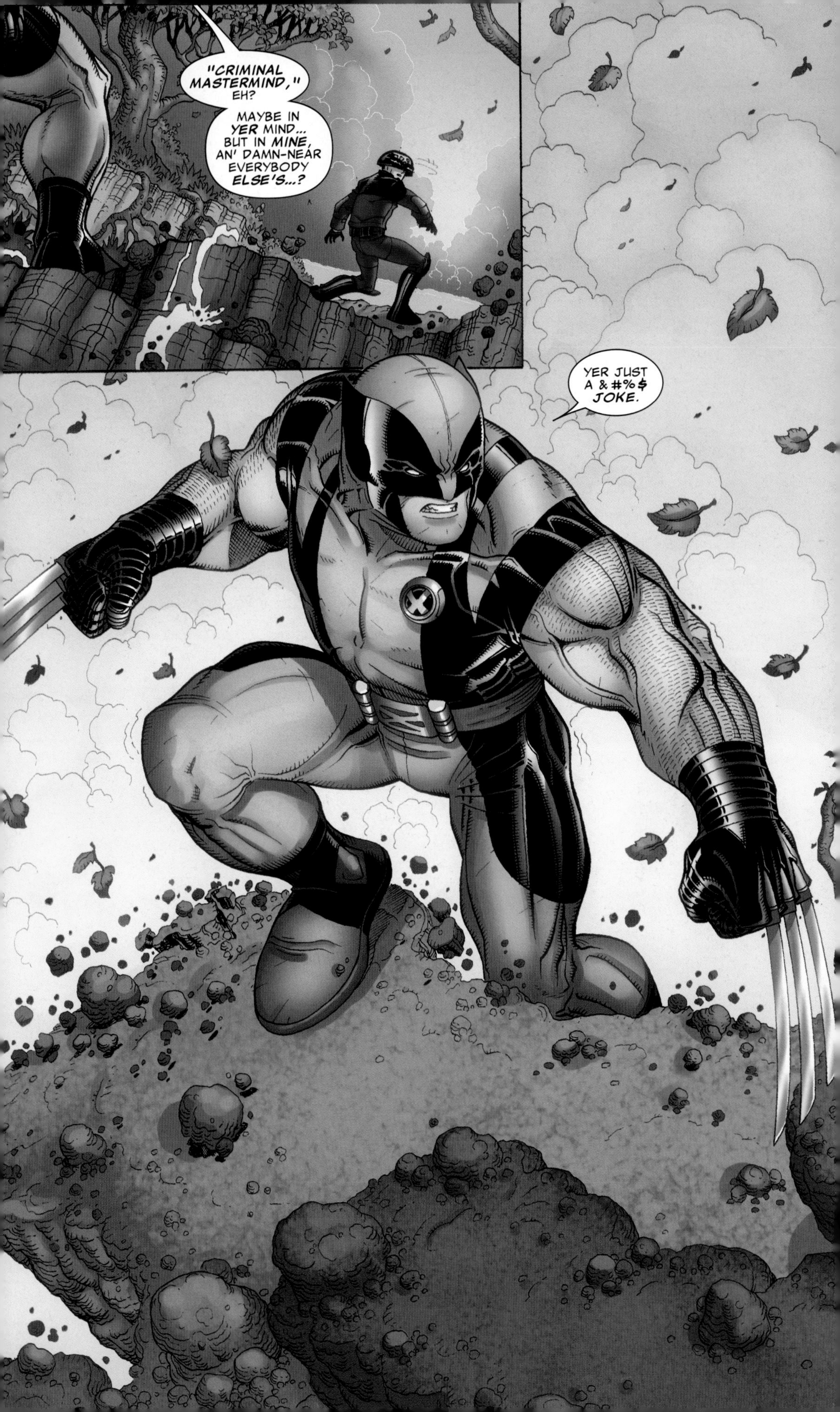
"CRIMINAL MASTERMIND," EH?
MAYBE IN YER MIND... BUT IN MINE, AN' DAMN-NEAR EVERYBODY ELSE'S...?
YER JUST A &#%$ JOKE.

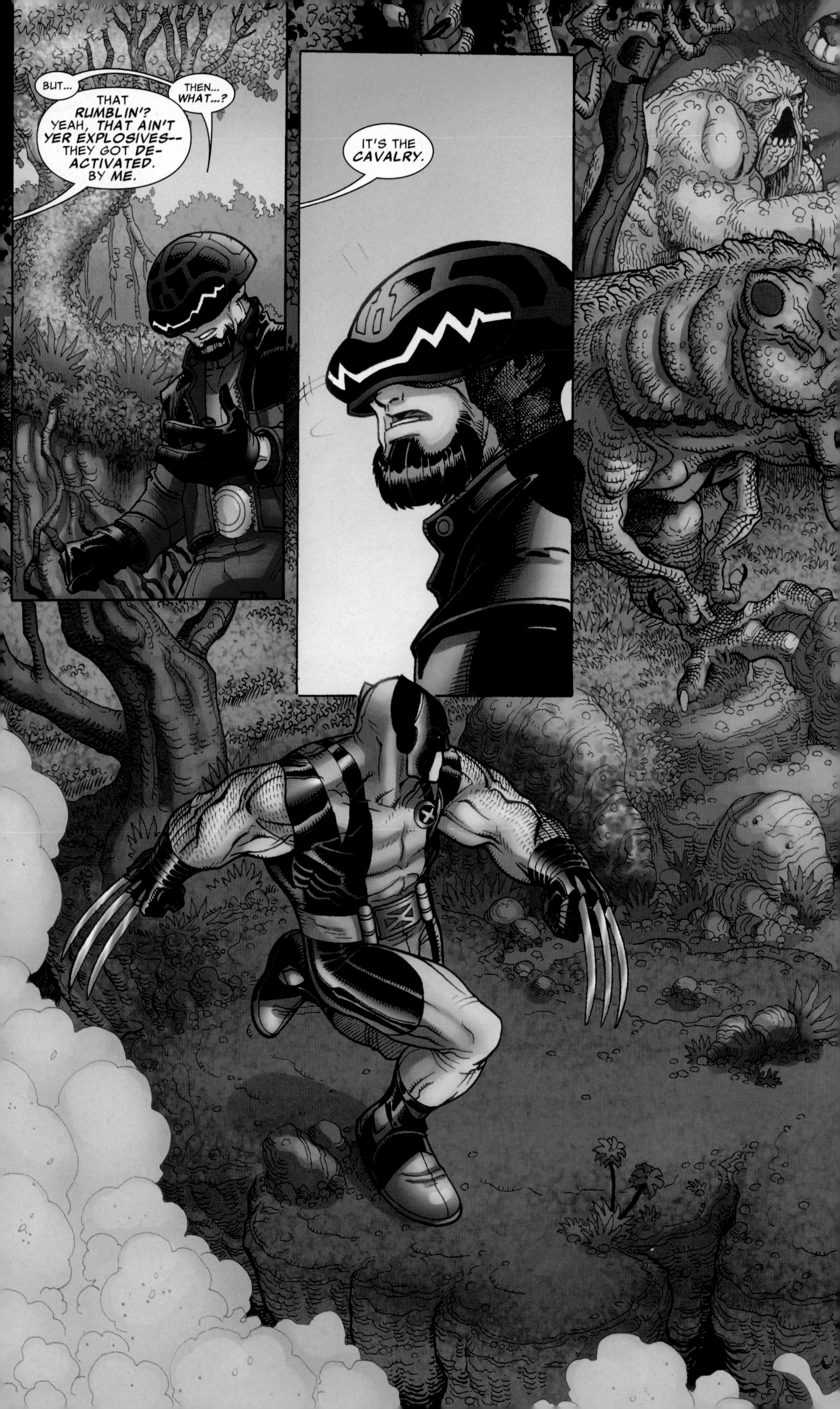

BUT...
THAT RUMBLIN'? YEAH, THAT AIN'T YER EXPLOSIVES-- THEY GOT DE-ACTIVATED. BY ME.
THEN... WHAT...?
IT'S THE CAVALRY.

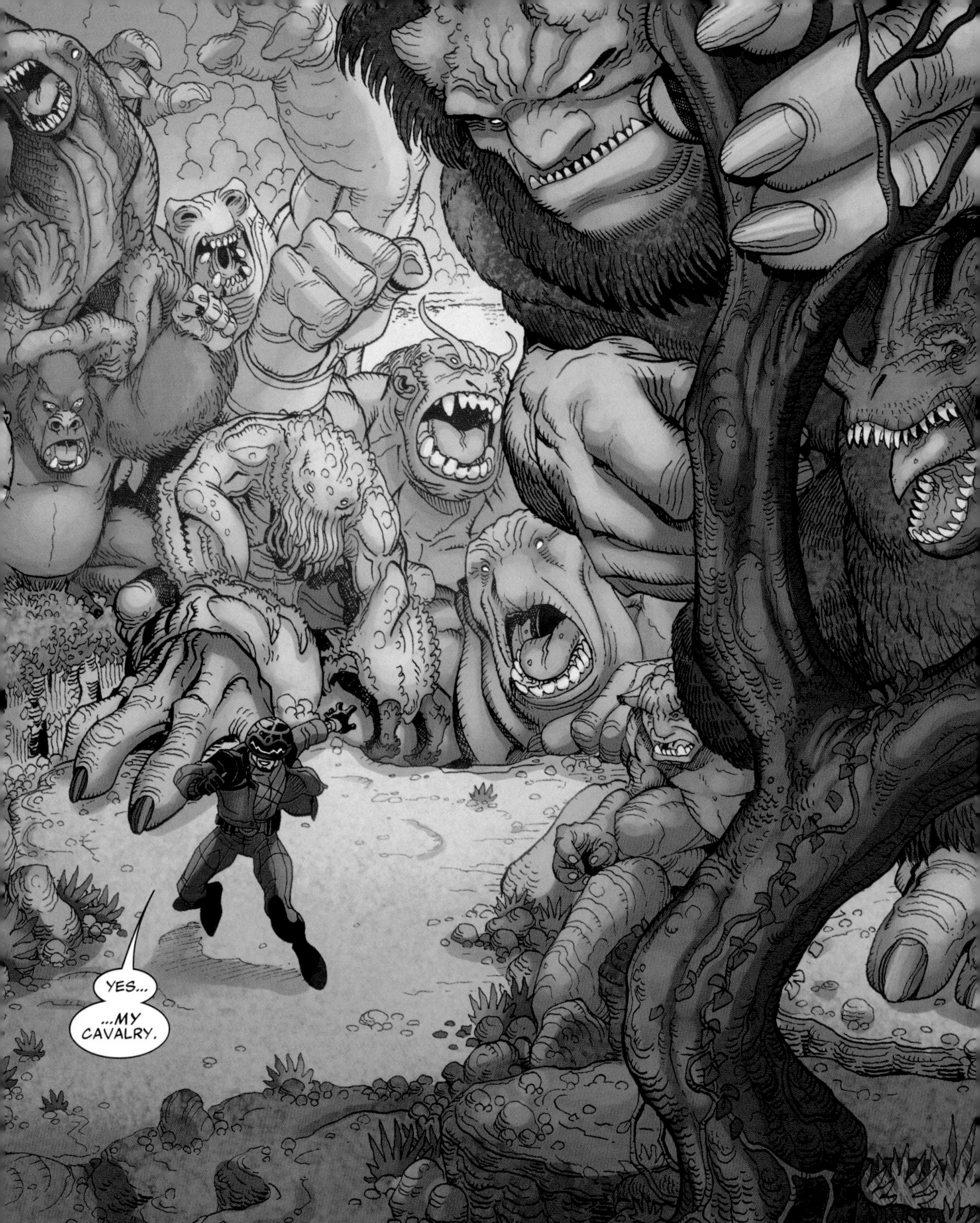
YES...
...MY CAVALRY.
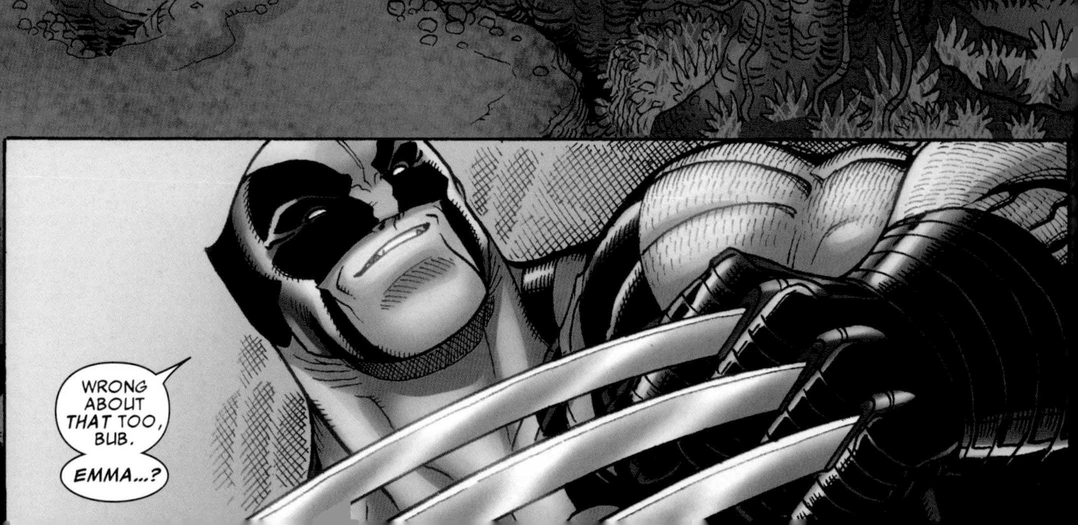
WRONG ABOUT THAT TOO, BUB.
EMMA...?

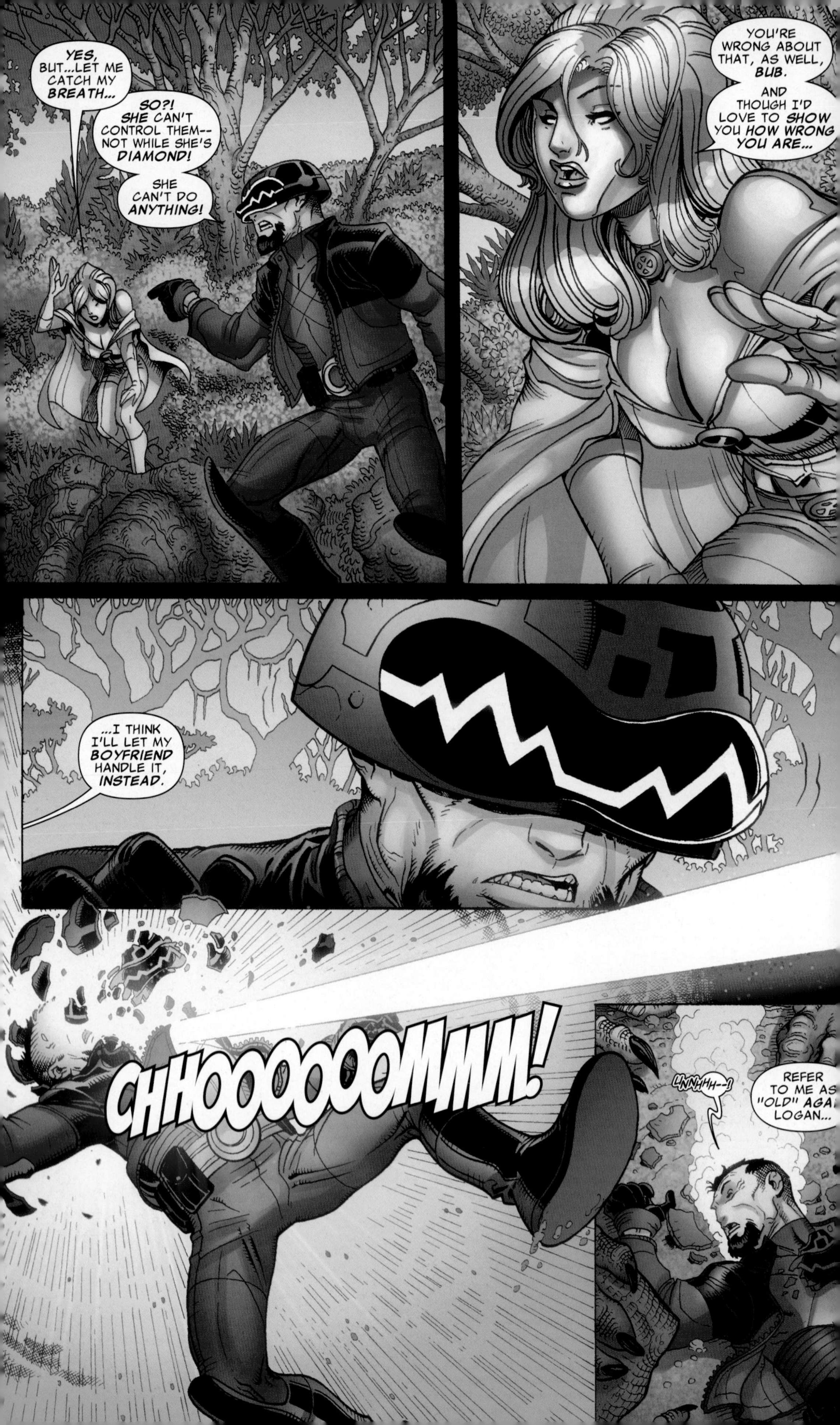
YES, BUT...LET ME CATCH MY BREATH...
SO?! SHE CAN'T CONTROL THEM--NOT WHILE SHE'S DIAMOND!
SHE CAN'T DO ANYTHING!
YOU'RE WRONG ABOUT THAT, AS WELL, BUB.
AND THOUGH I'D LOVE TO SHOW YOU HOW WRONG YOU ARE...
...I THINK I'LL LET MY BOYFRIEND HANDLE IT, INSTEAD.
CHHOOOOOOMMMM!
UNNHHH--!
REFER TO ME AS "OLD" AGA LOGAN...

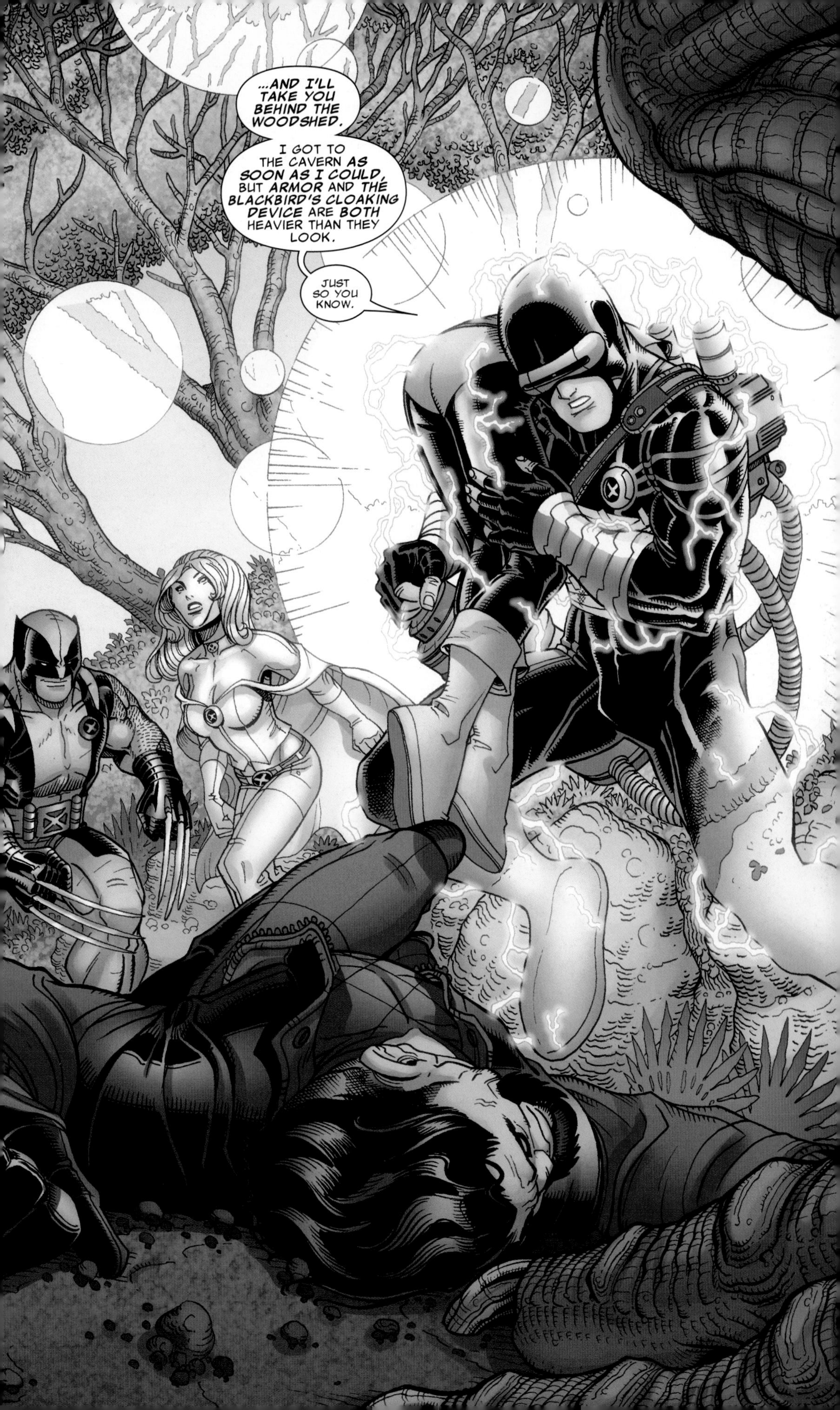
...AND I'LL TAKE YOU BEHIND THE WOODSHED.
I GOT TO THE CAVERN AS SOON AS I COULD, BUT ARMOR AND THE BLACKBIRD'S CLOAKING DEVICE ARE BOTH HEAVIER THAN THEY LOOK.
JUST SO YOU KNOW.

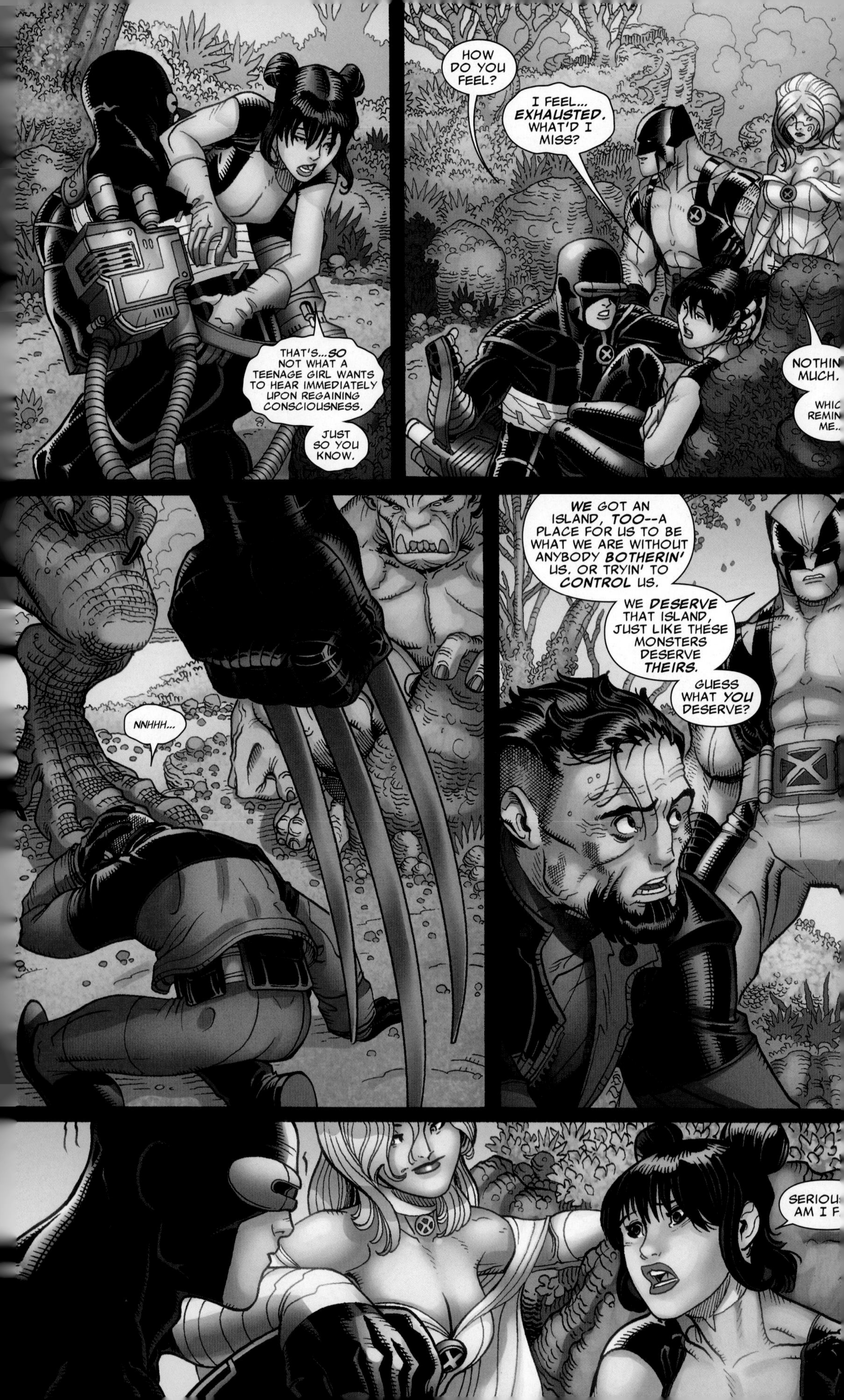
THAT'S...SO NOT WHAT A TEENAGE GIRL WANTS TO HEAR IMMEDIATELY UPON REGAINING CONSCIOUSNESS.
JUST SO YOU KNOW.
HOW DO YOU FEEL?
I FEEL... EXHAUSTED. WHAT'D I MISS?
NOTHIN MUCH.
WHIC REMIN ME..
NNHHH...
WE GOT AN ISLAND, TOO--A PLACE FOR US TO BE WHAT WE ARE WITHOUT ANYBODY BOTHERIN' US. OR TRYIN' TO CONTROL US.
WE DESERVE THAT ISLAND, JUST LIKE THESE MONSTERS DESERVE THEIRS.
GUESS WHAT YOU DESERVE?
SERIOU AM I F

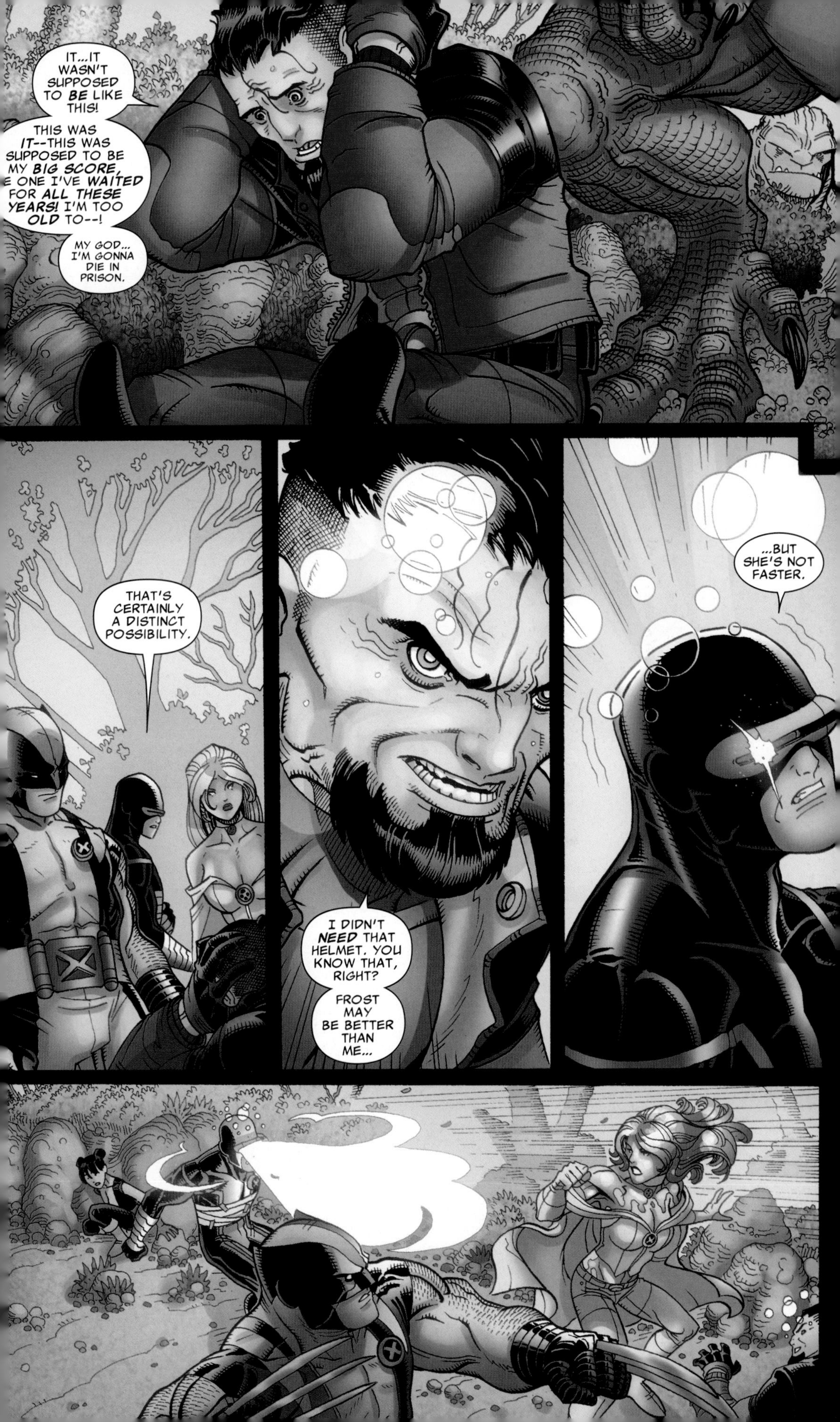
IT...IT WASN'T SUPPOSED TO BE LIKE THIS!
THIS WAS IT--THIS WAS SUPPOSED TO BE MY BIG SCORE, E ONE I'VE WAITED FOR ALL THESE YEARS! I'M TOO OLD TO--!
MY GOD... I'M GONNA DIE IN PRISON.
THAT'S CERTAINLY A DISTINCT POSSIBILITY.
I DIDN'T NEED THAT HELMET. YOU KNOW THAT, RIGHT?
FROST MAY BE BETTER THAN ME...
...BUT SHE'S NOT FASTER.

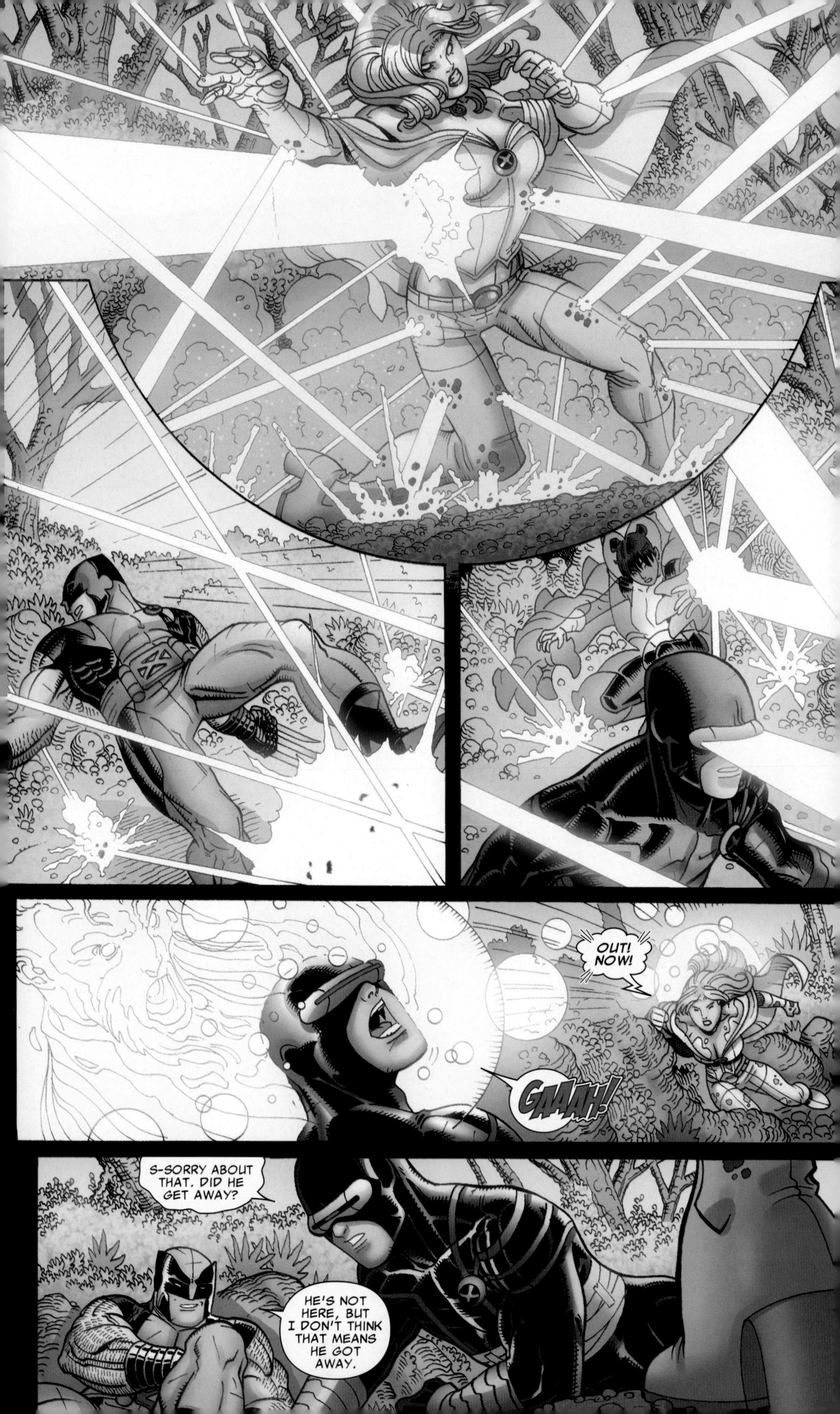
OUT! NOW!
GAAAH!
S-SORRY ABOUT THAT. DID HE GET AWAY?
HE'S NOT HERE, BUT I DON'T THINK THAT MEANS HE GOT AWAY.

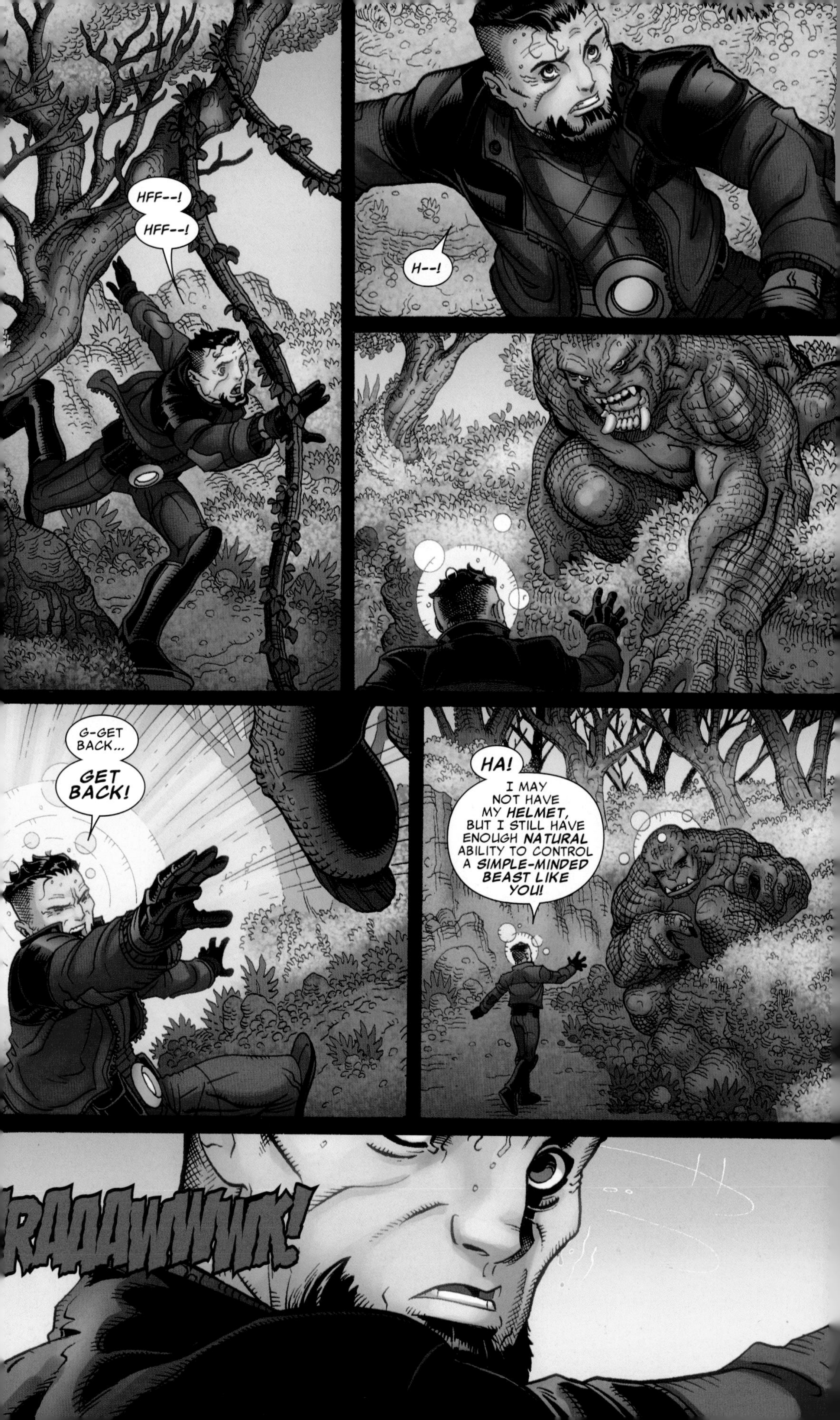
HFF--!
HFF--!
H--!
G-GET BACK...
GET BACK!
HA!
I MAY NOT HAVE MY HELMET, BUT I STILL HAVE ENOUGH NATURAL ABILITY TO CONTROL A SIMPLE-MINDED BEAST LIKE YOU!
RAAAWWWK!

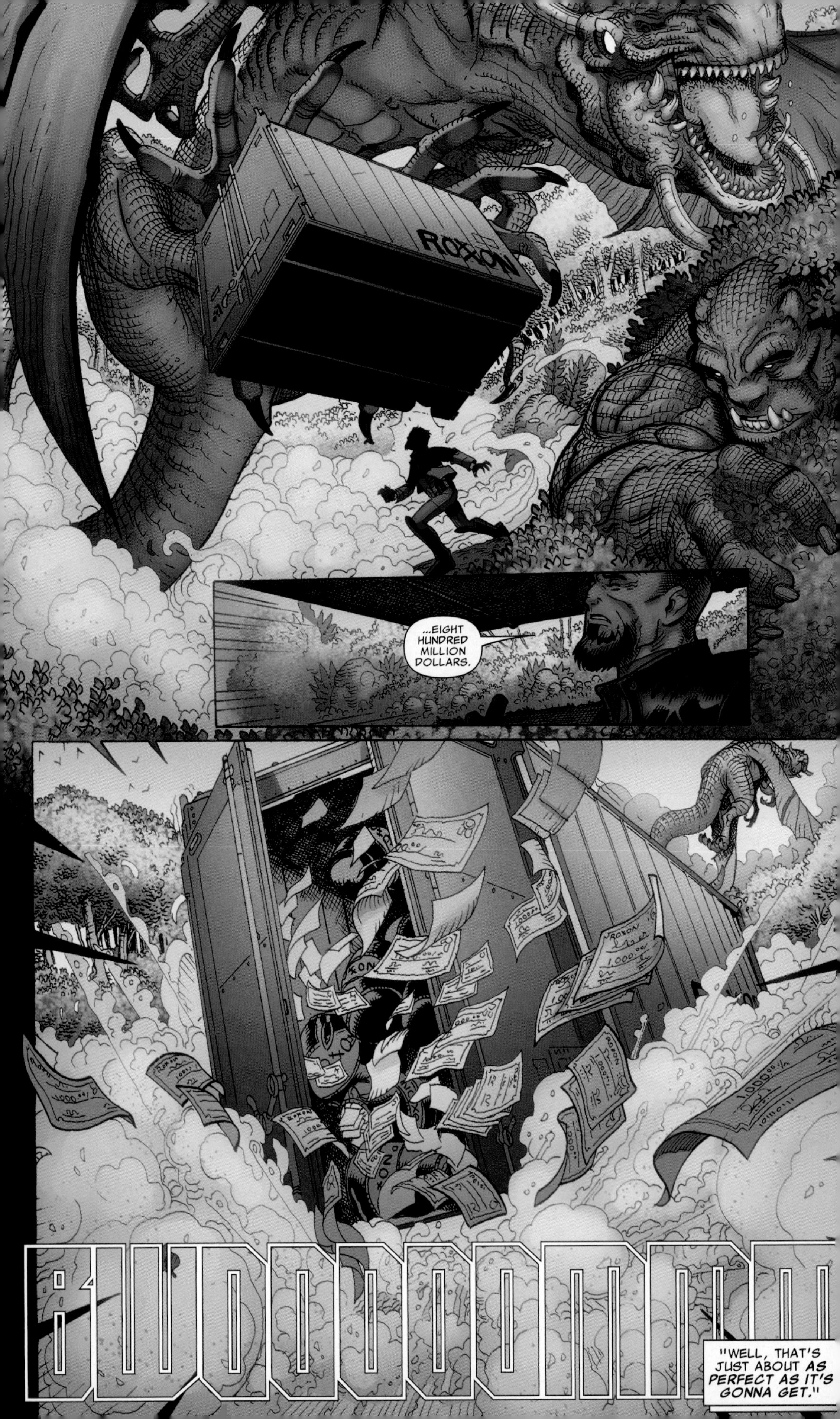

...EIGHT HUNDRED MILLION DOLLARS.
ROXXON
BUDOOOOMMM
"WELL, THAT'S JUST ABOUT AS PERFECT AS IT'S GONNA GET."

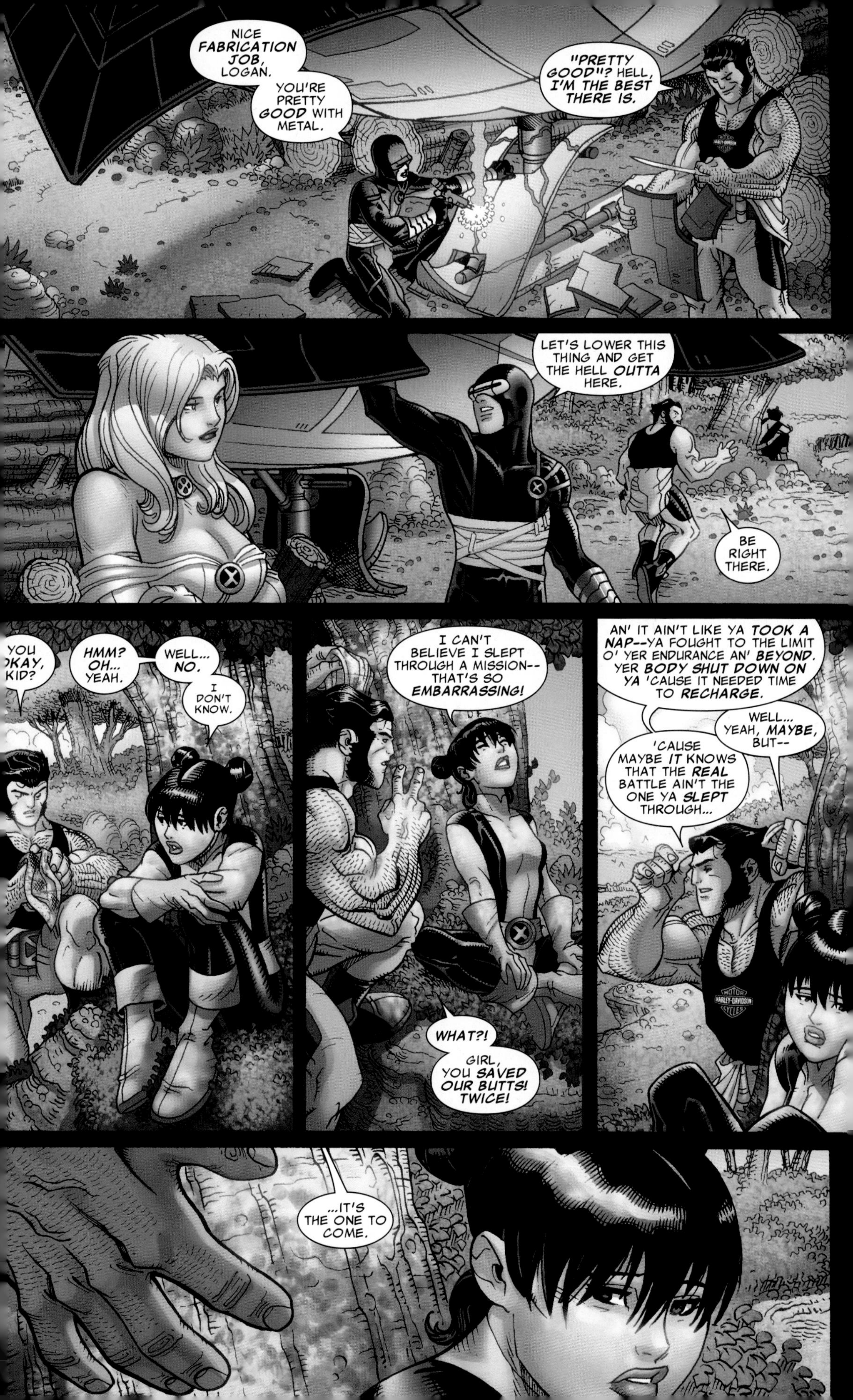
NICE FABRICATION JOB, LOGAN.
YOU'RE PRETTY GOOD WITH METAL.
"PRETTY GOOD"? HELL, I'M THE BEST THERE IS.
LET'S LOWER THIS THING AND GET THE HELL OUTTA HERE.
BE RIGHT THERE.
YOU OKAY, KID?
HMM? OH... YEAH.
WELL... NO.
I DON'T KNOW.
I CAN'T BELIEVE I SLEPT THROUGH A MISSION-- THAT'S SO EMBARRASSING!
WHAT?!
GIRL, YOU SAVED OUR BUTTS! TWICE!
AN' IT AIN'T LIKE YA TOOK A NAP--YA FOUGHT TO THE LIMIT O' YER ENDURANCE AN' BEYOND. YER BODY SHUT DOWN ON YA 'CAUSE IT NEEDED TIME TO RECHARGE.
WELL... YEAH, MAYBE, BUT--
'CAUSE MAYBE IT KNOWS THAT THE REAL BATTLE AIN'T THE ONE YA SLEPT THROUGH...
...IT'S THE ONE TO COME.

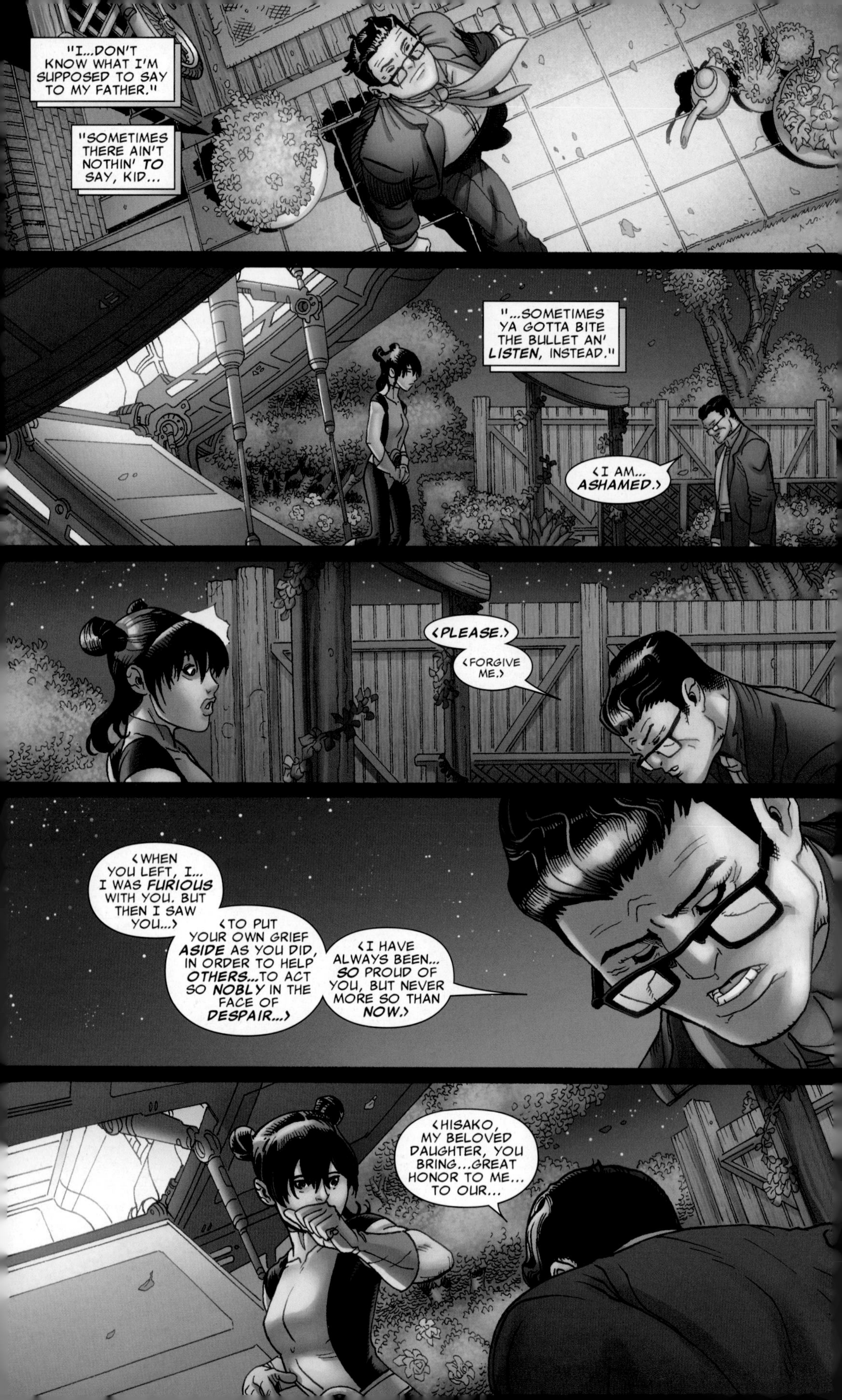

"I...DON'T KNOW WHAT I'M SUPPOSED TO SAY TO MY FATHER."
"SOMETIMES THERE AIN'T NOTHIN' TO SAY, KID...
"...SOMETIMES YA GOTTA BITE THE BULLET AN' LISTEN, INSTEAD."
‹I AM... ASHAMED.›
‹PLEASE.›
‹FORGIVE ME.›
‹WHEN YOU LEFT, I... I WAS FURIOUS WITH YOU. BUT THEN I SAW YOU...›
‹TO PUT YOUR OWN GRIEF ASIDE AS YOU DID, IN ORDER TO HELP OTHERS...TO ACT SO NOBLY IN THE FACE OF DESPAIR...›
‹I HAVE ALWAYS BEEN... SO PROUD OF YOU, BUT NEVER MORE SO THAN NOW.›
‹HISAKO, MY BELOVED DAUGHTER, YOU BRING...GREAT HONOR TO ME... TO OUR...

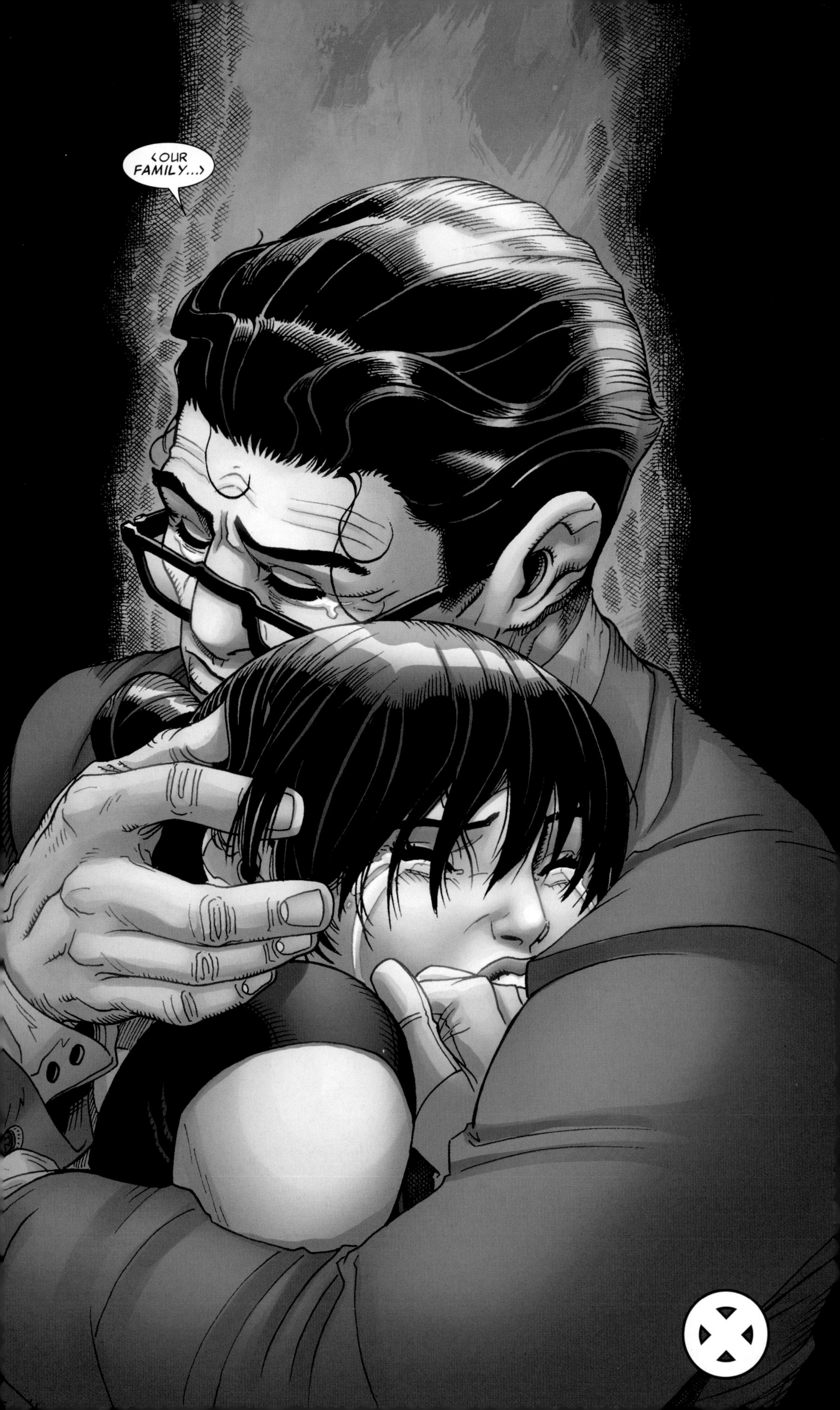
<OUR FAMILY...>

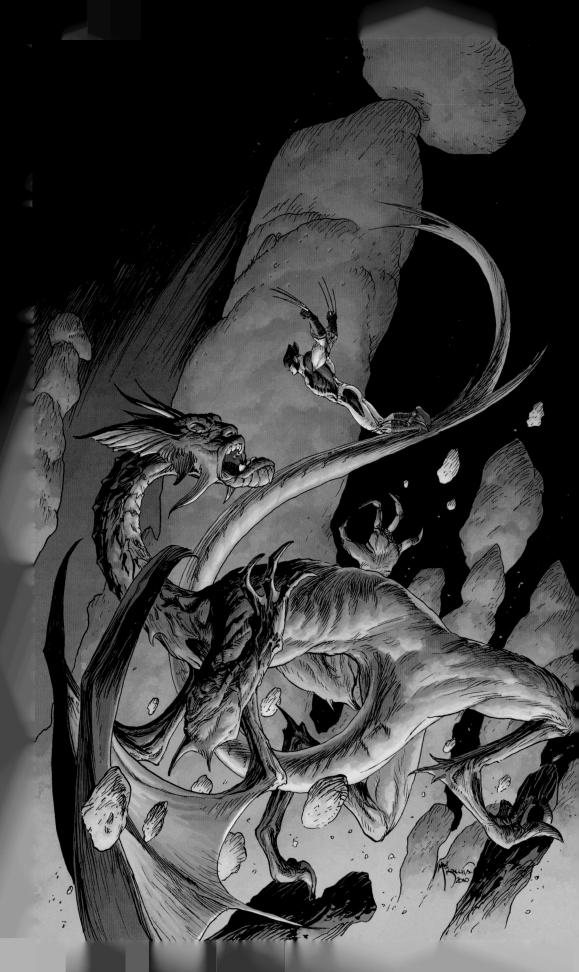

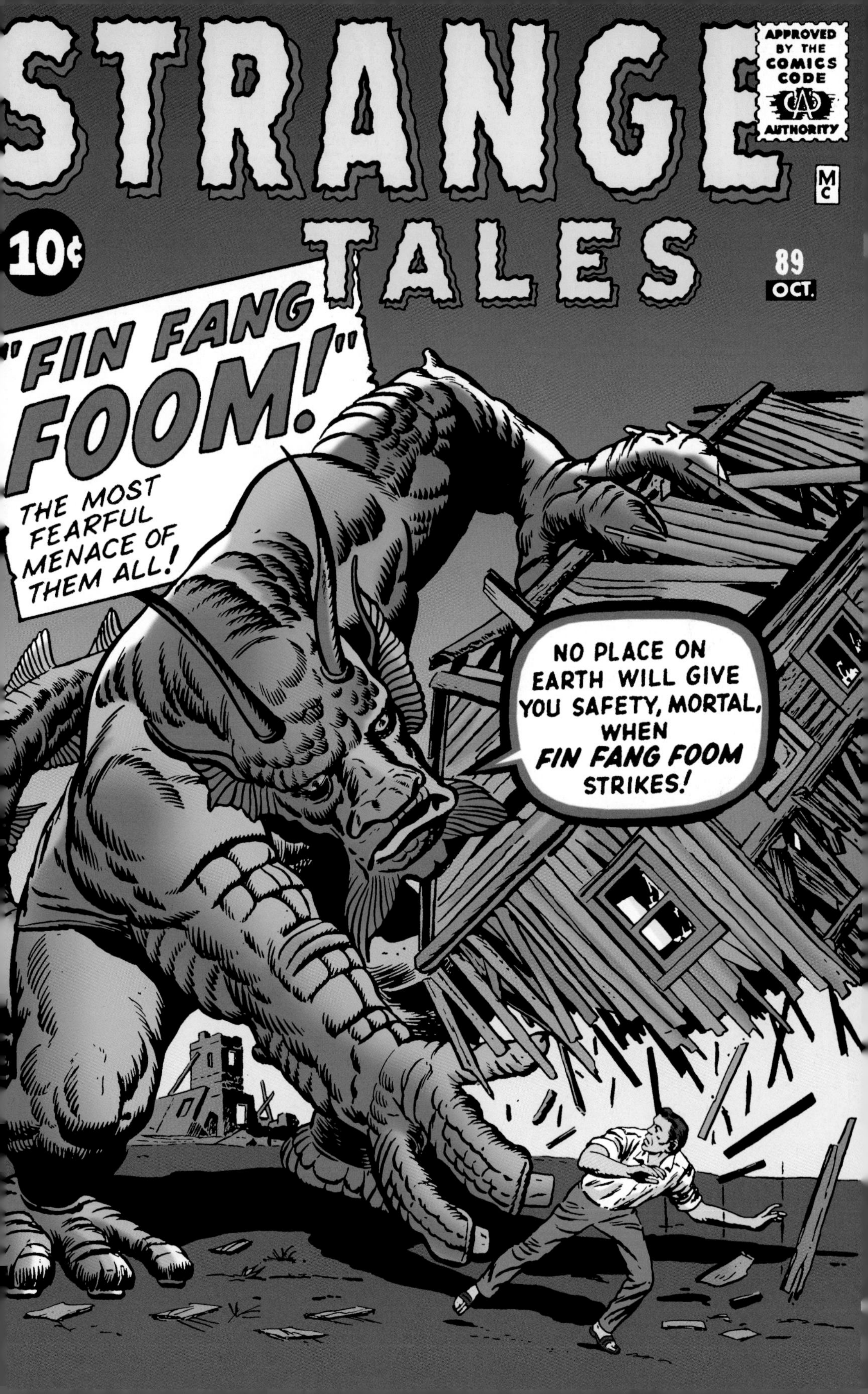
STRANGE TALES
APPROVED BY THE COMICS CODE AUTHORITY
MC
10¢
89
OCT.
"FIN FANG FOOM!"
THE MOST FEARFUL MENACE OF THEM ALL!
NO PLACE ON EARTH WILL GIVE YOU SAFETY, MORTAL, WHEN FIN FANG FOOM STRIKES!

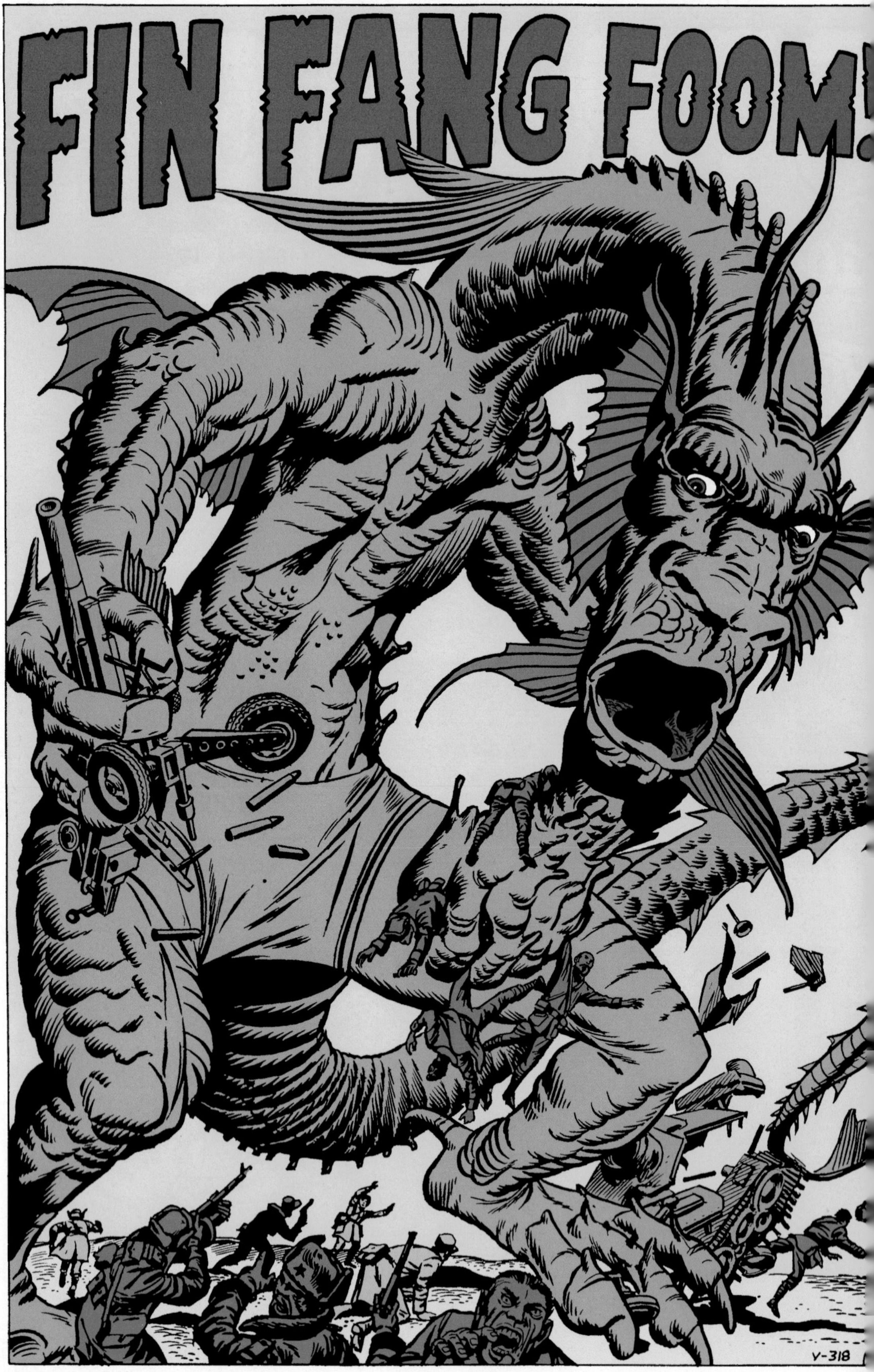
FIN FANG FOOM!
Y-318

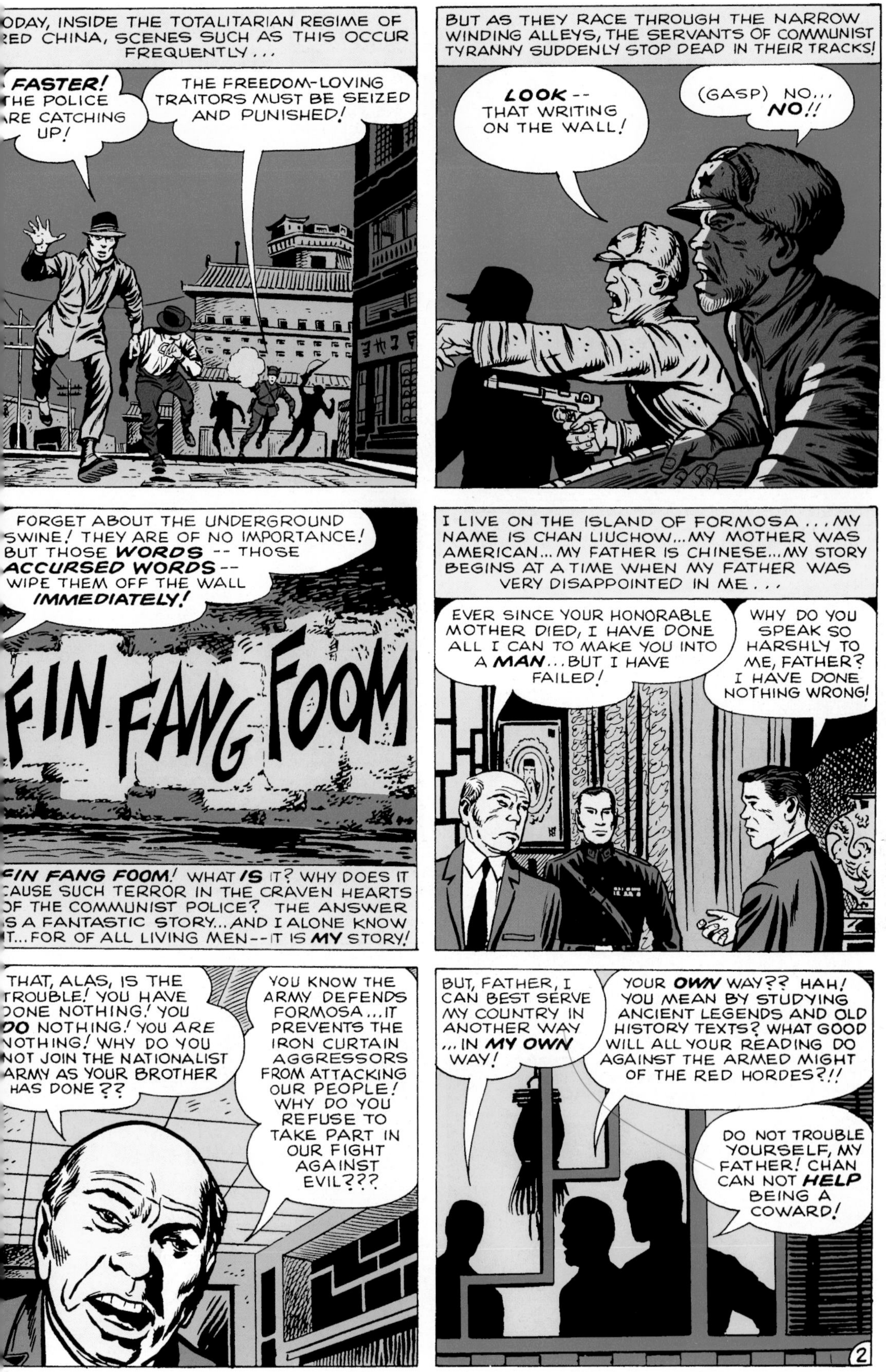

ODAY, INSIDE THE TOTALITARIAN REGIME OF RED CHINA, SCENES SUCH AS THIS OCCUR FREQUENTLY...
FASTER! THE POLICE ARE CATCHING UP!
THE FREEDOM-LOVING TRAITORS MUST BE SEIZED AND PUNISHED!
BUT AS THEY RACE THROUGH THE NARROW WINDING ALLEYS, THE SERVANTS OF COMMUNIST TYRANNY SUDDENLY STOP DEAD IN THEIR TRACKS!
LOOK -- THAT WRITING ON THE WALL!
(GASP) NO... NO!!
FORGET ABOUT THE UNDERGROUND SWINE! THEY ARE OF NO IMPORTANCE! BUT THOSE WORDS -- THOSE ACCURSED WORDS -- WIPE THEM OFF THE WALL IMMEDIATELY!
FIN-FANG-FOOM
FIN FANG FOOM! WHAT IS IT? WHY DOES IT CAUSE SUCH TERROR IN THE CRAVEN HEARTS OF THE COMMUNIST POLICE? THE ANSWER IS A FANTASTIC STORY... AND I ALONE KNOW IT... FOR OF ALL LIVING MEN--IT IS MY STORY!
I LIVE ON THE ISLAND OF FORMOSA... MY NAME IS CHAN LIUCHOW... MY MOTHER WAS AMERICAN... MY FATHER IS CHINESE... MY STORY BEGINS AT A TIME WHEN MY FATHER WAS VERY DISAPPOINTED IN ME...
EVER SINCE YOUR HONORABLE MOTHER DIED, I HAVE DONE ALL I CAN TO MAKE YOU INTO A MAN... BUT I HAVE FAILED!
WHY DO YOU SPEAK SO HARSHLY TO ME, FATHER? I HAVE DONE NOTHING WRONG!
THAT, ALAS, IS THE TROUBLE! YOU HAVE DONE NOTHING! YOU DO NOTHING! YOU ARE NOTHING! WHY DO YOU NOT JOIN THE NATIONALIST ARMY AS YOUR BROTHER HAS DONE??
YOU KNOW THE ARMY DEFENDS FORMOSA... IT PREVENTS THE IRON CURTAIN AGGRESSORS FROM ATTACKING OUR PEOPLE! WHY DO YOU REFUSE TO TAKE PART IN OUR FIGHT AGAINST EVIL???
BUT, FATHER, I CAN BEST SERVE MY COUNTRY IN ANOTHER WAY ... IN MY OWN WAY!
YOUR OWN WAY?? HAH! YOU MEAN BY STUDYING ANCIENT LEGENDS AND OLD HISTORY TEXTS? WHAT GOOD WILL ALL YOUR READING DO AGAINST THE ARMED MIGHT OF THE RED HORDES?!!
DO NOT TROUBLE YOURSELF, MY FATHER! CHAN CAN NOT HELP BEING A COWARD!
2

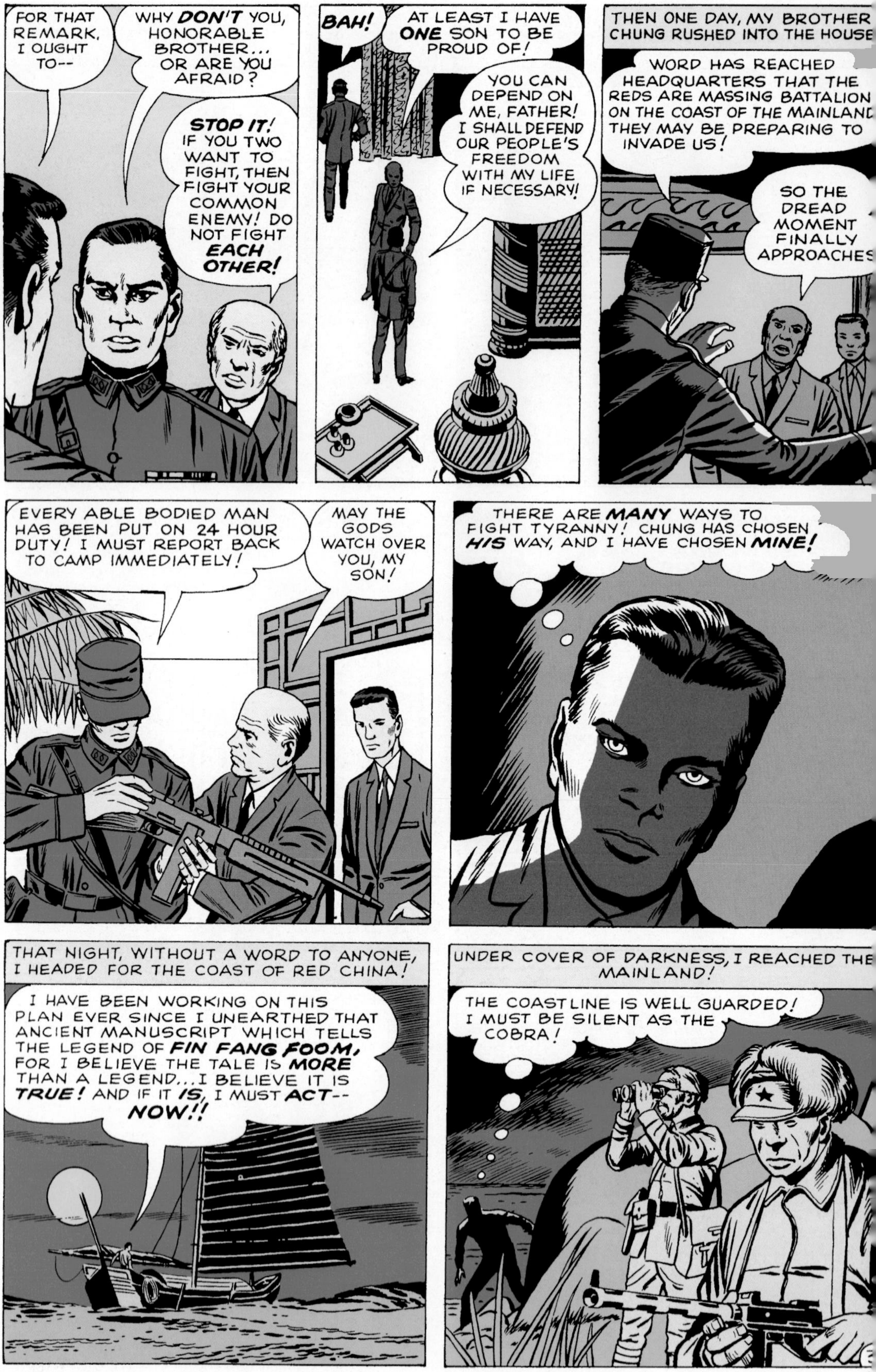
FOR THAT REMARK, I OUGHT TO--
WHY DON'T YOU, HONORABLE BROTHER... OR ARE YOU AFRAID?
STOP IT! IF YOU TWO WANT TO FIGHT, THEN FIGHT YOUR COMMON ENEMY! DO NOT FIGHT EACH OTHER!
BAH!
AT LEAST I HAVE ONE SON TO BE PROUD OF!
YOU CAN DEPEND ON ME, FATHER! I SHALL DEFEND OUR PEOPLE'S FREEDOM WITH MY LIFE IF NECESSARY!
THEN ONE DAY, MY BROTHER CHUNG RUSHED INTO THE HOUSE
WORD HAS REACHED HEADQUARTERS THAT THE REDS ARE MASSING BATTALION ON THE COAST OF THE MAINLAND THEY MAY BE PREPARING TO INVADE US!
SO THE DREAD MOMENT FINALLY APPROACHES
EVERY ABLE BODIED MAN HAS BEEN PUT ON 24 HOUR DUTY! I MUST REPORT BACK TO CAMP IMMEDIATELY!
MAY THE GODS WATCH OVER YOU, MY SON!
THERE ARE MANY WAYS TO FIGHT TYRANNY! CHUNG HAS CHOSEN HIS WAY, AND I HAVE CHOSEN MINE!
THAT NIGHT, WITHOUT A WORD TO ANYONE, I HEADED FOR THE COAST OF RED CHINA!
I HAVE BEEN WORKING ON THIS PLAN EVER SINCE I UNEARTHED THAT ANCIENT MANUSCRIPT WHICH TELLS THE LEGEND OF FIN FANG FOOM, FOR I BELIEVE THE TALE IS MORE THAN A LEGEND... I BELIEVE IT IS TRUE! AND IF IT IS, I MUST ACT-- NOW!!
UNDER COVER OF DARKNESS, I REACHED THE MAINLAND!
THE COASTLINE IS WELL GUARDED! I MUST BE SILENT AS THE COBRA!

MOVING CAUTIOUSLY AS POSSIBLE, I STOLE INLAND...

ONE MAN ALONE MAY DO WHAT AN *ARMY* CAN NOT...

BY MORNING, I HAD PENETRATED THE RED MILITARY DEFENSES...!

NOW TO HEAD FOR THE AREA DESCRIBED IN THE OLD MANUSCRIPT!

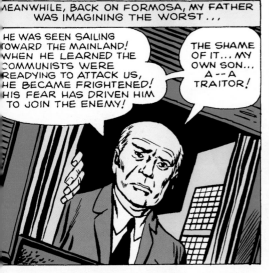

MEANWHILE, BACK ON FORMOSA, MY FATHER WAS IMAGINING THE WORST...

HE WAS SEEN SAILING TOWARD THE MAINLAND! WHEN HE LEARNED THE COMMUNISTS WERE READYING TO ATTACK US, HE BECAME FRIGHTENED! HIS FEAR HAS DRIVEN HIM TO JOIN THE ENEMY!

THE SHAME OF IT... MY OWN SON... A -- A TRAITOR!

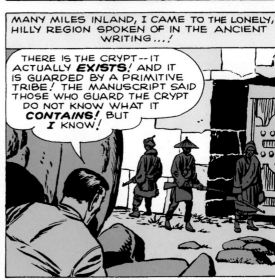

MANY MILES INLAND, I CAME TO THE LONELY, HILLY REGION SPOKEN OF IN THE ANCIENT WRITING...!

THERE IS THE CRYPT -- IT ACTUALLY *EXISTS*! AND IT IS GUARDED BY A PRIMITIVE TRIBE! THE MANUSCRIPT SAID THOSE WHO GUARD THE CRYPT DO NOT KNOW WHAT IT *CONTAINS*! BUT *I* KNOW!

HAD TO GET *INSIDE* THE CRYPT! ACCORDING TO THE MANUSCRIPT, THE GUARDS WERE FORBIDDEN TO ENTER THE UNDERGROUND VAULT, SO IF I COULD JUST RUSH *PAST* THEM...

AN INTRUDER!

STOP HIM!

SLAY HIM, YOU FOOLS!

NONE MAY ENTER THE SACRED VAULT!

I *MUST* GET THROUGH -- I *MUST*! EVERYTHING DEPENDS ON IT!

I *MADE IT*!

DO NOT ATTEMPT TO FOLLOW HIM! ACCURSED ARE THOSE WHO ENTER THE UNDERGROUND CHAMBERS!

4

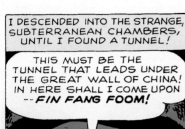

I DESCENDED INTO THE STRANGE, SUBTERRANEAN CHAMBERS, UNTIL I FOUND A TUNNEL!

THIS MUST BE THE TUNNEL THAT LEADS UNDER THE GREAT WALL OF CHINA! IN HERE SHALL I COME UPON --FIN FANG FOOM!

NOW, AS I NEARED THE END OF MY JOURNEY, I GREW TENSE AND FEARFUL! BUT TOO MUCH WAS AT STAKE! I DARED NOT BACK DOWN! I HAD TO GO ON AND ON ... UNTIL AT LAST...

THERE HE IS! THE DRAGON CREATURE HIMSELF-- FIN FANG FOOM!

THE ANCIENT MANUSCRIPT DESCRIBED TWO KINDS OF HERBS! ONE, TO MAKE THE MONSTER SLEEP ...AND THE OTHER TO AROUSE HIM, BY BRUSHING IT AGAINST HIS LIPS ... LIKE THIS!

HIS EYE -- IT IS OPENING!

I--HAVE--AWAKENED!

AFTER COUNTLESS CENTURIES, I LIVE AGAIN!

LIKE A TOWERING NIGHTMARE, THE HUGE DRAGON CREATURE LOOMED ABOVE ME!

YOU, MORTAL-- YOU HAVE BROUGHT FIN FANG FOOM TO LIFE AGAIN! I AM GRATEFUL TO YOU ...FOR TOO LONG HAVE I BEEN DEPRIVED OF AIR AND SUNLIGHT AND -- LIFE ITSELF!

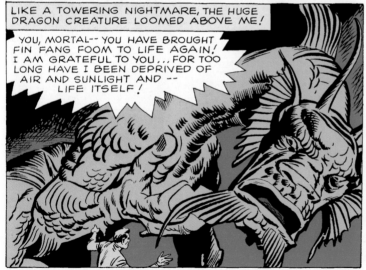

AND THEN CAME THE MOST DANGEROUS MOMENT OF MY LIFE...

HEAR ME, MIGHTY CREATURE! I BROUGHT YOU TO LIFE WITH A MAGIC HERB! BUT I HAVE ALSO ANOTHER HERB WHICH WILL PUT YOU TO SLEEP AGAIN! AND NOW THAT I HAVE SEEN HOW HUGE AND UGLY YOU ARE, I HAVE DECIDED IT IS BEST FOR YOU TO SLEEP-- FOREVER!

YOU WOULD TAKE THE GIFT OF LIFE FROM ME?! YOU-- YOU ARE MY ENEMY!!

...ES, I **AM** YOUR ENEMY--FOR I AM ...E ONLY MORTAL ON EARTH WHO ...OWS HOW TO PUT YOU TO SLEEP ...AGAIN! AND I SHALL **DO** IT!

NO!

I WILL **DESTROY** YOU!!

YOU CANNOT DESTROY ME UNLESS FIRST YOU **CATCH** ME--AND **THAT** YOU WILL **NEVER** DO!

...OWING THAT ONE MISSTEP WOULD ...EAN MY DOOM, I RACED BACK THRU THE DARK TUNNEL...

...THE TUNNEL IS TOO NARROW FOR ...ME! BAH! I SHALL GET TO THE SURFACE MY **OWN** WAY-- AS ONLY **I** CAN!

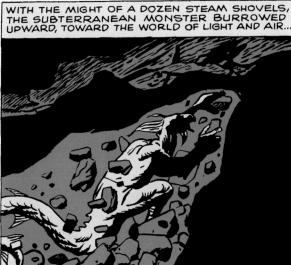

WITH THE MIGHT OF A DOZEN STEAM SHOVELS, THE SUBTERRANEAN MONSTER BURROWED UPWARD, TOWARD THE WORLD OF LIGHT AND AIR...

...NALLY THE FANTASTIC, MASSIVE FORM OF ...N FANG FOOM BURST THRU THE SURFACE!

A ...EMON ...ROM ...DER ...HE ...RTH!

HE RETURNS! AFTER AGES--HE **RETURNS!**

SLAY THE DEMON!

FOOLS! YOU DARE ATTACK THE ALL-POWERFUL **FIN FANG FOOM!!** I SHALL MAKE YOU REGRET YOUR IMPUDENCE!

NOW-- NOW IT IS ALL IN THE LAP OF THE GODS!

6

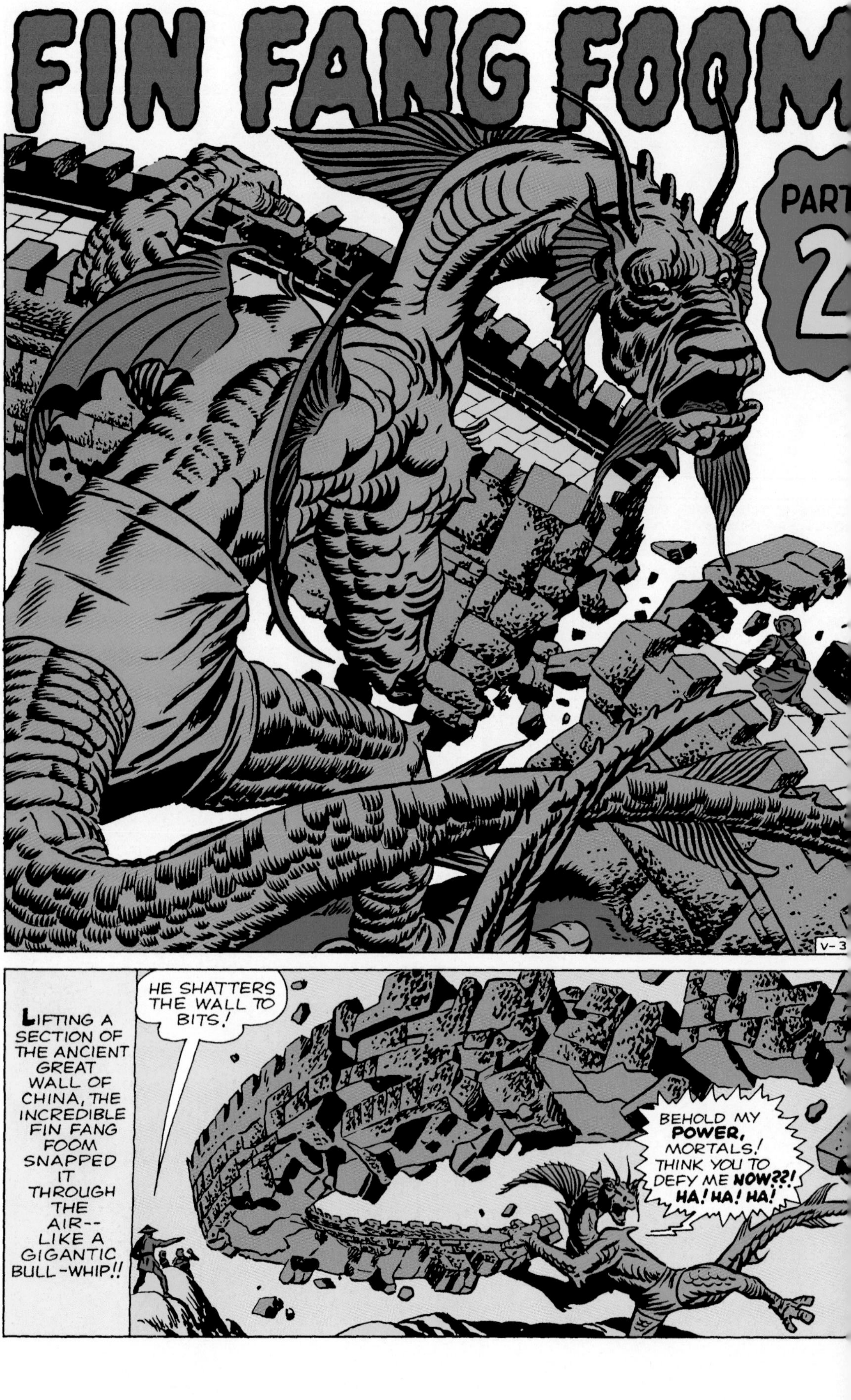
FIN FANG FOOM
PART 2
V-3
LIFTING A SECTION OF THE ANCIENT GREAT WALL OF CHINA, THE INCREDIBLE FIN FANG FOOM SNAPPED IT THROUGH THE AIR-- LIKE A GIGANTIC BULL-WHIP!!
HE SHATTERS THE WALL TO BITS!
BEHOLD MY POWER, MORTALS! THINK YOU TO DEFY ME NOW??! HA! HA! HA!

HAVING CAUSED THE HILL PEASANTS TO FLEE IN TERROR, THE MIGHTY FIN FANG FOOM NOW TURNED TO HIS MAIN CONCERN!

WHERE IS MY ENEMY? THE ONE WITH THE POWER TO MAKE ME SLEEP!

HERE I AM, DEMON!! CATCH ME IF YOU CAN!

I SHALL CRUSH YOU LIKE AN INSECT!! FOR I AN FIN FANG FOOM!

MUST STAY FAR ENOUGH AHEAD OF THE MONSTER SO HE CANNOT CATCH ME... BUT NOT TOO FAR, FOR HE MUST NOT GIVE UP THE CHASE!

USING MYSELF AS HUMAN BAIT, I LURED FIN FANG FOOM FOR MANY MILES IN THE DIRECTION OF THE COAST! BUT THEN, WHEN I CAME TO A RIVER...

THIS ACCURSED RIVER! I MOVE TOO SLOWLY! THE MONSTER IS CLOSING THE GAP! FASTER, MY STEED-- FASTER!!

BUT BEFORE MY MOUNT COULD REACH THE OTHER SHORE, THE MONSTROUS FIN FANG FOOM REACHED ME!

NOW SHALL YOU PERISH, MORTAL!

FIRST, I REMOVE YOU FROM YOUR CHARGER! HA! HA! HA!

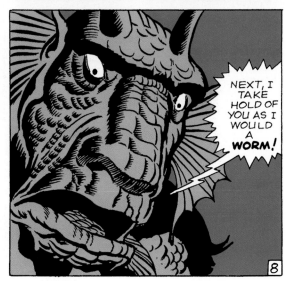

NEXT, I TAKE HOLD OF YOU AS I WOULD A WORM!

8

BUT I PROVED TO BE AS **SLIPPERY** AS A WORM, AS MY WET BODY SLITHERED THRU HIS GIGANTIC FINGERS!

YOU MERELY PROLONG YOUR FATE, FOOL! THERE IS **NO ESCAPE** FROM ME!

I SWAM A SAFE DISTANCE DOWN STREAM, WHERE I AGAI TOOK ON THE GRIM ROLE OF DECOY!

IT IS EASY TO **THREATEN,** DRAGON! LET US SEE IF YOUR **CUNNING** CAN MATCH YOUR WORDS!

THE TITANIC MONSTER CONTINUED THE PURSUIT! BUT NOW WE WERE NEAR THE COAST-- NEAR MY DESTINATION!

MY STRENGTH FADES! MY LEGS GROW WEARY! I CANNOT ENDURE MUCH LONGER... HE COMES CLOSER--CLOSER--

DOWN BELOW!!! **THE RED INVASION FORCE** PREPARING TO SAIL AGAINST FORMOSA I HAVE TRIUMPHED! I HAVE REACHED MY GOAL!! AND NOW-- LET FATE GUID MY FOOTSTEPS!

SUMMONING ALL MY REMAINING STRENGTH, I RACED TOWARD THE BATTALION OF ARMED TROOPS!

THE MEN DON'T EVEN **NOTICE** ME! THEY'RE TOO BUSY WATCHING THE MOST INCREDIBLE CREATURE THEY'VE EVER SEEN!

BEHOLD-- A LIVING **DEMON!!**

EEEAA!! IT IS-- **FIN FANG FOOM!!**

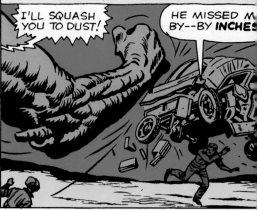

THERE WERE THOUSANDS OF HUMANS THER ...BUT FIN FANG FOOM WAS INTERESTED IN ONLY **ONE**... THE HUMAN WHO HAD TH POWER TO PUT HIM INTO THE SLUMBER FROM WHICH HE HAD BEEN AROUSED

I'LL SQUASH YOU TO DUST!

HE MISSED M BY-- BY **INCHES**

FOOL! YOU THINK TO ESCAPE ME BY HIDING UNDER A **BUILDING**!!

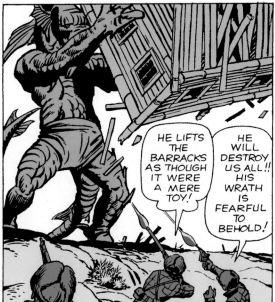

HE LIFTS THE BARRACKS AS THOUGH IT WERE A MERE TOY!

HE WILL DESTROY US ALL!! HIS WRATH IS FEARFUL TO BEHOLD!

THE RED TROOPS OPENED FIRE ON FIN FANG FOOM... AND AGAIN I WAS SAVED!

WHILE THE MONSTER IS BUSY WITH THEM, I SHALL HEAD FOR THE PIER!

OUR BULLETS CANNOT INJURE HIM!

KEEP FIRING! PERHAPS THE **NOISE** WILL DISMAY HIM!

BUT **NOTHING** COULD HINDER FIN FANG FOOM! THEY COULD ONLY ANGER HIM... UNTIL FINALLY, WITH ONE SWEEP OF HIS MIGHTY ARM, THE COLOSSAL CREATURE SENT MEN AND MACHINES SPRAWLING AND FLEEING!

OUT OF MY WAY, INSECTS!!

HE SEES ME! HE'S COMING **AFTER** ME AGAIN! IT IS ALL HAPPENING JUST AS I HAD **PLANNED**!

FIN FANG FOOM APPROACHES!! WE ARE **DOOMED**!!

I WAITED UNTIL THE GIANT DRAGON REACHED THE SHIP! THEN, AS THE CREATURE FROM THE PAST STRUCK, I LEAPT TO SAFETY!

SMASH!

THUD!

JUST IN TIME!

FIN FANG FOOM MISSED **ME**... BUT HE COMPLETELY WRECKED **THAT SHIP!** I PRAY I MAY SURVIVE THIS GAME OF CAT AND MOUSE, UNTIL THE MONSTER HAS DESTROYED THE ENTIRE INVASION FORCE!!

AGAIN THE NIGHTMARE CREATURE ATTACKED ME, AND AGAIN IT WAS A RED VESSEL THAT WAS THE VICTIM!

I'LL SMASH YOU!! DO YOU HEAR--**SMASH** YOU!!

THE CARNAGE CONTINUED UNTIL ALL THE SHIPS WERE WRECKED! THEN, AROUSED BY MY TAUNTS, AND BY HIS OWN INABILITY TO SEIZE ME, FIN FANG FOOM TURNED HIS WRATH AGAINST THE VERY PIER ITSELF!

THEIR SHIPS WRECKED, THEIR EQUIPMENT RUINED, THE TERRIFIC RED TROOPS FLED IN PANIC.

THE INVASION IS **FINISHED!** BUT MY WORK IS NOT YET DONE! I MUST NOW RETURN THE DRAGON-CREATURE TO THE PLACE FROM WHENCE HE CAME!

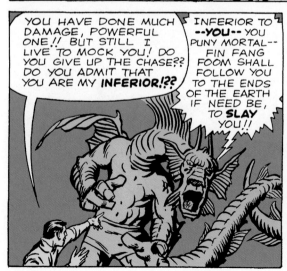

YOU HAVE DONE MUCH DAMAGE, POWERFUL ONE!! BUT STILL I LIVE TO MOCK YOU! DO YOU GIVE UP THE CHASE?? DO YOU ADMIT THAT YOU ARE MY **INFERIOR!??**

INFERIOR TO --**YOU**-- YOU PUNY MORTAL-- FIN FANG FOOM SHALL FOLLOW YOU TO THE ENDS OF THE EARTH IF NEED BE, TO **SLAY** YOU!!

FRUSTRATED AND ENRAGED BEYOND ALL REASON, THE UNIMAGINABLE CREATURE MADE THE VERY EARTH TREMBLE BENEATH THE FORCE OF HIS DESPERATE CHARGE!

TIGHTER AND TIGHTER DOES FATE DRAW HER WEB! WE HAVE AGAIN COME TO THE PLACE WHERE I FIRST FOUND THE MONSTER!

WHEN I BREATHLESSLY REACHED THE CRYPT, I FOUND THAT THE AREA HAD BEEN DESERTED BY THE FEARFUL PEASANTS!

THEY WERE SO PANICKED BY FIN FANG FOOM, THAT THEY LEFT WITHOUT TAKING MOST OF THEIR POSSESSIONS!

QUICKLY SEIZING THE ONE THING I NEEDED, I RE-ENTERED THE FEARFUL DUNGEON!

EACH SECOND COUNTS! FIN FANG FOOM IS RIGHT AT MY HEELS!

THE MORTAL HIDES WITHIN THE TUNNEL BELOW! NOW THERE IS NO ESCAPE FOR HIM, WITHOUT PASSING ME!

AH! YOU CAN FLEE NO FURTHER! YOU ARE TRAPPED! LONG HAVE I WAITED FOR THIS MOMENT OF RECKONING! NOW SHALL YOU PAY FOR YOUR INSOLENT TAUNTS!

I OFFER YOU NO MERCY--NO PITY--NOTHING BUT DOOM!

12

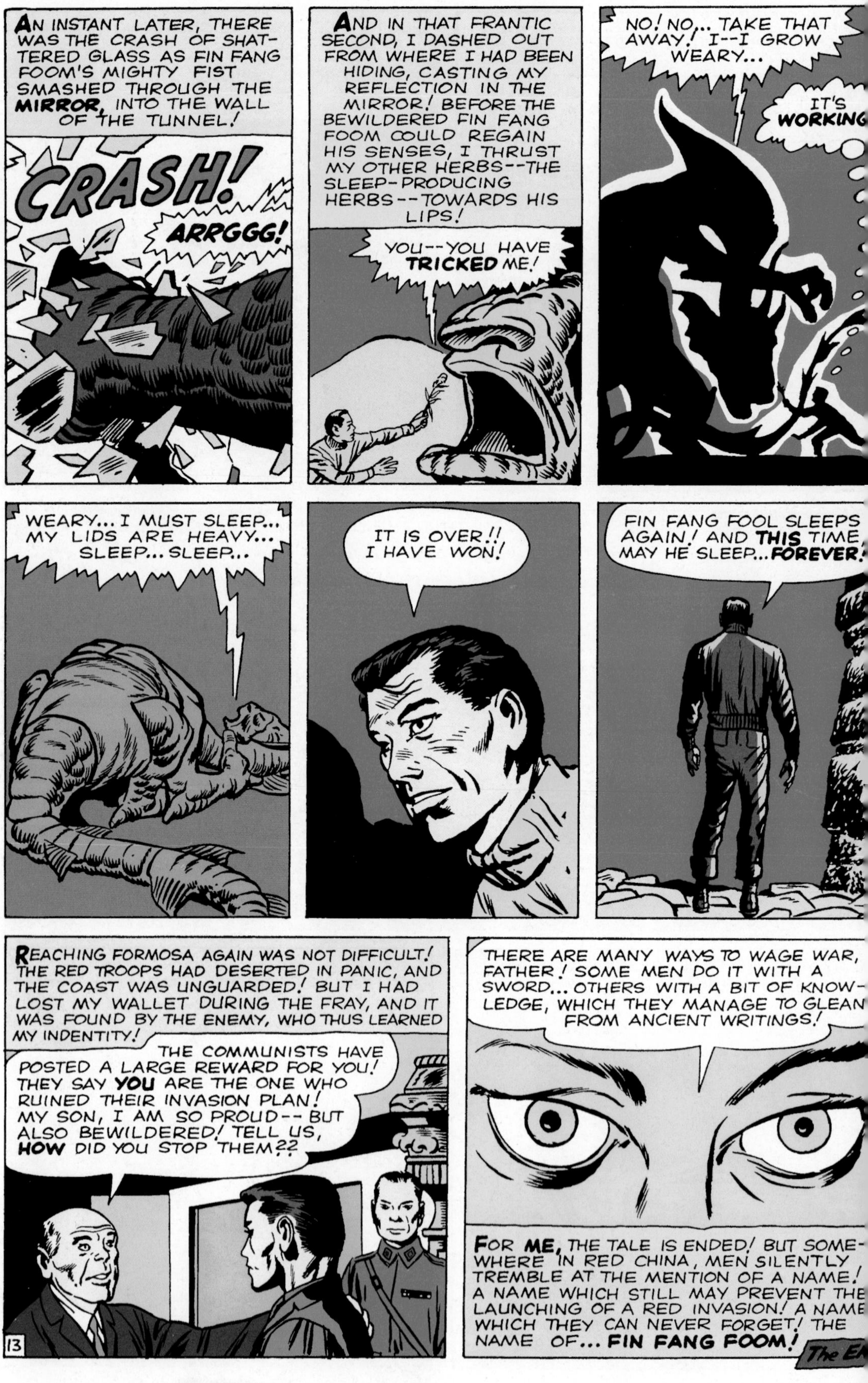

AN INSTANT LATER, THERE WAS THE CRASH OF SHATTERED GLASS AS FIN FANG FOOM'S MIGHTY FIST SMASHED THROUGH THE MIRROR, INTO THE WALL OF THE TUNNEL!
CRASH!
ARRGGG!
AND IN THAT FRANTIC SECOND, I DASHED OUT FROM WHERE I HAD BEEN HIDING, CASTING MY REFLECTION IN THE MIRROR! BEFORE THE BEWILDERED FIN FANG FOOM COULD REGAIN HIS SENSES, I THRUST MY OTHER HERBS--THE SLEEP-PRODUCING HERBS--TOWARDS HIS LIPS!
YOU--YOU HAVE TRICKED ME!
NO! NO... TAKE THAT AWAY! I--I GROW WEARY...
IT'S WORKING
WEARY... I MUST SLEEP... MY LIDS ARE HEAVY... SLEEP... SLEEP...
IT IS OVER!! I HAVE WON!
FIN FANG FOOL SLEEPS AGAIN! AND THIS TIME, MAY HE SLEEP... FOREVER!
REACHING FORMOSA AGAIN WAS NOT DIFFICULT! THE RED TROOPS HAD DESERTED IN PANIC, AND THE COAST WAS UNGUARDED! BUT I HAD LOST MY WALLET DURING THE FRAY, AND IT WAS FOUND BY THE ENEMY, WHO THUS LEARNED MY INDENTITY!
THE COMMUNISTS HAVE POSTED A LARGE REWARD FOR YOU! THEY SAY YOU ARE THE ONE WHO RUINED THEIR INVASION PLAN! MY SON, I AM SO PROUD-- BUT ALSO BEWILDERED! TELL US, HOW DID YOU STOP THEM??
13
THERE ARE MANY WAYS TO WAGE WAR, FATHER! SOME MEN DO IT WITH A SWORD... OTHERS WITH A BIT OF KNOWLEDGE, WHICH THEY MANAGE TO GLEAN FROM ANCIENT WRITINGS!
FOR ME, THE TALE IS ENDED! BUT SOMEWHERE IN RED CHINA, MEN SILENTLY TREMBLE AT THE MENTION OF A NAME! A NAME WHICH STILL MAY PREVENT THE LAUNCHING OF A RED INVASION! A NAME WHICH THEY CAN NEVER FORGET! THE NAME OF... FIN FANG FOOM!